The gift of kinship

Structure and practice in Maring social organization

Edward LiPuma

Department of Anthropology, University of Miami

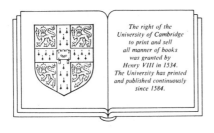

The right of the
University of Cambridge
to print and sell
all manner of books
was granted by
Henry VIII in 1534.
The University has printed
and published continuously
since 1584.

CAMBRIDGE UNIVERSITY PRESS

Cambridge

New York   New Rochelle

Melbourne   Sydney

Published by the Press Syndicate of the University of Cambridge
The Pitt Building, Trumpington Street, Cambridge, CB2 1RP
32 East 57th Street, New York, NY 10022, USA
10 Stamford Road, Oakleigh, Melbourne 3166, Australia

First published 1988

Printed in Great Britain by
Redwood Burn Limited, Trowbridge, Wiltshire

British Library cataloguing in publication data
LiPuma, Edward
The gift of kinship:
structure and practice in Maring social organization.
1. Maring (New Guinea people) – Social life and customs
2. Ethnology – New Guinea
I. Title
995   DU739.42

Library of Congress cataloguing in publication data
LiPuma, Edward, 1951–
The gift of kinship.
Bibliography.
Includes index.
1. Maring (New Guinea people)
2. Social structure – Papua New Guinea.
I. Title.
DU740.42.L57 1988   306'.0995'3   87-20883

ISBN 0 521 34483 2

Contents

Illustrations

Preface

This book is about the social organization of the Maring people of Highland New Guinea. I intend this study both as an ethnography of Maring social life and a theoretical contribution to the understanding of Highland social systems. Equally, the study is about the connection of structure and practice, since without a view of this connection there is no understanding of Maring social organization. The theoretical points I wish to make have texture only in relation to the ethnography itself, and so they are inter-woven throughout the text. I place equal emphasis on theory and ethnography because I see the creation of theory and a theory of ethnography as inseparable, their co-development being the means of generating an account adequate to its object.

Twice I have conducted fieldwork in the Maring area. In 1974, I spent four months with the Tuguma of the Simbai Valley. From 1979 to 1980, I resided with the Kauwatyi of the Jimi Valley. The latter stay was conducted under a research grant from the National Science Foundation.

The most important person in the writing of this manuscript has been Dr Sarah Keene Meltzoff, my wife and colleague, whom I met fortuitously walking in the mountains of New Guinea. She edited the manuscript, was a source of inspiration, and provided innumerable ethnographic insights. Sarah is an incomparable ethnographer, and some of her sensitivity has surely rubbed off. Most important to the making of this text are the many Maring who took me into their homes, aided me even as I mangled their language in my attempt to learn, and so patiently shared their experiences and laughter with me. Most important is Barnabas Gou who was my housemate, co-gardener, and companion for the duration of my stay among the Kauwatyi. We lived and slept side by side in our own "men's house" and much of what I could ever come to know about the emotional underside of Maring life I know from the numerous evenings when Gou and

I and his friends would sit beside the night fire talking about the practical concerns of everyday life. A good deal of my field technique consisted of situating myself inside one of the men's houses and recording people's humor, discussions, and arguments about gardening, land tenure, pig husbandry, the quality of plumes, the merits of war and aggressive behavior, health and sorcery, and much more. The Maring were a bit surprised that I did not spend most of my time interviewing, as they had come to see this as the proper work of the ethnographer. But after several months with my "nothing" technique, I blended into the pandanus leaves and pitpit siding of the men's house. Another crucial dimension of my field method was to take an active role in the exchange system. Both alone and in the company of friends, I made exchanges in clothes, pigs, taro, money, medicine, bushknives, and much more.

Marshall Sahlins contributed mightily to the making of this account, by virtue of his theoretical insight and as importantly by his respect for and knowledge of ethnographic data. His comments have improved the manuscript. I also wish to thank David Schneider who taught me much about kinship and about the courage to speak up theoretically in a clear and undisguised voice. In many respects, the theory which I propose herein is a result of my encounter with the anthropology of Marshall Sahlins and David Schneider, and the writings of Michael Silverstein and Pierre Bourdieu. Important as well in the making of this account are Skip Rappaport and Cherry Lowman, fellow Maringologists. Both gave much time, energy, and intelligence in an unselfish way that made me feel particularly good about doing ethnography in their company. Skip and Cherry shared in the true Maring sense of the word, in a way that leads not only to good anthropology but lasting friendship. The theory and ethnography which I present would have been impossible without their integrity and pioneering work. I would like to thank them and Roy Wagner for reading the book and offering their insights. In addition, discussions with Pierre Bourdieu were an important asset during the final stages of formulation. I am deeply grateful to the Anglican mission staff at Koinambe, principally Father Brian Bailey, who became a good and trusted friend. I would like to thank my colleagues – especially Benjamin Lee and Moishe Postone – at the Center for Psychosocial Studies for creating an intellectually rich environment. Finally, I owe thanks to Marilyn Jorge and Beatriz Figueroa for their diligence and wit during the final stages of preparation.

Introduction

When in the 1920s and 1930s gold prospectors, missionaries, and Australian patrol officers first entered the Highlands, they discovered that nearly half of the island's population, some 1 million people, lived on the slopes and plateaus cradled in the high mountains. It was at the close of World War II that anthropologists began to pour into the Highlands, their arrival and departure becoming as perennial as the torrential rains of the wet season and the sun of the dry.

Inspired by the writings of Fortes and Evans-Pritchard, they set out to describe the social structure of Highland societies, somehow confident that while ritual, exchange, and land tenure were not to be ignored, the essence of the social order lay in kinship and descent. But in 1962, Barnes drew together the implications of the then published studies, and seriously questioned whether the models based on descriptions of corporate lineage structure made sense when exported to New Guinea. Twenty years of analysis have more than confirmed Barnes' suspicion, though no new candidates have succeeded to the throne. Indeed, left high and dry by the failure of descent theory, New Guinea analysts have leaned toward piecemeal approaches. Yet the difficulties that ethnographers have experienced in producing a comprehensive interpretation seem only to have intensified the hunt. There is an unspoken feeling that just as descent models from Africa and exchange models from India have permanently enriched our understanding, so an adequate analysis of a Highland social system will have a similar effect.

Even before embarking on the current project, I felt that many of the newer accounts remained trapped within the design of descent theory. Though they emphasized exchange, local groups, and ideology, and thus immeasurably enlarged our understanding, they still retained the distinctions between descent and exchange, ideology and practice, and kinship versus descent groups. All were basic presuppositions of descent theory. Thus the content of the works changed more than their founding principles.

In line with tradition, the spirit and data of my analysis centers on the elements of social organization. It describes how the interaction of cultural categories, principles, and practices defines Maring social relations and groups. The express aim is to generate a theory which can account for both the structure and reproduction of Maring society. So, for example, I am interested in explaining not only how the basic opposition between male and female orients the division of labor, but how gardening practices reproduce this opposition in people's day to day experience. My argument is that the inseparability of the symbolic and material, norm and action, structure and practices, should be the basis of analysis.

There are three interconnected objectives which orient the study. The first is the making of an ethnography which accurately portrays Maring social organization. I seek to give an account which is adequate to its object because (1) it is constructed on the basis of cultural categories and generative schemes; (2) it is able fully to encompass the range of practices (e.g., food taboos and bridewealth) constitutive of the social system; and (3) it demonstrates how the society symbolically and materially reproduces itself. Accordingly, the analysis depicts social phenomena such as land tenure, kinship, clanship, reaffiliation, marriage exchange, and commensality in terms of their interrelationship. The unifying analytical thread is the local conception of social reproduction – embodied in the flow of substance through the reproduction cycle – and a structural understanding of group formation grounded in the opposition between sharing and exchange. The essential argument is that this is the primary generative scheme for the construction of the social system, and that it is only in practice that this structure is brought to life in such a way as to reproduce the clan and other social units. I am trying to develop what might be called a generative theory of Highland social organization.

My second objective is to identify some of the ways in which the situation of the ethnographer informs the production of ethnography and making of theory. The idea is to begin to understand how the ethnographer's relationship to his/her object of study shapes his/her explanation of kinship and exchange. Participant observation, much more than setting anthropology apart from other disciplines, grounds its interpretation of the Other. But only recently has anthropology begun to locate fieldwork and the ethnographic experience in the epicenter of its theoretical discourse (Fabian 1983). This issue is paramount, particularly so in New Guinea where there is a great epistemological and social divide between observer and observed. The practical interests of the ethnographer are far removed from the interests of New Guinea practice; the deductive and totalizing logic of ethnography is never the cultural logic of practice.

The interplay between method and theory enters the analysis from several directions. Most important, it enters through a detailed look at how Maring represent their own practices, and the social functions of these representations (ideology). Although ideology is just one moment of practice, it is that moment which impresses itself upon the ethnographer who, bearing no birthmark other than that of the stranger, and lacking mastery of the social process, frequently gathers information by asking informants to represent their own practice. In this sense, theory may follow method, the ethnographer reading into his object of study his relationship to that object. The issue of method implies that we need a theory of Highland ethnography, an explicit account of the epistemological and social conditions which make an ethnography possible. With this in mind, I try to indicate some ways in which the conditions of ethnography have misdirected the creation of Highland social theory.

The third objective is to develop through the ethnography an analysis of the relationship between structure and practice. My aim is to account for both the structure of the social system, and the way social strategies and practices reproduce this structure. I try to show how the opposition of sharing and exchange guides the formation of the clan, and how its embodiment in the clan fashions a generative scheme for practice. By turns, analysis centers on how practice, by animating certain generative schemes and practical strategies, reproduces the clan and the oppositions it embodies. I argue that the reproduction of the clan is based on a dialectical relationship between the power of structure – flowing from cultural categories and principles – to set the objective terms of reproduction, and the authority of practice to forge the production of the structure. This view confers no special privilege on structure or practice (ontologically). What motivates social action is a cultural logic of practical necessity. In this sense, the material concerns and strategies of clansmen (e.g., to acquire more garden land or achieve greater prestige) produce the structures which define their realization. So against mainstream interpretation, I maintain that the Maring social system – which bears a strong family resemblance to that of many other Highland societies – is "loosely structured" only in the shadows of those theories which separate (as exclusive) exchange and descent, native model and statistical reality, symbolic and material. Successful ethnography overcomes these separations, theoretically and socially.

Structure and practice

By focusing on the specifics of production, this ethnography commits itself to a theory of the relationship between structure and practice. The issue is that if social relations have a true structure and are thus systematic how do they reproduce themselves under conditions which the structure could never anticipate, but must necessarily encompass. The two structuralisms, British and French, were both founded on an opposition to history and thus to practice. In the view of Bourdieu (1977) and later of Sahlins (1981), the individual actions and concrete practices which move reproduction were reduced to the execution of the system in place. This formulation is clearly inadequate for New Guinea, where the social structures do not march to descent and the cultural categories are embedded in practice itself. Indeed, each historical realization of the social system is that of a transformed form. I would argue that an adequate account of a Highland social organization entails a theory of how the reproduction of the structure is also its transformation.

Disabused of the notion that a social structural account was sufficient, and impressed by the power of practice, ethnographers opted for ecological or materialist accounts of Highland social systems. But they have been similarly unable to provide a good understanding of social practices and reproduction. Insofar as practices are dissolved and reformulated according to utilitarian interests, there is no vision of the organization of practices or of their coordinated reproduction. The social system is simply a result of the way people put resources into use.

What I want to establish here is that there is not only a received cultural order, and an organization to social relations, but a structure of reproduction. The interests and strategies of individuals and groups mediate the relationship between cultural concepts of the social order and the reproduction of this order in and through material production. That is, it is by illuminating the structure of reproduction that cultural principles (like the opposition between male and female) are brought into congruence with practical activities (of men and women).

It may seem that an account of Maring society, or for that matter, any Highland social system, is of limited relevance. My argument is the reverse: that New Guinea Highland social systems – by virtue of

4

their design – provide a special opportunity for coming to terms with the structures in practice and the practical reproduction of structures.

The direction of the analysis

The Maring social system is based on a fundamental opposition between the relations of sharing, exchanging, and commerce. These relations are the significant terms for the creation of different forms of relatedness. Sharing is the basic intra-clan relationship. This is exemplified in the sharing of land, food, and bridewealth, and is carried out daily in an infinite number of routines. Exchange is the primary relationship between clans. Thus affines exchange men, women, land, cultigens, and other goods according to the laws and strategies of reciprocity. The exchange defines the difference between clans and at the same time unifies them through the transfer of agnatic resources. Commerce is the relation between clansmen and outsiders, that is, those who do not participate in the kinship of sharing and exchanging. Insofar as the principal purpose of this account is to show the formation of groups it has only touched lightly on this latter category.

As one moves from the center of the system – the point of view of the clan – to the periphery, the economic dimensions of a transaction increasingly dominate the social. Paradigmatically, Maring share with their own clansmen, exchange with their affines, and see outsiders such as the Anglican mission in commercial terms. The ethnographer begins his stay on the periphery and then gradually, by establishing himself as a social person capable of employing the proper schemes and strategies, moves into the more social sphere of exchange. Local concepts about the purpose and truth of the gift, as given in particular contexts, are the pragmatic means of sorting out this relationship. Commerce beyond the sphere of kinship signifies a break with the other two categories insofar as it alienates and depersonalizes the objects. It removes the dimension of time, the essence of true reciprocity, by reducing the transaction to a simultaneity. There is a continuum and intergrade between the sociality of sharing and exchange and the economics of commerce.[1]

---

[1] Commerce as a social relationship antedates contact with the West. People have always engaged in trade with foreigners – *yindok ndemi* or wild people – giving and receiving kina shells, salt, stone axes, pigs, bird plumes, clays, and magic. What is now significant is that commerce is becoming more important with passing years and is part and product of the incremental commercialization of the Maring local economy. One of the reasons why Maring, like other Highlanders, have fared well in the face of political and economic development is that the possibility of a desocialized economy was already a dimension of the indigenous system.

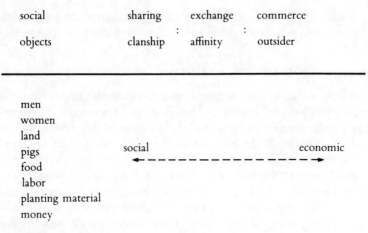

Figure 1 Primary social oppositions

For the Maring, the gift of kinship lies in the sharing and exchange of land, pigs, planting material, food, labor, and money, as well as the attributes of men and women (i.e., strength and fertility). These objects stand out as instruments of social relations because they are primary elements of the reproductive cycle of the clan. They are the material signs by which clansmen reproduce themselves as social beings, blessed with a sense of clanship, alliance, and self-identity. In and through practice, people combine these material signs with generative principles to produce social groups and relations. For instance, the pork which passes from wife-taker to wife-giver is an index of that relationship and a means by which it is reproduced.

The objects of reproduction are linked to a kinship system which is based on co-substance rather than pure genealogy (i.e., kin typing). An individual is related to his parents and to the larger universe of clan relations through transmission of male and female substances – grease and blood respectively. The substance of clanship is shared substance, and each clan member shares clan grease. Maring conceive this in both physical and spiritual terms. Within the realm of sharing, and thus within the orbit of clanship, the practices and actions of clan members transmit grease through a natural cycle of reproduction. Substance flows from the bodies of clansmen into clan lands, from there (through the use of labor and magic) into taro, pigs and other foods, and then ultimately returns to clansmen through eating food. This cycle defines the relationship between the elements, creates their values, and makes them the practical terms in which the culture regiments clanship. Land, food, and other material signs are where the kinship system

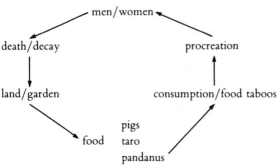

Figure 2 The cultural construction of the natural reproductive cycle

interlocks with the mode of production. Thus, it is in terms of land tenure, commensality, food taboos, co-gardening, and ritual sacrifice that clansmen create and define clansmen. It is the point where the social system expresses itself practically and openly, and thus where ethnography must look for its account of social organization. The Figure 2 outlines the natural cycle of reproduction.

Two modes of exchange complement the natural cycle; that is, the cultural construction of how nature is organized and operates with respect to human society. The first mode of exchange is the propitiation of clan ancestors (and occasionally, nowadays, Jesus Christ). The centerpiece of ancestor worship is the ritual sacrifice and communion of pig in return for which the ancestors assist their descendants in reproduction and (formerly) in the prosecution of war and peace. Ritual sacrifice explicitly defines the linkage between clansmen and their ancestors as one of total continuity. Moreover, ritual sacrifice is the functional analogue within the clan of the exchange of women between clans. Insofar as each subclan possesses its own sacred groves and conducts separate sacrifices, but to all of the clan's ancestors, the ritual both differentiates the subclans and specifies their unity.

Within the clan the terms of identity are the co-sharing of a clan substance, rather than descent from a common ancestor. It is participation in the same rituals and reproductive cycle which maps membership. Hence, Maring conceptualize clanship in terms of clan brotherhood, rendering the calculation of precise genealogies and biological connections irrelevant.

The second mode of exchange is that of marriage, including the attendant set of compensation payments. Successful reproduction demands that clans exchange men, land, labor, pigs, food, and, most of all, women – if they are to survive economically and politically. There is an interplay between the reproductive cycles of different clans, for clansmen mobilize a variety of strategies to reproduce the clan against the odds of prevailing conditions and in accordance with their image of clanship. For the clan, marriage exchange serves two functions. In the external realm, marriage allies exogamous clans by transporting women (i.e., female blood, fertility, and labor-power) in one direction, while moving pork, money, and like prestations in the other. In the internal arena, marriage exchange and distribution of bridewealth defines the boundaries of the clan through contrast between sharing and exchange. The two modes of exchange in concert with the reproductive cycle determine the structure of social groups. The formation and dissolution of groups, as well as the processes of recruitment and reaffiliation, become intelligible on their own terms.

This constitutes a brief rehearsal of the basic theory which I develop herein. The ethnography of the Maring social system which follows is intended to pursue and elaborate this viewpoint within the context of the total system.

Theoretical framework

On several counts, the Maring material is significant for both the theory of social structure and structuralist theory. The richness of the ethnography as well as the diversity of ethnographers (at least eight) provides favored conditions for a theoretical assessment of the basis of social organization in the Highlands. Such assessment, I will claim, argues for the development of a revised theory: namely, a pragmatic structuralism.

Time and again, my analysis shows that agnation and affinity are linked at the level of practice. They are of telling importance because they are never simply affairs of kinship, but involve all of social reproduction. Elements of the economic, political, moral, social, and religious domains enter into the reasons and motives which impel people to act in a given way. In essence, it becomes evident that agnation and marriage concern the functional relationship between domains.

Consideration of social reproduction reveals that exchange links seemingly disparate practices. There is constant formation not only of lineal relations, expressed in the clan's history and continuity, but lateral relations which slice across boundaries. These generate kinship by way of practices which encourage the exchange of reproductive objects between non-agnates. For example, when affines exchange land or garden rights, they create kinship. There is a dialectical movement between structure and practice. On one side, cultural categories and principles organize the form and content of giving. The opposition of sharing and exchange, the principle which invites wife-givers to request land rights, and the cultural sense of how clans reproduce, all define the exchange. On the other side, it is in practice that a given relationship becomes salient and pragmatic. Though marriage may create the possibility of exchanging land rights, it is only actual gifts of land (as well as other material signs) which define the practical value of this marriage, bring to light the communion of interests, and therefore inspire clansmen to reproduce the alliance. The totality of such actions produce the Maring social system in a way that is both determinate and constantly changing.

As the union of kinship and economy illustrates, Maring practice owes no allegiance to the analytical segregation of phenomena. Ritual and religion, land tenure, territoriality, production and consumption, and marriage are all integral components of social organization. Their relationship is instrumental to reproduction of social groups and relations at all levels of social organization. This is manifest in the role of ancestors in the well-being and continuity of the clan and in the link between consumption and the renewal of male substance. It surfaces in the relationship between foods, land tenure, and reaffiliation, and in the ritual processes by which non-agnates are converted into *bona fide* clansmen. It appears in the concept of spiritual essences, in the model of vegetable growth used to envision agnatic identity, and in the making of gender and sex roles. It is inscribed in the principles, norms, and procedures which govern marriage relations, particularly the collection and disembursement of bridewealth and the interests realized in the marriage system. Analytical concepts of genealogy – such as those underlying Kelly's study of the Etoro (1977) and Meggitt's study of the Mae Enga (1965) – do not order Maring kinship or play a part in the determination of clan identity. While concepts of substance (deceptively) resemble those of genealogy,[2] they have markedly different implications for clan and subclan formation. That recruitment to the clan ignores the presence or absence of common ancestors and focuses instead on the consubstantial effects of sharing gardens and foods exemplifies this reality. These relations of co-substance support Schneider's view (1968; 1972) that kinship and descent enjoy no phenomenological status apart from native constructs. Specific to the Highlands, Maring concepts of substance and how they work show that it is not simply the empirical facts of living and working side by side which produce agnation, but a cultural logic of relationship and group formation. Hence I aim for an analysis which reveals how prac-

---

[2] This resemblance occurs at the egocentric level of kinship, although even here there are a number of salient differences.

tice integrates material and social (e.g., prestige) interests while recognizing that both types of interests are culturally constituted.

The sharing and exchange of substance generates social units bearing a recognized identity. It is the movement of substance within the social field which governs unit definition and unit relationship. The basic units of Maring society are of two types: exogamous clans constituted by a principle of recruitment based on the sharing of clan grease, and clan clusters constituted by a principle of recruitment based on the sharing of blood. However, the intergenerational passage of grease within the clan and the transportation of blood across clan boundaries ride on reproduction and exchange. Clan members are co-recipients of clan substance insofar as they have participated in the same reproductive cycle. That is, they have been conceived and/or nourished by substances from the same land. In the same vein, the alignment of clans into a named cluster that maintains and defends a common territory, arises from a pattern of restricted exchange that assures that all clans are related through women. In essence, at any given time, the clan appears to be organized in terms of patrilineality, when, in fact, the making of the clan is contingent on reproduction and exchange. This is the practical equation binding the substantive links of the social system.

My account of Maring social organization calls into question two of the founding presuppositions of Highland ethnology. The integration of clanship and economy undermines the common presupposition that analysis can treat them as independent phenomena. For Maring at least, there is literally a production of kinship and agnation. Principles of co-substance tie the formation of clans to the making of gardens and the husbandry of pigs. This rules out the anthropological thinking which separates the social from the economic, and then understands each as a discrete variable, most frequently by trying to show how production or ecological stress (the independent variable) command the formation of the social group (the dependent variable).[3] My account also challenges the presupposition that "descent" determines the composition of the patriclan while exchange determines alliance between patriclans. The hand of exchange in the construction of the Maring clan means that exchange and clanship differ only in that they represent different moments of group formation.

The revised theory, by reversing the entropy of received distinctions, brings to the fore significant issues concerning the structure of clan reproduction. The Maring case illustrates that the formation, development, and transformation of the clan lies in the integrated move-

[3] In the Highlands, this viewpoint is enshrined in the hypothesis that pressure on agricultural resources, such as land, leads clansmen to stress patriliny.

ment of agnation, exchange, and the mode of production. Reading Highland ethnography from this revised viewpoint indicates that the theory has wider applicability. Throughout the text, accordingly, I have called upon other ethnography to enlarge the theory and support the ethnographic reading. My analysis – and the social theory which it proposes – offers a resolution to the classic problem of "flexible" or "loose structures," the apparent disjunction between norm and reality which purportedly disorganizes Highland societies.

Ethnographic framework

The preceding sections briefly describe the theoretical tack taken in this ethnography, including where my analysis parts company with more mainstream accounts. Nonetheless, my theory and method is an extension and development of existing ethnography. It attempts to reformulate the relationship between phenomena already inscribed in the literature; and it intersects at many points with the theories of social organization now current. Most elements at the heart of the analysis (e.g., the link between food taboos and kinship) have been reported previously, albeit in an unsystematic way and often without notice of possible linkages. It is useful, then, to adumbrate how existing ethnography foreshadows the theory of structure and practice which elucidates the Maring social system.

For more than two decades, Schneider (esp. 1968, 1972, 1976) has roundly criticized the notion that kinship and descent can be appreciated in analytical terms. Salisbury added the ethnographic coda that "there should be an examination of different peoples' conception of the category 'kinship'" (1964:170). Wagner's study (1967) of the Daribi was the first major attempt to penetrate indigenous views and to understand kinship on its own terms. His study, perhaps most akin to the one envisioned here, illustrated that Daribi base kinship and agnation on concepts of co-substance. According to Daribi canons, confluence of two substances, mother's blood and father's semen, is necessary to produce a child. Wagner also suggested that the Daribi emphasize the transmission of semen thus generating a principle of agnation. He proposed that local concepts of substance and their lineal transmission are influential in organizing social relations. In this vein, Strathern (1972) noted that the Melpa similarly conceptualize kinship in terms of semen and blood, and that the transmission of paternal substance is inseparable from membership in the lineage. He related that "the idea of *ndating* is a cultural dogma which expresses not only the notion of continuity in lineage membership but also the notion that

males are different from females. It explains why only males can theoretically transmit lineage membership" (1972:11). These are the most
well-documented accounts. However, almost all ethnographies which
focus on social organization mention concepts of substance somewhere along the way: Siane (Salisbury 1965:59), Hua (Meigs
1976:395), Kainantu and related groups (Berndt 1962:190), Mae Enga
(Meggitt 1965:193), Huli (Glasse 1968:60), Etoro (Kelly 1977:137),
Wiru (Strathern 1971:456), Kuma (Reay 1959:75), Foraba (Wagner
1970:94).

Accumulating evidence also kindles the view that Highland social
structures encompass practices and institutions which a classical model
cannot account for. In theoretical overviews and ethnographic
writings, the interrelationship between food, sharing, locality, and
exchange is a persistent theme. In questioning the use of African
models Barnes (1962) set the stage for the presentation of other components besides descent. He wrote that descent operates "concurrently
with other principles" and suggested the value of pursuing their interconnection. Ryan (1961:303) underlines the power of exchange, and
identifies it as the governing principle; he wrote that "it is the system
of exchanges, not the descent system, that delineates the socially significant relationships between individuals and groups." De Lepervanche (1967) maintains that bonds arising from common residence
and working side by side in production led to the formation of groups.
She argues that locality is the operative principle and that "a change of
group affiliation with all the corresponding implications" resulted
from a change in residence (1967:145). Brown and Brookfield (1959)
observe that social units at various levels of the social structure
emerged from the interaction of several components. They discern
that units may conceptualize their relationship in terms of common
descent and/or siblingship, as their pairing is simultaneously a result of
agnatic concepts and exchange relations (1959:37-40). Wagner (1967:
xxvi) characterizes this integration of components:

Unit definition and interrelationship, in this sense, are the functions towards
whose fulfillment the entire complex of interrelated elements – descent, marriage relationship and so on – is oriented. They order or organize the relationships of those elements to one another, or more accurately, they subsume a
complex of relations and rules which we variously identify as "descent" or
"marriage."

Schwimmer (1973) has built a model of Orakavia exchange which is
definitive of social units and encompasses several spheres of social relations. He analyzes in some detail the link between exchange and land

tenure and the place of food in the construction of social relations. A number of Highland ethnographers have likewise noted the relationship – though more often than not it is not reported – between the sharing of food, especially meat, and social identity. Lowman (1971:322) and Meggitt (1965:32) both report that individuals who have been born on agnatic lands and nourished by its products are *ipso facto* certified members of the patriclan. Strathern (1972:29) has commented on the prevalence of this link:

Food creates substance, just as procreation does, and forms an excellent symbol both for the creation of identity out of residence and for the values of nurturance, growth, comfort and solidarity which are associated with parenthood. In cultural terms what we often find in the Highlands, I would suggest, is a combination of filiative rules and ideas based on upbringing, nurturance and the consumption of food.

In this context, Wagner (1967), Strathern (1972), and Kelly (1977) have all pointed out instances in which male substance is thought to be depleted by sexual intercourse and replaced through the consumption of pork and other types of meat. In the external domain, Newman (1965:51–71), Meggitt (1969), Rappaport (1968), and many other analysts have observed that prestations of pork play a prominent role in marriage exchange. Kelly concludes his study of Etoro social structure by suggesting that it is through the interplay of descent and exchange that siblingship emerges as "both the organizational basis of local groups and the mechanism of their alignment" (p. 28).

I could marshal other testimony to support the theory that the formation of social groups depends on indigenous concepts of reproduction and exchange. For extant theory, however, the essential point is that no theory has been developed which can assimilate the full range of data exhibited by Highland societies, and as importantly do so without committing violence to their cultural conception of life.

1 The ethnographic context

Linguistic, social, and geographic setting

The Maring are a distinct linguistic and cultural group living in the interior Highlands of Papua New Guinea on the island of New Guinea. They number upwards of 7,000 people and are situated just south of the equator at approximately 5 degrees south latitude and 145 degrees east longitude in the Bismarck mountain range that bisects central New Guinea. The Maring territory consists of roughly 350 kilometers of steep, rugged, heavily forested terrain that is characteristic of the Highland fringe, which, in contrast to the more central areas with their broad valleys and relatively level lands, is one of great topographic relief. The Maring people are split into two segments defined by geographical and political boundaries. Nine of the major groups of about 2,000 people reside on the northern fall of the mountain range in the Simbai Valley which is included in the Madang Province. Twelve major groups are located on the southern fall of the range in the Jimi Valley which is part of the Western Highlands Province. The political boundary reflects the fact that the Maring occupy the Highland's border and incorporate some features of intermediate stepland societies lying between the Highlands and the coast. For the most part, however, their cultural, linguistic, and social affinities are with the Highlands, especially as regards social organization.

The Maring language is classified within the Central Family of the Eastern New Guinea Highlands Stock (Wurm and Laycock 1961; Bunn and Scott 1962). The Central Family includes at least fifteen distinct languages and extends in a curved band through the Southern, Eastern, and Western Highlands Provinces. Consistent with its location on the Highland fringe, Maring is the most northerly outpost of this stock. Analysts further classify it as belonging to the Jimi subfamily of the Central Family which is comprised mostly of tongues from Eastern Highlands groups (Wurm 1964). Cultural affinity is expressed in the "genetic" relation between languages in the area and their geographical location in relation to Maring. Narak, lying to the south and the Highlands proper, is most closely related to Maring. In adjoining communities, the two languages may approach the dialect level (cf. Cook 1967).

There is sufficient continuity in grammatical structure and the presence of enough cognates so that most speakers can achieve intelligibility if they so desire. Maring maintain that there are telling differences between Narak and Maring and are not hesitant about professing their linguistic distinctiveness. There is much less social and linguistic integration with neighbors to the north and south. Gunt to the north and Kalam to the west are distantly related languages and are not classified within the same Eastern Stock. With the advent of regional representation in the national government, however, Simbai Maring must pass through Kalam country on their way to the Simbai patrol post. There is a growing degree of relatedness and they have begun to hold joint dance festivals. Association in this context invites increasing intermarriage, such festivals being a central forum for contacts between marriageable men and women. Undoubtedly, this will promote linguistic, social, and political integration in the future (see Map 1).

The Maring people are divided up into twenty-one clan clusters whose member clans are integrated through a history of extensive intermarriage. Prior to pacification in 1955, most clan clusters were not named groups, although those assigned by the government have been readily adopted, in no small part because Maring have always been able to give definite descriptions of a given clan cluster. Clusters should maintain a single territory and cooperate in production, warfare, and performance of certain crucial ceremonies. Almost all clan clusters share at least one border with an old enemy, defined by a history of conflicts and quarrels that may range over many generations, and a border with a cluster with whom they are allies. The configuration of enmity and alliance serves to localize warfare and Maring neither engage in long-distance warfare nor align themselves as a body against other societies. This type of social organization and pattern of warfare has two major consequences for ethnographic studies. The first is that the relationship between the Maring and adjoining societies must be analyzed on a case by case basis, particularly in terms of the political structure of the clan cluster at points of contact. The second is that the clan cluster is the largest political and economic unit. There-

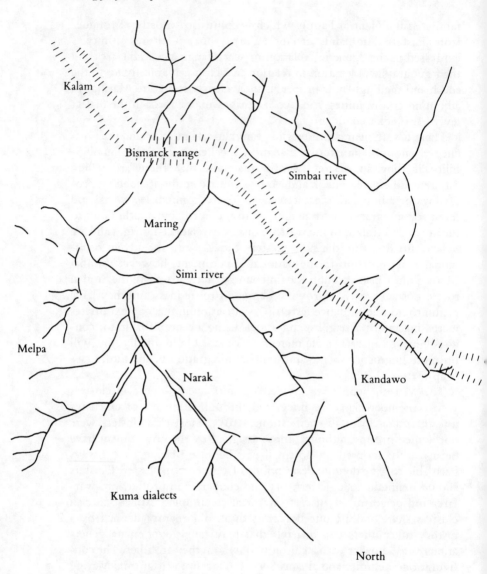

Map 1 Linguistic boundaries in the Jimi Valley

fore, ethnographic studies of the Maring have focused intensively on a number of specific clan clusters.

Maring ethnography was part of the ascendancy of ecological anthropology and it has, for the most part, centered on the biological and ecological factors which defined the structure of the population and its temporal continuity. The natural result has been an extensive body of etic data on the means and techniques of production; the ecological effects of warfare and ritual; and the demographic, genetic, and nutritional factors determining the size and health of populations. This agenda has informed field methods, researchers systematically collecting data on social organization only as it bears on these concerns. Theoretical concerns have also influenced ethnographic output in that the ecological model calls for etic information which centers on the functional relationship between components in a system. Vayda (n.d.) has completed a Pan Maring Survey that provides census material and certain oral history for each of the clan clusters. In the far western end of the Simbai Valley, Roy Rappaport (1967; 1968; 1969; 1971; 1979) has been studying the Tsembaga, devoting some attention to cultural matters but mainly interested in the ecological functions of their behavior. I have studied the Tuguma, the eastern neighbors of the Tsembaga (LiPuma 1980). Tuguma have also been researched by Buchbinder (1973; 1974; Buchbinder and Rappaport 1976) as part of a coordinated effort to document the biological forces that influence the ecology. Her work focuses on the genetic, demographic, and nutritional factors that determine the profile of Maring populations. As part of the same project, Lowman (1971; 1974; 1980), who investigated the Fungai in the eastern end of the Simbai Valley and the Kauwatyi in the Jimi, has submitted a thesis that analyzes health and population statistics. In the Jimi where, until recently comparatively less research had been done, Healey (1977; 1979; 1985a) has contributed a description of trade in bird plumes and settlement patterns for the Kundagai. Maclean (1984) has produced a dissertation on the modernizing forces now defining the course of Tukmenga political economy. In addition to anthropologists a team of geographers has conducted a study in the area (Clark 1971; Street 1967; Clark and Street 1967; Manner 1976). The intersecting interests and skills of the various investigators has generated a concentrated body of data on a diversity of clan clusters over a time span of more than two decades. I have drawn on important cultural data interspersed in previous studies to provide a more comprehensive account of social organization (see Map 2).

My ethnography features the Kauwatyi clan cluster, although the account aims for a more catholic view of social organization. The

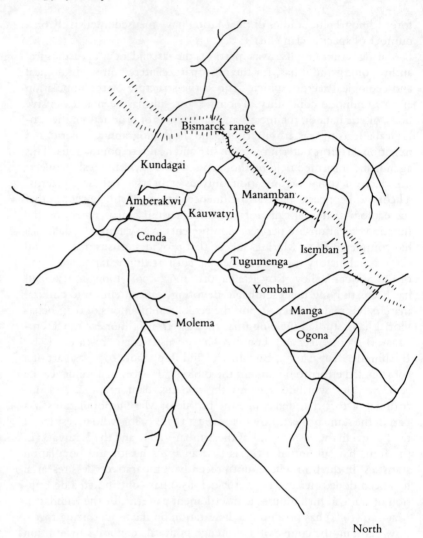

Bismarck range

Kundagai

Amberakwi

Kauwatyi

Manamban

Cenda

Tugumenga

Isemban

Yomban

Molema

Manga

Ogona

North

Map 2 Jimi Valley clan clusters

Kauwatyi are flanked on their western border by the Cenda and Amberakwi, on the north by the main Kundagai cluster, and on the east by the Manamban. The Kauwatyi maintain active alliances with the groups of the western Simbai, specially the Tuguma and Tsembaga who live on the adjoining face of the mountain range. The Kauwatyi number in excess of 900 people, being the largest and most powerful of the Maring groups; their political and economic influence reflects this standing. Political considerations encourage population expansion since clansmen correlate political muscle with unit size. Despite the political and economic pressures to remain roughly equal in popu-lation, clan clusters vary considerably, ranging from 150 to 900 people. More than a function of access to fertile land, the variation stems from epidemiological, demographic, and ecological forces which intervene in the social process. Desire to augment the population is seriously undercut by epidemics, the demographic disruption that ensues, and the long-term repercussions of such disruption on social relations, par-ticularly marriage exchanges. On the social side, variations in clan cluster size arise from the lack of manifest structural limits on expan-sion. Fragmentation that might conceivably result from the dilution of kinship ties is forestalled by a concept of clan substance that does not recognize collateral lines, and the potential for greater intra-cluster marriages. The latter is a function of an increase in the number of avail-able women and a political reality where size minimizes the need to cultivate external alliances. There is a statistical correlation here be-tween cluster size and endogamy.

Maring society is bordered by the Kalam in the western Simbai and by the Manga in the eastern Jimi. Natural boundaries separate other nearby peoples and thus social intercourse involves travel. Maring have their strongest cultural and linguistic affinities with the Manga. Nevertheless, they take pride in pointing out what they see as telling differences between the groups. They comment on the distinctiveness of Maring language, mainly the proper pronunciation of key words (e.g., pig), and the fact that Manga food preferences sometimes run counter to their own. Clearly, the level of differentiation is more indi-cative of similarities than differences. Most importantly, their respec-tive concepts of spiritual qualities, which are central to social identity, are cultural and linguistic cognates (cf. Cook 1967; 1968). Now that intertribal warfare does not discourage travel, intermarriage is common.

Prior to pacification, the Kauwatyi were the most militant and aggressive Jimi cluster. They have waged at least five wars in the past century, several in recent memory. In the late 1940s, they fought against the Cenda, their western neighbors. The fighting produced only a handful of casualties and by 1979 relations were relatively amicable (i.e., they cooperate with little fanfare when both parties stand to benefit). The same cannot be said of their war against the Manamban cluster in the early 1950s which was a holocaust by local standards. Kauwatyi launched an assault on the Manamban settlements that left their compounds in flames, sent them fleeing to safety with Simbai allies, and claimed an uncharacteristically large number of lives; the Manamban suffered more than 100 casualties if local estimates are reliable. Peace was not restored easily. It was not until the government intervened on behalf of the Manamban that they were reinstated on their territory. Time has done little to mend these wounds to body and pride, and relations between combatants are sensitive as many of the participants and kinsmen of those slain are still alive. In fact, there has been no formal truce ceremony to mark the end of hostilities and technically a state of war is still in effect. At present, social distance is indicated by a discontinuity in the spacing of settlements along the borders.

Social economy

Production, exchange, and consumption – what anthropologists usually consider the spheres of economic activity – are conceptually and materially instrumental in the formation of social groups. The use and distribution of crops, the allocation of labor, etc., are all components of the social system. It is thus useful to outline the general structure of the social economy as it has a bearing on the discussion of agnation and exchange which are the primary concerns of the subsequent chapters.

Production

In contrast to the central Highlands, the Maring environment has greater variation in altitude and heavier forestation. Social exploitation of these features contributes to greater variation in resource distribution and the practice of a more classical regime of swidden agriculture (slash and burn). Production revolves on cultivation. This encompasses a complex of interrelated social practices, including magic spells, designed to propagate certain plants and animals and to utilize them for social purposes. Materially, the most important is shifting horticulture since people derive most of their subsistence goods from the garden. Gardens are usually made in secondary forest and abandoned after a single planting, although this is not always the case. Gardens are cut in the wet season, burned in the dry, and planted with a temporary association of cultivated plants. Cropping continues for up to two years, after which the garden is permitted to revert to secondary growth and to lie fallow for at least a decade. Such horticulture is labor extensive and entails a great amount of useable land.

Men and women cooperate in making gardens, though there is a salient division of labor along sexual lines. Men fell and pollard trees, build fences to keep out marauding pigs, and distribute logs to act as plot markers, planting guides, and soil retainers. Male activities are limited in scope and duration, with a great amount of energy expended on these tasks. The burden of production falls on women, as evidenced by the substantial amounts of time and labor they put into gardens. They are responsible for the second firing of the garden to dispose of refuse, and sometimes for the initial burning also. Women do most of the actual planting of taro, yams, sweet potato, manioc, the important tubers, and other staples. Men plant sugarcane, bananas, and *manap* (Pidgin: pitpit). After women plant the garden, they weed to insure unimpaired growth of crops. Such weeding is a continual and essential chore for the maintenance of the garden. Harvesting also falls largely on women, and to this extent they devote considerable time and labor over an extended period of time. Apart from cultivation of crops, women gather a variety of edible greens, leaves, stems, and insects. One social implication of this division of labor is that people do not make gardens by themselves.

Maring organize gardening units around specific kin relations and the norm that they be comprised of at least one male and one female. The stipulation results from the division of labor; the clear separation of production tasks defines and reinforces sexual identity, being its most visible expression. For Maring, gardening pairs composed of unrelated persons are a structural anomaly that is suspicious and no doubt slightly incomprehensible. Similarly, it is shameful for a person to garden alone (though this sometimes happens) because it signals an absence of kinsmen and therefore low status. A woman is urged, and generally does, make gardens with her widowed father and her own and/or husband's brothers, provided they are unmarried. Bachelors prefer to marry their sisters near to home for this reason, especially in the case of delayed exchange. Indeed, a brother conceptualizes a wife as a replacement for his sister, a view inscribed in the ideal of sister exchange and the explicit parallels clansmen often draw between wives and sisters. By way of contrast, a man is likely to make gardens with certain female kin in addition to his wife, specifically his unmarried sister or his widowed mother. Thus, during the same season, an individual participates in making several gardens and gardening pairs invariably overlap. On a more inclusive level, the compound also functions as a unit of production. Basically, the compound is a residential group composed of several families of the same clan but frequently different subclans. Clansmen from separate subclans will form a unit on the basis of matrilateral kin ties. This prefigures a point that will appear repeatedly in the ethnography: exchange in the external sphere influences the internal configuration of clan relations. The compound includes also the houses of non-agnates, especially when the processes of reaffiliation are well advanced. At the heart of the compound is a men's house which contains any number of men, on a temporary or permanent basis. Residence in the men's house is not restricted to clan members; women may enter but not sleep there.

Many productive tasks benefit from cooperation and members of the compound readily assist one another. This is especially true with respect to house construction and building of fences, rather arduous toil, and the sharing of planting material, the circulation of which insures that each family will enjoy a balanced distribution of crops in the forthcoming year. The women of the compound often work together, rotating their attention from one garden to the next. Such cooperation constitutes an exchange at the level of production that not only underwrites social relations but creates them; Maring assume this as a fact of life and practice. There is a moral obligation to help compound members that is reinforced by relations of substance.

The location of the compound is a social and moral statement about the relationships within the clan and clan cluster. At the epicenter of the clan cluster territory is the dance ground, the magic house: the public political forum that is the domain of male clan relations. Further out from this space at the center of the social universe are the gardens: the more private economic forum that is the domain of male–female relations. There is a tension or opposition between male/male relations on one hand, and male/female relations on the other. The tension is underlined by the formation of the compound itself which is frequently the product of matrilateral ties. It is also revealed in the social meaning of the location of different compounds. Some are situated close to the dance ground and male center, and thus represent spatially the integration of male/male relations. All the leading figures of the community are within easy yodeling distance. Others are situated progressively further from the center and represent the ascendancy of male/female relations. Men who live far away are morally as well as spatially distant from their fellow clansmen.

In the social economy, territory is a dimension of agnatic organization and is treated as such. Clansmen share land much the same as they share certain foods and land transfers within a clan are usually consummated routinely and fluidly. Reasons for the structure of land tenure and transfer will become evident in light of the future discussion of modes of exchange. For present purposes, it is sufficient to note that there is a hierarchy of rights conforming to the contours of the social structure, with more inclusive levels having priority over less inclusive ones. Clan interests have precedence over those of the subclan and the subclan over those of the individual. Rappaport (1967:116) is correct in his assessment that this amounts to a stewardship for both the subclan and the individual. Males have privilege in the entire estate of their clan lands by virtue of co-substance ties. However, because the cultivation of crops and animals is a link in the transmission of paternal substance, there is an inclination for individuals to claim titles to particular sites that were used by their father or grandfather. This replicates on a personal plane the continuity between a clan and its territory that is at once a sign and source of successful social reproduction. Nevertheless, clan interests supersede individual claims, making gross inequities adjustable. If an individual is strapped with insufficient land, he requests grants in perpetuity from better endowed landholders. Subclans whose numbers expand more rapidly than brother lines are ceded garden sites and entire tracts of land if necessary. Within the orbit of the clan, agnatic principle stipulates that those who share clan substance must share land (see Table 1). As land is related to substance so the serial transfer of garden sites is a vector of agnatic identity and constitutes a temporal counterpart to the spacial intermingling of garden sites. Inversely, failure to respond to requests for land undermines the clan's structure, and, according to Maring, is a forecast of its dissolution. The cultural integration of agnation and territoriality is explored more fully in chapter 3.

Second in material importance to horticulture is animal husbandry. Maring raise and domesticate to varying degrees four kinds of animals: pigs, cassowaries, chickens, and dogs. These animals are valued differentially on the basis of their role in social exchange. This valuation is most evident in the treatment accorded the different species and the extent to which they are incorporated into human society. Chickens and dogs are considered marginal and as a result are usually left to fend for themselves. Serious attention is reserved for cassowaries and pigs which are the most highly valued animals. Cassowaries are relatively rare because they do not breed in captivity and chicks are difficult to capture (Healey 1985b:154–5). Maring use the feathers as quills and

Table 1 Conveyances of land titles

Level of transfer	Number of grants	Percentage of total	Principle of transfer	Perpetuity	Percentage of total	Usufruct	Percentage of total
			Types and principles of land grants			Types of land grants	
Subclan members	490	63.7	Agnation	490	100.0	—	—
Clan members	180	23.4	Agnation	146	80.0	34	20.0
Clan cluster	78	10.0	Affinity	20	25.7	58	74.3
Members of different clusters	22	2.9	Affinity	4	18.2	18	81.8
Totals	770			660		110	

trade cassowaries to non-Maring groups. In terms of numbers, contribution to consumption, and social import, pigs are the most significant domestic animal. Pigs are the centerpiece of social exchange. Both the propitiation of the ancestor and the making of marriage ties demand their ceremonial slaughter and presentation. For this reason, pigs have preferential status in Maring society that is mirrored in their treatment, residence, and nomenclature. So pigs are given proper names to identify them; they live, sleep, and feed in the houses of their mistress (pig stalls are a major feature of women's house design); and they are treated with personal care and concern.

The number of pigs owned by a clan is a measure of wealth among the Maring as it is among other peoples of the Highlands. They compare the quality of pigs and determine relative value on the basis of several features, frequently summarized in terms of size. People maintain that larger animals are more desirable and afford greater prestige when ceremonially presented. Clansmen judge pigs suitable for exchange only after they have attained a sufficient size (by cultural standards). Small ones are considered unfit for ceremony and such offerings are likely to arouse the ire of ancestors and affines. Those who would sacrifice small animals are denigrated, often humorously, as rubbish men able to meet their obligations only in the most niggardly fashion. To insure that domestic pigs grow large, owners encourage them to forage in abandoned gardens and provide additional rations when possible.

Table 2 *Demographic structure of a pig herd*

Months	No. of pigs	Wamba nak	Wamba ank	Baka	Yondoi	Yondoi mai	No. of litters
				Size of pigs[a]			
Oct.–Nov.	82	11	24	24	14	9	6
Dec.–Jan.	91	11	20	28	17	15	4
Feb.–Mar.	90	10	16	24	21	19	2
Apr.–May	107	9	17	34	26	21	3
June–July	116	7	13	29	40	27	0
July 27	114	7	13	27	40	27	0

[a]Pig sizes: *wamba nak*, under 40 pounds; *wamba ank*, 40 to 80 pounds; *baka*, 80 to 120 pounds; *yondoi*, 120 to 160 pounds; *yondoi mai*, over 160 pounds. See Rappaport 1968:60 for similar but less comprehensive data.

Clansmen will intensify their efforts to increase the size of their pigs in preparation for ceremonial slaughter. Long-term schedules seem almost infinitely flexible, and it is not unusual for participants to reschedule a payment many months running. It is judgement of the herd's readiness that triggers the invitations to guests. Table 2 illustrates how the Kakupogai clan altered the demographic profile of their herd in anticipation of a *kaiko* (that was subsequently postponed). There is a demonstrable change in the porcine population in favor of more mature animals suitable for a presentation. Efforts to prevent sows from becoming pregnant (and thus losing their fat) reduced fertility successfully, this despite the increase in numbers. During this period clansmen put affinal payments in abeyance, sometimes by giving a nominal gift and the assurance that more would be forthcoming during the *kaiko*. Other than this, accidents, the destruction of pigs caught uprooting a garden, and pig sacrifices in times of illness accounted for the only deaths. Table 3 shows a twofold alteration in commercial traffic in pigs. Note that imports greatly exceeded exports and that there was a greater concentration on the purchase of mature pigs as the deadline approached (supposedly July 1980). With this strategy in mind, owners sold only small to middle sized pigs and retained those of any size.

Table 3 *Pig purchases*

| Months | No. of pigs bought | Size of pigs[a] | | | | | No. of pigs sold |
		Wamba nak	*Wamba ank*	*Baka*	*Yondoi*	*Yondoi mai*	
Oct.–Nov.	7	3	3	0	1	0	4
Dec.–Jan.	8	2	3	3	0	0	2
Feb.–Mar.	7	1	3	3	0	1	3
Apr.–May	9	2	1	3	3	0	0
June–July	10	0	1	3	4	2	1
Totals	41	8	11	12	8	3	10

[a] See note to Table 2.

Owners generally keep meticulous mental records where their pigs are concerned and they maintain that they consciously strive for such goals. Tuguma, for example, recall that prior to summer 1974 they attempted to produce enough large pigs to coincide with the ceremonies that would be held for men returning from contract labor. Similarly, Kauwatyi cited the ritual slaughter itself as evidence of having most successfully manipulated the pig herd in the social interest. Thus, in order to meet the ceremonial timetable clansmen try to delay affinal payments, prevent sows from becoming pregnant, and provide extra rations for the herd. All this is part and product of a calculated effort to coordinate production with ritual.

Producers employ a number of techniques to optimize the size of their pigs. Perhaps the most important is the castration of all male pigs before they are old enough to breed (at three months of age). People aver that this practice insures a larger animal with a greater proportion of fat. They note that boars are more active and aggressive than castrated males, and have less fat. Together with its effect on boar size, castration helps prevent domestic sows from becoming pregnant. The prevention of pregnancy is said to be especially important when the herd is being readied for an impending ceremony. Should it occur a considerable amount of the mother's body weight is diverted to nourishing her young. In fact, the decision to delay the *kaiko* originally scheduled for July 1980 was prompted in part by a rash of pregnancies in the herd of the largest clan. People contend that this substantially diminishes the size of the animal, thus rendering it unfit for ritual.

A major effect of castration is that producers must rely on feral pigs to impregnate domestic sows. Matings are infrequent, however, as feral pigs are relatively scarce and are likely to avoid human habitation. As important, Maring deliberately lower the chances of mating even further. They house pigs in the high region (above 4,000 feet), knowing that feral pigs are inclined to stay in the lower bush (below 3,000 feet). In addition to these measures, they use magic spells to prevent pregnancy and solicit the help of ancestors.

The effectiveness of production practices is evident in the reproductive rate of the pig population (Rappaport 1968:70) and the fact that the majority of pigs are obtained via trade in the regional exchange system. Overall, Maring are willing to sacrifice numbers for size because size is the key quality in ritual presentations. The general point is that cultural concepts and practice set the goals of production. Whether local producers meet these goals or not depends on environmental and ecological conditions, as well as the intrigues of domestic politics.

Beliefs concerning the size of ritual pigs motivate certain production practices which in turn inspire production in other areas. In particular, the suppression of the pig herd has the subsidiary effect of encouraging men to hunt for bird plumes and other items of exchange in order to obtain piglets to replenish the herd. Healey (1977) has shown that there is a coordinated regional relationship between the trade in bird plumes and pigs. In general, however, the hunting, trapping, and gathering of wild animals ranks third in material significance behind gardening and animal husbandry. Women and young boys pursue small game such as birds and insects while men hunt cassowaries, marsupials, and wild pigs, and trap eels and snakes. Food from wild animals forms only a minute part of the diet although one that people consider to be culturally important. The paucity of game reflects environmental constraints, the fact that hunters were not (at least before the advent of shotguns) very effective hunters, and food taboos which prohibit certain species of animals. While hunting is the least rewarding in terms of material benefits, it is counted the most prestigious production activity. As in other Highland societies, it is charged with social rather than material significance, being symbolically linked to warfare and manhood (see Bulmer 1968).

Exchange

Exchange in Maring society is a total social phenomena. It is a fundamental dynamic of social relations, for exchange mediates the communication between clans and/or members of distinct clans. The ubiquity of exchange makes it impossible to disengage the circulation of goods and services, a traditional staple of economic analysis, from the formation of social relations. Social exchange centers on transactions based on marriage and the practices arising therefrom. In large measure, these transactions have the express function of making a statement about the relationship between the parties to the exchange. Individuals also negotiate transactions based on their needs and ambitions. The center of gravity of such exchange is the ego-oriented network of non-agnatic ties, commerce at this level having its most direct bearing on personal fortunes. It expands an individual's social universe, and when extended to more distant communities is the first step in the construction of relations of social exchange. Individual traders are perceived as representing their clan in the sense that those who offer gifts of poor quality are imputed to belong to clans of less value.

Several types of exchange can operate simultaneously in one context insofar as they are pegged to distinct levels of social structure. Affinal payments set in motion by marital unions are always consummated as a relationship between the opposing clans. This level of involvement rests on the fact that the clan is the maximal agnatic unit, formally underwriting marriage arrangements and the concomitant flow of goods and services. That the groom plays a minor role in brideprice ceremonies reflects the nature of the exchange. On an individual plane, exchange has special significance for the principals in the marriage ceremony. This is signaled terminologically and by the fact that they offer the prestation not only on behalf of the subclan and clan but also in their own name. Insofar as structural parity is a condition of exchange (i.e., clans oppose one another) it can vary in terms of inclusivity or the levels of structure it encompasses. The effect of this hierarchy is that exchange between clans is co-occurrent with exchange on subordinate levels. Two crucial features result: first, exchange acquires different functions at different levels of the social structure; and second, a specific act of exchange can have more than one function. It is the perceived functions of the give and take which imbue it with a particular meaning or signification; and more importantly, they give rise to an understanding as to the social relations under material discussion. This understanding permits the participating actors to evaluate the prestation and (ideally) reach an unspoken agreement on the obligations that are satisfied or brought into being.

Maring make a distinction between social exchange and trade or commerce. Such commerce has a utilitarian moment. But what interests the Maring is that it permits individuals to index and create social relations on a personal level. Commerce is to the individual what social exchange is to subclan and clan; however, a trader represents his clan (being perceived as an index of the quality of its land, people, and resources) as well as himself. The result is that social exchange and commerce are inseparable and reciprocal. The extension of a trading network into a new region suggests the possibility of intermarriage while marriage ties promote and foster trade. Indeed, the extension of a man's trading network is through the affines of his affines, and the pragmatic handling of kin terms of which the Maring system is so adept (see chapter 4).

The axes along which most goods circulate are an outgrowth of affinal ties. A man usually engages in commerce with agnates of his wife, mother, sister's husband, and others. Trade relations thus imitate the pattern of intermarriage, the flow of material objects following in step with that of women. The consequence is that the degree to which two clans are intermarried is of a piece with economic interdependence; and, conversely, a clan's material concerns inflect its marriage pattern. The clan cluster is itself constituted by intermarriage and thus material exchange achieves its greatest density within its borders. My figures indicate that almost 70% (360 of 564 cases) of all transactions are within the clan cluster (cf. Healey 1985b). While this exceeds the rate of intermarriage by about 15%, it reflects the cultural concept that commerce is the means of building a personal relationship between kinsmen. Trade is one instrument through which the relationship between individuals made possible by kinship and marriage between groups acquires practical value and force.

The reins placed on exchange fabricate a zone in which the density of affinal ties promotes integration and interdependence. A man juggles

Table 4 *Structural basis of exchange relations*

Exchange relationship with agnates of	Number of axes of exchange	Number of dual axes of exchange[a]	Nature of agnatic relation		
			Father or brother of	Same sub-clan as	Same clan as
Wife	46		22	18	6
		16	9	5	2
Sister's husband	31		18	7	2
Mother	21		12	9	0
		9	6	2	1
Daughter's husband	18		9	7	2
Other	6				

[a]This heading expresses the fact that categories of affines may not be in complementary distribution. Two forms of overlap are possible given the structure of marriage practices. In sister exchange, wife's agnates and those of sister's husband are the same; similarly, this holds for mother's agnates and those of daughter's husband in the case of patrilateral second cross cousin marriage. Replication is indicated in that it is an index of strength and is related to the volume and kind of goods that are transported.

exchanges with at least three sets of affines and possibly a fourth. These encompass the agnates of his wife, his mother, both/or his sister's husband and daughter's husband. The net effect is the concentration of exchange within the limits of the marriage system. Or, to recast this in different terms, there are no formal channels for initiating exchanges with more distant affines (e.g., FFM agnates) because ideally an intermarriage should reoccur in a more immediate generation thereby renewing the original contract. The flow of goods and services between clans tends to lapse or substantially diminish after two generations in which they have failed to intermarry (the initial generation is subject to prohibition). Only special circumstances such as mutual access to scarce but valuable resources or personal friendship can sustain an axis of exchange in the absence of marriage. Under the heading of "other," Table 4 depicts just how infrequently men enjoy trade relations with more distant affines. But if marriage can be said to secure the passage for goods and services then the reverse can also be spoken for. Material transactions bridge the generation in which there is a prohibition on marriage. During this interval it serves as the functional equivalent of marriage and the exchange of women in succeeding generations directly hinges on the material flow along this axis. Should the economics be productive for both parties, the gifts given truthfully, the future exchange of women is guaranteed. Especially in the clan cluster this generates a symbiotic relationship that indefinitely perpetuates the cycle of exchange in that neither side (assuming for the sake of discussion that they might want to) could extricate itself without suffering a severe setback on both fronts. Conversely, failure to maintain economic ties is a breach of contract. Almost surely it arouses resentment, sometimes outright hostility, and forecloses the option to intermarry in the conceivable future.

While it would certainly be the best of all worlds in Maring eyes, it is usually economically unfeasible for a man to cultivate all possible affinal relations. Still, strategy dictates that he support as many as he can bear because death, migration, warfare, or some other unforeseeable event might extinguish a particular relationship and its benefits. Relationships with affines derive their impetus from three sources: the advantages gained from the exchange of agricultural land, labor, and products; the leverage that flows from access to habitats and products which are locally unavailable; and the safety secured by establishing alliances that can be tapped in case of war and that provide a place of refuge in the event of defeat. The last motive has evaporated with pacification and does not now present a lure to exchange – though this may change as violence is spreading through the Highlands again.

While specific relationships will ideally confer numerous benefits, expectations are rarely so heady and one motive is often outstanding. The geography of exchange circumscribes ideals as some goods and services are not mobile and depend on proximity for effective use (e.g., land), for others distance itself becomes an important feature (e.g., refuge). Still, men strive to consolidate as many benefits as possible in a single relationship, trade-offs being weighed with no little interest. It is, for example, quite judicious to initiate a connection that provides not only a port on a regional exchange route but refuge in the misfortune of defeat. Men carefully consider their competing interests and needs and opt for what they hope will prove a winning strategy. Ultimately, success or failure has a bearing on the future of the individual and the subclan and clan. Maring sum up this philosophy in the aphorism that "a man who makes wise exchanges is sure to have a strong name." That is, those who have profited from his work will assist him in gardening, political causes, and making exchanges.

Indigenous economic concepts and their conjunction in practice crystalize in decisions concerning which exchange relationships are the best bet. These decisions reflect a man's current or anticipated needs in the acquisition of desired goods and services. More than a calculus of simple quantity, their intention is to endorse existing avenues of exchange or inaugurate new ones. Given that production and exchange are oriented by culturally defined goals, needs are determined by three forces: ecological constraints on cultivation, the structure of production, and the geography of the regional exchange systems. Because clans are spread over a variety of ecological zones which favor the growth of some products and militate against others, there is a differential availability of prized goods. Some clans, for example, are rich in products requiring high altitude terrain and poor in those that flourish in the low altitude. More crucial is the way in which production manufactures needs. Recall that practices used in pig husbandry are geared to the ritual exchange cycle and that this severely retards the expansion of the herd. Evidence indicates that this scarcity is filled by an exogenous source – many pigs arriving via foreign exchange. The structure of production had the subsidiary effect of stimulating the accumulation of valuables (e.g., bird plumes or fur) which men may barter for pigs. With these economic conditions in mind, men often choose to maintain relations with affines who have access to sources of pigs or who reside in clan territories known to favor pig husbandry. Those situated on a regional exchange route along which bird plumes travel are also good candidates. Or, a man will fuel exchanges with those who can extend grants of land. Within the orbit of marriage exchange and the possibilities for commerce it provides, decisions about which relations are to be kept active and which are to remain dormant devolves on the role of exchange as an intermediary between consumption and production.

Movement of goods and services dominates certain practices. These practices are dimensions of the structure of exchange. They provide the ostensible motive for the transaction and the social stage upon which events unfold. In line with the organization of the agnatic units, practices which feature relations between clans and subclans take precedence over those that concern individuals only. Social exchange is founded either on payments that arise directly from intermarriage or those that come into play once the link is established. Such exchanges represent compensation, that is, payment for the transfer of procreative substance or material, nurturance, and more generally the complex of relations generated therefrom. The ethnography enlarges the received idea of exchange insofar as it encompasses not only the transfer of women but the complementary distribution of reproductive goods and services. It is the most visible outcropping of an ethnographic definition of exchange, one that understands this structure in indigenous terms. Transactions on the individual level also serve as contexts for material flow. And, with the modernization of the economy, their frequency climbs with each passing year. Exchanges of this caliber are casual except for a careful inspection of the merchandise and negotiation of exchange value. These relations demand a minimal amount of planning and cooperation and can occur at virtually any time, even a chance encounter. Nevertheless, both strategy and convenience urge that men coordinate personal ventures with social exchange, and they often occur in the same context.

Maring have a category of vital wealth or valuables (*mungoi*) which they contrast to subsistence goods. Valuables have preeminence because they are not merely consumable goods, but those used in social reproduction. The structure of demand, deployment of means of production, and strategies of exchange all reflect the ranking. For example, a desired aim of exchange is to convert subsistence goods into luxuries and valuables, especially pigs and money. In this respect, people often value the ethnographer as a means for converting subsistence goods into those of superior categories. Clansmen concur that pigs are the most important valuable (though certainly in recent years money seems to be gaining ground). This valuation derives from the fact that pork mediates all social exchanges between affines and between the clan and its ancestors. Women sometimes say the value of pig derives from the time and energy and care they devote to husbandry. The two viewpoints are of course one, and whatever else may comprise the prestation, it is judged altogether unsatisfactory unless donors include generous portions of pork.

Trade between individuals occurs as the participating parties see fit. The one exception is the trade in pigs which, in so much as it threatens to subvert the prevailing system of distinctions, is subject to special stricture. Recall that production practices induce men to acquire pigs from foreign sellers, and that this runs counter to the convention of reserving pigs for affinal prestations. There is thus an emergent contradiction between the manner in which men procure pigs and the practices in which they use them. But the symbolic opposition between raw and cooked pig resolves the contradiction. Between individuals a commerce in live pigs is encouraged whereas cooked pigs are banned; conversely, in social exchange with affines cooked pigs are presented and live ones are precluded. One implication is that the presentation of roast pork in an invariant index of the nature of the exchange and is understood this way.

Pig and cassowary are the only meats whose apportionment is a public act and the prerogative of the clan/subclan. Cassowaries while highly valued are relatively scarce and few ethnographers have even witnessed its consumption. More important are the pigs that men sacrifice in ritual to compensate ancestors and affines. Broadcast of the sacrifice in concert with the prohibition on private use of pork effectively socializes its consumption. The apportionment of pig rests on the orientation of the sacrifice: if clansmen direct it to the spirits (*rawa mai*) who inhabit the lower territorial and conceptual strata then only the kinship system and the size of the prestation offered circumscribe its disembursement. In the latter instance, clansmen share pig and strategically allocate some to affines. Conversely, if they dedicate pig to spirits of the high territory (*rawa mugi*) then this limits consumption to the clan and subclan.

Most domestic pigs are killed to meet marriage payments and the set of compensations that ensues. Clansmen define themselves as those who partake in the same bridal pork (*ambra konch, ambra koins*), and use the phrase to refer to this dimension of clan formation. Recipients of gifts of pork circulate the share they receive to other members of their clan and also to non-agnates who live in their men's house. If quantity permits, non-agnates will in turn give a part of their share to their own agnates and so the distribution continues along ordained lines. It is significant and indicative of closer ties that co-residents receive their share before agnates who have taken up residence with another clan and do not participate in the functions of their natal one. This ordering gives substance to reports of their distance and ultimately distance to their ties of substance.

In summary, Maring economic relations are of a piece with the formation of social units and the development and use of kin ties. There is no separation of economy and society other than that imposed by the analyst in the art of translation. The study of the economic is the study of the social system in terms of its material order; for the value of objects and services, their movement in the social field, and their production on the natural one derive from their coordinates within the social structure just as the social structure is reproduced in time through the operations the clan performs with these objects. Indeed, women, land, pigs, and taro will appear at every turn, this insofar as people's true and only interest is the reproduction of a way of life.

2 Substance and social exchange

Gou explained: Women come to our line and sometimes men. The women have children and old people pass away. It has been this way since before the time of my grandfather and his ancestors. That is why the clan is like this land – and we are one people who share land and pork.

The statement captures the social fact that though the clan (or line) undergoes constant change, it preserves its continuity and identity. The people of today share a consubstantiality with their ancestors that neither death nor marriage exchange can ever efface. Without trying to make a statement about the principles of social life, indeed simply trying to explain the world with the concepts at hand, the wording calls our attention to the functions of marriage exchange and the possibility of recruiting new members through birth and reaffiliation, the incorporation of death into the clan's lineality, and the virtues of sharing. To explain why people are what they are, the primary cultural categories need be invoked.

The oppositions of Maring society

Maring society is founded on three principal oppositions: that between men and women, the ancestor spirits and their living descendants, and sharing and exchange. These cultural oppositions give rise to the primary generative schemes for structuring practices and interpreting events. They provide the cultural scheme for the structure of social organization.

The first opposition between male and female is pervasive. Everything from kinds of plants and spiritual characteristics to psychological dispositions and types of behavior are imbued with meaning in terms of the opposition. There are discrete male and female lines of substance and the transmission of patriclanship through one sex. Society is reproduced through the distinction yet complementarity of male and female, and Maring apprehend their world in terms of the separation of sexes (e.g., to divide the domestic from political) and their union (e.g., the making of a garden). There are, in different words, cultural principles of relationship between specific oppositions and domains of social practice.

The critical feature of gender relations is the alternation between differentiation in the act of production and reproduction and complemen-

35

tary or unity in its product. What this means is that the opposition between male and female is an objectification of one moment of this alternation. The other moment is objectified as one of sexual duality. This generates two modes of conceptualization: the lineal continuity of the clan is defined in terms and through relations among men, whereas the clan's reproduction is defined in terms of relations among men and women, such as those involving exchange or complementary action. Maring ideology takes two corresponding forms: a referential ideology which depicts the clan in all male terms, and a pragmatic ideology which recounts the mobilization of cross-sex relations.

The second opposition divides the cultural universe into the domain inhabited by living clansmen and that inhabited by spirits of clansmen. The opposition recognizes that even in the event of mortality, and thus the separation of kinsmen, the clan/subclan/family maintain their continuity over time. This is embodied in the concept of personal existence after death, and the corollary belief that the soul that transcends death is the repository of a person's personality, will, and wisdom. It represents a cultural negation of the death, decay, and natural transformation of matter presupposed and entailed by the natural cycle.

The final opposition between sharing and exchange is used to define the kinship universe. It divides the world into those who share reproductive resources and those who exchange them. Thus, clansmen share pork when they sacrifice to the ancestor spirits, and exchange pork with other clans. In this way, the opposition represents the dual dimensions of clan and subclan reproduction: its internal reproduction via perpetuation of a shared identity, and its alliance to other clans via the exchange of reproductive materials. Sharing and exchange correspond and stand in reciprocal relation to types of people, ritual participation, modes of cooperation, spatial location of houses, social manners, ways of speaking and addressing people, and much more. As such, division of those who share from those who exchange is overdetermined and generally transparent. Ambiguities which can and do arise are always resolved through transactions with ancestors and affines.

Importantly, the opposition between sharing and exchange is of a different order than the other oppositions. The opposition between male/female and ancestor spirits/clansmen represent the cultural appropriation of nature – of the realities of gender and death respectively; the opposition between sharing and exchange is culture's appropriation of its own activities to create kinds or classes of people. It is recognition that the clan persists in spite of its continual change through the cultural valuation and valorization of practical activity.

In other words, the clan reproduces itself in history; the cultural definition of the concept and sense of limits provides basis for defining the clan's limits in practice. To paraphrase Sahlins: social relations are signs that are set in various and contingent relations according to people's instrumental purposes – purposes that are socially defined even as they are individually variable. Social relations have a functional value in projects for action which subject them to review and reformulation, from which arise unprecedented forms and meanings. Clansmen use and experience social relations as inseparable from their encounter with others and the world. Hence, their engagement with social relations is itself a valuation, and potential revaluation, of these relations (1981:5–6).

Substance and social exchange

The interrelationship between principles of co–substance and social exchange is the principal dynamic of Maring social organization. It constitutes the very foundation of social relations and practices and their ideological representations, the repercussions of this interrelationship subtly influencing even those practices that at first glance look far removed. Analysis of Maring social organization thus begins with the dimensions of social exchange and co–substance, and a paradigm for their interplay. My objective is to describe the elements of social identity, including the dominant images, spiritual qualities, and mythological bearings. All foster the coexistence of lineal and lateral dimensions to clan/subclan formation. Consideration of these two dimensions reveals the same enduring theme: social relatedness arises from the principles of co–substance as they articulate with prevailing modes of exchange. Clansmen express this relatedness in terms of siblingship and other forms of practical knowledge. The revitalization and transmission of substance, and hence social identity, is connected to two cycles of social exchange. The first centers on the clan and the reproduction of clanship through ritual transactions with the ancestor spirits. The exchange knits an interdependency between the clan, its land, physical and material reproduction, and clan ancestors. The other type of exchange centers on marriage and the attendant set of compensation payments which follow. Because both cycles of exchange are integrated and coordinated, neither could operate in the absence of its counterpart; a transformation or fluctuation in one cycle instigates a response in the other, people's strategies often capitalizing on this interdependency.

The circulation of male and female substances, as embodied in people, goods, and services, defines and motivates these circuits of exchange. And it is not only the direct passage of substance between people – through procreation – which engenders relatedness, exchange transforms every instance of social reproduction into an occasion of social definition. Making new relationships, pruning old ones, and especially managing existing ties are based on gifts of labor, cultigens, tools, knowledge, etc. used in producing the social body. In this respect, the conventions, preconditions, and pragmatic manipulations of gift-giving infuse it with meaning for personal and clan reproduction. As my friend, Kaiya, explained to me in order to impress its virtues, "Giving is to my line as money is to yours, our thoughts and customs are made for them."

Principles of substance

Concepts of procreative substance as a means of organizing social relations seem ubiquitous in the New Guinea Highlands, not to mention many coastal societies. Maring concepts fall squarely within this tradition; available accounts show they most clearly resemble those of the Daribi (Wagner 1967; 1972) and the Melpa (Strathern 1972) and I have tried to organize my presentation to facilitate comparison. The relative strength of this resemblance probably reflects ethnographic more than actual conditions, for Wagner and Strathern alone have published anything approaching comprehensive accounts. There appear to be certain marked regional differences especially with respect to mechanisms of transmission. Only further and more detailed ethnography can disclose the nature of this pattern.

For clarity, it is necessary to situate indigenous concepts of substance within the flow of practical concerns and interests. The process of written analysis has the makings of an ethnographic distortion in which all of culture appears as objectively codified in practice as it does on paper. But principles of co-substance seldom rise to consciousness and there is no compelling reason why they should do so. It is a false intellectualism to conceive them as abstract or well-articulated formulas ready to furnish clansmen with a set of conceptual guides or blueprints for behavior. More accurately, they are premises about the nature of social relations and the formation of groups, subject neither to speculation nor revision. For all practical purposes there is nothing to discuss or contemplate, except for those who wish to reflect critically on the makings of their own society. The embodied state of substance enters as a given social condition and surfaces, if at all, during discussions of food or sexual conduct, situations in which bodily substances pass between boundaries. One of the clearest occasions for the expression of concepts that are both unquestionable, and, because they are tied to sexuality, unspeakable, is the profanity hurled during adultery accusations. In essence, cultural beliefs about substance are unfailingly contextualized (in the non-trivial sense of context) and the reader should bear in mind that local knowledge thereof is inextricably embodied in practice.

Principles of co-substance are embodied in social relations, actions, and objects built up in terms of such principles. They appear as a sense of kinship, a comprehension that a particular food is taboo, a certain tract of land is worth fighting for, or a woman from a specific clan is marriageable. This understanding is not given over to conceptualization or awareness of underlying connections. It is a disposition to act along particular lines, favored by an analogical awareness which may, for example, equate rice and taro because of their similarities in color and texture. The different practical embodiments of substance occur in separate practices which, for most practical purposes, are self-contained. There is thus no way for clanspeople to relate them to one another systematically; to explain, for instance, the linkage between food taboos and burial procedures. But the linkages exist and certain informants will acknowledge this systematicity if the ethnographer points it out. Certainly for the Maring, one of the few contexts in which the interconnection between practices had practical value was in their interaction with me.

Equally, the diverse fields of practice, from land tenure to burial ceremonies, are more or less integrated because they are all generated from the same principles of substance. The coordination of principles and a degree of systematicity appears in practice as a sense of what should or should not be done. Maring do not have explicit mastery of co-substance principles or how such principles determine the nature of kinship. These principles are what people are; these actions are what people do; and these objects are what objects are. A person is socialized when that person possesses, in its incorporated state, the system of generative schemes ordering the world and organizing practice. To understand practical acts, ethnography must thus, as Bourdieu (1977:123–4) recommends:

reconstruct the principle generating and unifying all practices, the system of inseparable cognitive and evaluative structures which organizes the vision of the world in accordance with the objective structure of a determinate state of

the social world: this principle is nothing other than *socially informed body* with
. . . all its senses, that is to say, not only the traditional five senses – which
never escape the structuring action of social determinisms – but also the sense
of necessity and the sense of duty, the sense of direction and the sense of reality, the sense of balance and the sense of beauty, common sense and the sense
of the sacred, tactical sense and . . . the sense of propriety, the sense of humor
and the sense of absurdity, moral sense and the sense of practicality, and so on
[Bourdieu's emphasis].

The very nature of substance is that it is inseparably and simultaneously of the body and thinking subject. It represents a Maring refusal to elevate the distinction between mind and body into an
ontological postulate. What this implies, and the point that cannot
possibly be overemphasized, is that the Maring concept of subjectivity
and the self does not perceive thought and praxis as contrasting or
opposed. The concept of thought as a discrete category, and the belief
that there is an invisible mind that is separate from the body, are things
which the Maring believe they have learned through contact with
Europeans.

In an egalitarian society, like the Maring, where differences in
wealth, political power, and knowledge are important but rarely decisive, it is hardly surprising that sexuality is one of the main generative
schemes for structuring social relations. The opposition between male
and female is used in very different contexts spanning many separate
domains. The same is true for the opposition between sharing and
exchange, and to a lesser extent the opposition between the living and
the dead. The wide variety of uses of these schemes makes them practical and manageable, and enriches the possibilities of meaning since one
application of a scheme simply means that all other applications remain
virtual. Actors may retrieve them when contemplating alternative
courses of action, or for other reasons. By economizing on its generative schemes, Maring culture increases semiotic possibilities because
the repeated use of a single scheme produces different levels of relationship, i.e., relations between relations. This means that the various contexts structured by the same opposition can remain implicit, such
knowledge contributing to a particular situation only by way of creating another pragmatic strategy.

The logic and economy of generative schemes impresses itself on the
ethnographer in several ways. The first is that in separate contexts the
same object may have different complements and therefore different
and/or opposed properties. So the following equations are all used:
men are to animals as women are to plants; men are to plants that grow

above the ground (pandanus) as women are to plants that grow below the ground (tubers); and men are to cooked tubers as women are to raw tubers. This could be extended further to include the fact that men are to cooked tubers used in ceremony as women are to cooked tubers eaten domestically. That the same opposition between male and female can appear on distinct structural levels simultaneously creates integration and separation, distinction on one level is a commonality on another and more specific level. For example, plants are female but some plants are male.

The logic and economy of generative schemes also appears in the fact that abstract knowledge about practice has no practical value. For a Maring to know about the relationship between the equations cited above is esoteric knowledge. I have seen this clearly in terms of Peng, an intellectually gifted person and informant. He sometimes seizes upon such knowledge in the course of our talks, and uses it in conversation with others. But, few people take notice or even recognize this as knowledge. They sense that it has no implications beyond the context of the discourse. It is significant that ethnographers and informants, such as Peng, who possess the ability to objectify practices, are drawn to one another. Such informants entice ethnographers into giving a lopsided account of practice which unduly stresses its intellectual dimension; their reflective understanding of their own culture appeals to the intellectualism of anthropology.

Procreation and substance

Beliefs about the process of conception provide a favorable point of departure for describing concepts of substance. People know that children are the product of coitus and there is little mystery surrounding the respective roles of men and women. Conception occurs when semen commingles with female blood. Both men and women are said to carry the child, recognition that each has a complementary and essential part in conception. "To carry" a child is to assume responsibility for it, and the phrase is a statement of parenthood. Conception progresses as semen envelopes the blood in the womb and binds it (*nukum mangla*, blood-tying). The adhesive qualities of semen working within the enclosed space of the uterus effect this binding process. Nobody feels a single insemination is sufficient to induce conception. Binding takes anywhere from four to eight weeks depending on the frequency of intercourse and what steps parents take to bolster their procreative fluids. People view the speed of conception and the close spacing of children as a sign of fertility, and relate them to gender identity.[1]

Extramarital trysts do not cause paternity problems unless the culprits protract the affair over many months. When a couple engineers such an affair and a child results serious problems of heredity ensue, not to mention the real possibility of violence. The child's paternity may be mixed, both the offended husband and the adulterer contributing substance, or it may be the fruit of one man exclusively. This is determined by observing if the child bears a facial resemblance to its legitimate father and/or the adulterer. Such judgement may turn on the interdependency between the parties. If, for example, the relationship is between true siblings, the case might be quietly disposed of, the husband claiming the child as his alone, both to save the relationship and face. In any event, the adulterer pays compensation (in 1979, 3 pigs and 200 kina) and the child belongs to the offended husband. If a child is illegitimate, a woman should feed it from her left breast as public notice of their moral failing.

Maring make a distinction between the inside and outside of the human body, this generative scheme applying to both physiology and psychology in the widest sense. Their epistemology associates the inside with truth, the essence of an idea, action, or object, and the outside with the aura of falsehood. The interior body is the true or genuine article, while interchanges with the external world always involve an element of uncertainty and danger, such as pollution. The interior divides into two kinds of morphology: that which is solid or hard (*anc*) and that which is soft or fluid (*nak*). The first encompasses the bone and muscles of an organism; the latter includes blood, semen, mucuses, oils, and bone marrow. The fluid or soft substances reside in the two major circulatory networks. The first is the *nukum kekla* or blood system which includes the principal arteries as well as the smaller vessels extending to the appendages. In local theory, blood does not circulate throughout the body as part of a natural physiological process. Circulation occurs when people bleed, eat pandanus nuts, or agitate the blood by rubbing their skin with stinging nettles. The second

[1] Some men say that the fertility of one's partner is a source of eroticism. It is evidence that the man and woman exemplify their respective sexes with opposition between them at its zenith; hence, union entails greater risk, augmenting sexual excitement. Repeated insemination, however, is necessary not only to fasten the blood but to feed the embryo once it begins to develop. A woman's vagina is said, metaphorically, to eat a man's penis; indeed, in one myth a vagina armed with teeth does precisely this and later gives birth to fruits and vegetables (cf. Buchbinder and Rappaport 1976). The homology between sex and food – that is, between the intake of substance in two of its principal manifestations – is a recurring theme in humor, art, and myth.

and independent circuit carries *imbana* or grease, that is, the viscous, semi-transparent fluids that the body harbors and occasionally expels through certain orifices.[2]

The central physiological difference between men and women is that men's genitals are connected to the *imbana* system whereas those of women are connected to the *nukum* system. Vaginas bleed and penises issue semen. When men engage in sex, the stimulation funnels the grease dispersed throughout the body into the penis. This accounts for its swelling and rigidity during intercourse and its relaxation following ejaculation. A man's failure to have an erection or ejaculate indicates that he has not accumulated enough grease.[3] Ejaculation drains a man's *imbana* system and consequently his skin becomes slack and then recovers in due time, especially if he eats meat. The effects of intercourse are cumulative, so the skin of young men is taut and sleek and that of old men hangs wantonly from their bones. This creates a tension that is visibly played out in sexual relations: young men desire women but want to avoid frequent sex whereas older men frequent women but with an ebbing sexuality. Men's fear about exhausting their bodily substances, or, more consciously, their strength, is one reason wives are usually younger than their husbands. Given these beliefs about the human body, more than one ejaculation during intercourse is thought risky, despite being a sign of male virility and power; and local gossip reports that it is more likely to occur in illicit affairs.

The womb is the one place where people allow blood and grease to conjoin[4] and coitus is the means of bringing them together. This initiates an intricate process built on the crucial though always implicit distinction between *conception*, the primary union of male and female substances; *development*, the process whereby they foster a child's growth; and *transmission*, the inheritance of and ability to transmit substance. Blood and semen play distinct roles in the conception of the

[2] The *imbana* network corresponds in most respects to what we would call the lymphatic system.

[3] When a wife is angry at her husband because he has not had sex with her she may accuse him of masturbation. The not too subtle implication is that rather than using his grease to produce children, thereby increasing the strength of his family, subclan, and clan, and incidentally, the prestige of his wife, he squanders it narcissistically. I might add that the sexual shortcomings of others were always shorter than those of my informants, and that everyone I talked to claimed to know about sexual problems only secondhand.

[4] During these menses women should not prepare food for fear that some of their blood may inadvertently (or deliberately) trickle onto the food and contaminate it. By the same token, Maring look on the consumption of blood-sucking insects as a kind of cannibalism, and shudder at the habits of coastal people whom they believe are uninhibited in their dietary preferences.

child creating specific organs and external features, as well as the separate network of vessels containing them. The blood of the mother, once bound by semen, forms the bones, the musculature, and the other hard tissue. This plus the synthesis of the blood vessels occur irrespective of the sex of the fetus. Once the conceptual phase has run its course, a mother feeds her baby by passing milk through her umbilical cord. This continues until birth whereupon the midwife (usually a sister-in-law) severs the cord and the infant starts to feed directly from the breast. The development of bone, muscle, and blood stems from the nutritive properties of milk. Speakers use the term umbilical cord in several contexts to suggest an essential attachment, especially one mediated by women (e.g., matrilateral kin tie).[5] While a father's semen binds the blood and creates the vessels of the *imbana* network regardless of the sex of the child, it conceives the genitals, facial and genital hair, and countenance only in the male. In the developmental phase, repeated inseminations nourish the male child and create the distinctive male features: greater size and musculature, deeper voice, oratorical propensity, superior intelligence, etc. People believe that failure to produce a male child, or to produce one that is unmanly, is due either to insufficient introduction of semen or an external force, like sorcery, which can block its effect.

In a sense, women create the fundamental person, with the aid of male semen of course, and men supplement their effort to produce a male child. Men have the essential humanness of women plus additional qualities which make them superior. Maring myths, dreams, and fantasies depict men as affixed women, not women as castrated men, a Western image. In one myth, a woman bathing in a stream turns into a man when an eel enters her vagina and transmutes into a penis of extraordinary proportions as well as origin. Naturally, she assumes the roles, stature, and bearing of a man. Men express sexual fears in dreams when they encounter women, living solitary in the forest, who are incipient hermaphrodites. These are but two more transparent expressions of a refrain in which women become men through an addition of socio-physical features that properly belong to males. I stress this imagination to cast light on the fact that the perpetual oscillation between male and female modalities, the language and practices of sexual segregation and conjunction, and the uses of

---

[5] The mother or midwife hides the umbilical cord and placenta both to prevent men from seeing them and to keep harmful spirits that lurk in the woods from stealing these liminal organs, and using them to harm the child. Usually they are buried or tucked into the hollow of a tree.

this generative scheme have conceptual and psychic roots in the indigenous view of procreation.[6]

Table 5 *Relations of substance*

Process	Male child	Female child
Conception	Blood and semen	Blood and semen
Development	Semen and milk	Milk
Inheritance	Blood and semen	Blood and milk
Transmission	Semen	Blood

Semen, blood, and milk participate rather differentially in the process of procreation, and this has profound implications for the unfolding of social relations. The primary division is along sexual lines as this spearheads a wealth of further distinctions.

While the process of conception is the same for siblings of either sex differences occurs in subsequent phases. In contrast to his sister, a brother develops through the intercession of both parents, semen and milk acting cooperatively. These differences between brother and sister are played out in notions of physical appearance, personality, and attachment. Thus a woman's physique, temperament, attitudes, etc., will resemble her mother and maternal grandmother. Kibitzers at a trial, for example, will often stretch their imaginations to trace the illicit actions of a daughter back to her mother, even if the latter is seemingly virtuous. Equally, a father's character is visited on his sons, and people find same sex siblings with divergent deportment to be incongruous.

An interesting example is Kama who is an industrious man with a keen political mind and an eloquent sense of timing which someday will carry him to government office. People praise his judgement, honesty, generosity, and views which are penetrating yet delivered in a modest, almost self-effacing style. His eldest brother, Row, is conversely boisterous, ill-mannered, and a compulsive thief. He has spent a turn in jail and been spared further incarceration only because Kama has made restitution on his behalf. After another court hearing where Row was again convicted, this time for stealing a shirt, post-mortem discussion centered on how two true brothers could possibly be so different. Suggested hypotheses were that the two men were of different parents or that a sorcerer had interfered with Row's mother while she was pregnant with him or perhaps had even implanted the child.

[6] Maring associate "Sepik people" with the practice of introducing semen into young boys via oral intercourse to spur growth; and even if the practice occasions heartfelt horror, they appreciate its logic and entertain a certain fascination about its effects.

45

Maternal and paternal substance generate not only the socio-physical character of a child but its spiritual qualities, which develop over a person's lifetime. This accords with the cultural premise that these qualities are central to the social identity of an individual, and that the construction of this identity is an ongoing process. Volition, cognition, intentionality, reason, etc., – the wisdoms that set humans apart from and above nature – are not inherent human propensities. Rather, procreation culturally transmits them, a mother passing her attributes to her daughter and a father to his son. They then blossom with socialization, especially language-learning and the rites of passage in which ancestors convey knowledge to descendants. The concept of *nomane* embodies these qualities, it embraces the social sentience of an individual and practice itself, and speakers may use it to mean social essence, belief, custom, or culture.[7] The implantation of *min* which occurs during early stages of a pregnancy (presumably after the sex of the child is determined although informants are vague and indifferent about the precise point) follows the same lines of transmission: males inherit from their father and females from their mother. *Min* is the life-force or spirit being which dwells in a person's body during their life (although it departs temporarily in dreaming). As a result of patrilineal transmission, the individual *min* of clansmen derives from a common source and is thus a salient point of clan identity.

The differential inheritance of spiritual qualities is one limb of a body of relations based on the principle of sexually segregated lineality. As long ago as 1949, Levi-Strauss noted, though few took note, that in New Guinea societies there is "a differentiation of status between brother and sister, the brother following the paternal line and the sister the maternal line" (1969:465–6). His observation fits the Maring material to a T, for males and females transmit different substances from one generation to the next. From a sibling perspective: a brother inherits the blood of his mother and the semen of his father but can transmit only semen to his sons; his sister inherits only her mother's blood but transmits it to both her sons and daughters. The result is two descending lines of substance that form a dual pattern of heredity. The lineal flow of substances is entirely asymmetrical. A father's co-substance tie to his daughter, and ultimately her tie to his clan, is weaker than a mother's tie to her son and thus his relationship

---

[7] When a male child reaches his teens he undergoes a kind of communion service in which he eats the ears of a ritual pig so he might hear the talk of ancestor spirits more clearly. Informal instruction (chiefly by an initiated father and senior males of the subclan) in the clan's customs and history often accompany the ritual. Details of these teachings range from tales of sorcery and heroism to specification of preferred marriage partners.

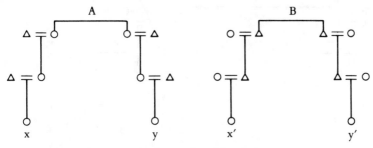

Figure 3 Relationships stemming form male and female ties

to her natal clan. Virilocal residence and the practice of burying women on the land of their husband's clan expresses the relative weakness of the father–daughter bond. A son inherits not only his father's semen but his mother's blood which creates a co-substance link with his mother's natal clan. In more specific terms, he will be of one blood (*nukum rungyi*) with his mother's brother, and the enduring significance of this relation flows from that connection. Observe also that the two modes of connection differ in scope and power: men may be related (by blood) through women but women may not be related (by semen) through men. Examine Figures 3 and 4.

In frame A the rules of relationship decree that x and y are of one blood; this is given voice in the reciprocal use of sibling terminology. In B, neither blood nor semen affiliate x' and y' directly, that is in the sense of inheritance, though they are of course members in the same patriclan.[8] If women were substituted as the connecting link in the first ascending generation x' and y' need bear no relationship whatever. Were I to carry out a mirror program in frame A and substitute men the effect would only be to transmute the relation from one of maternal to paternal substance.

Another crown of this arrangement of bloodlines is its powers of integration. A simple dispersal of marriages will in two generations forge extensive ties among several clans. Examine the following pattern which is common, especially as marriage practices promote it.

Two women born of separate clans can establish a blood bond between two sets of siblings who are members of yet two further unrelated lines. So do female cousins in the first ascending generation link x and y and their brothers and sisters from clans D and E respectively. Moreover, one exchange sequence of this sort binds persons from all four clans shown inasmuch as individuals s through z are all related by

---

[8] Clan sisters also use sibling terms. However, the application of such terms across clan lines has a different instrumental value.

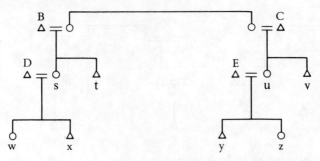

Figure 4 Bloodlines stemming from the marriage of two sisters into different patriclans

blood. Where clan boundaries insulate the flow of semen, bloodlines wind like garden paths across the boundaries that delimit clans. Blood is like a trace element charting the practice of exchange and relationship, and thus the see-sawing of alliances so familiar to the political and economic history of any clan.

The passage of substance begets more than filial networks, for the two descending lines of substance do not produce the same type of social relatedness. Maring fasten the transmission of semen, in contrast with blood, to the concept and principle of agnation. All male clansmen share and convey to their sons the paternal substance inherited from the clan's ancestors. While the material flow of semen is always between individuals, as part and product of procreation, it derives from a common source. That Maring clans archtypically descend from two or more brothers expresses this fact. Brothers, having one father, epitomize the co-substance bond, so it follows according to cultural logic that all of their descendants will bear the same relation. One big-man, trying to impress this point upon me, struck at it this way: "All of my clansmen since the time of the ancestors have but one grease and today we may be called 'men of one grease.'" The insulated flow of semen defines the patriclan in reproductive terms thereby differentiating it in both past and present terms. The composition of the terms for male substance reflect this patrilineality, the inseparability of kinship and descent (to fall back on the argot of anthropology). Semen may be called *yu kai wunga, yu kai imbana,* and an assortment of other names usually having a strong iconic motivation (e.g., the clear viscous sap which seeps out of certain trees). *Yu kai* means men-base/root, it signifies that the men in question claim common roots or origin, and speakers use this term to refer to the clan. The origin myths of autochthonous or indigenous clans relate that clan ancestors emerged, like plants, out of a hole in the ground. Such myths underline the founding relationship between landedness, gardening, and agnation, locating

48

them at the birth of clanship, and thus culture itself. *Wunga* refers to branching, the point at which the limbs of a tree fork out in different directions. Certainly this is an apt metaphor to describe the process of procreation. *Imbana* denotes grease, the substance which flows in the *imbana* system. Thus terms for semen convey the notion that male substance is shared and transmitted by all clansmen and is the basis of their consubstantial identity. Insofar as these terms are rooted in land, vegetable growth, and grease they engage a whole universe of other relationships and help create the creativity of social life.

Mythology of social exchange

Certain myths of origin provide an excellent introduction to exchange cycles, for they place the gift at the heart of social reproduction, and more the birth of culture itself. Clanspeople consider such myths to be factual in form if not in substance and classify them apart from tales of imaginary beings and happenings. They are the social recollection of portentous events and have a perceived historical presence. For example, they may be cited in legal disputes, most appropriately in litigation over land title. That until recently Maring kept these myths secret is an indication of their eminence, and more generally the significance they attach to origins. I should make it clear that variation abounds in myths of origin to the point where it is often impossible to tell whether two myths are simply variants or altogether different. Further, given creativity and the evolution it fosters, it is unreasonable to expect to find lines of demarcation. Narrators have discretion to edit myths to serve their purpose or fancy, emphasizing aspects which seem apropos and deleting or downplaying others. In addition, as myths of origin are usually related in terms of specific clans there tend to be regional variants which stress certain locations, themes, events, etc., and let others lie fallow.

I have chosen to relate the following myth because, more than others, it concisely assembles many structurally crucial elements. My intention here is not to discover the myth's hidden meaning but rather the cultural knowledge or presuppositions which lie behind it.

A man traveling from Hagen [an appellation used to describe the region to the southwest] arrived at the water Yimi, a river running along the valley floor. In the distance he spied a woman's fire which glowed like a star and lured him. He traveled towards this brightness over barren ground stopping to rest at various points along the route. When he discovered the woman, who was living alone at the place that is now called Kiama, he suggested that she follow him home. But she protested saying that she would agree to marry him only on the condition that he settled here [she pointed to the barren territory with her digging stick]. The man wavered, however, noting that there was no food to eat and no women for his brothers to marry. The woman retorted that her sisters would marry the man's brothers but first they must make a garden. So he went down to the lower bush and gathered some wild taro, bananas, and pitpit, and after he cleared and burnt the land [following her instructions] she did the planting. When the garden was sown the man invited his "tamboo line" [her father and brother] to a feast in which they ate taro and pig. Yet, the land remained infertile, the transplanted cultigens grew poorly and disease claimed many pigs. The man, fearing that his ancestors were angry at being abandoned, sacrificed a pig in their honor. During the ceremony he called out their names in a strong voice and they responded immediately by migrating to his new homeland. Soon after, the pigs thrived, the taro came up bountifully, and his brothers joined him. [The myth then goes on to relate how the married couple had three sons who went separate ways after a dispute over the owner-ship of a *komba* tree (pandanus) that led to bloodshed.]

Condensation, economy of style, and straightforward elegance seem to characterize Maring mythology. This myth is no exception, encod-ing an entire theory of social organization and a model for its replica-tion. It depicts exchange, and specifically the gift of food, as the basis of culture. The circulation of objects is the means of perpetuating a way of life, a realization of the social order at the level of concrete distinctions. Consider that land becomes a source of social reproduc-tion only after a sacrificial offering solicits the assistance of the man's ancestors. Their intercession is responsible for transforming wild plants into cultigens and once barren soil into life-giving earth. The gift persuades them to abandon their old homeland for the promise of their descendants. Similarly, and in a different modality, the gift con-summates the marriage between man and woman by forging a link be-tween him and his in-laws.

The myth locates food, epitomized by the prestation of pork and taro, at the center of exchange and thus social reproduction. They are the instrument of mediation that bridges the oppositions, the gifts which repay in kind, and so the means by which clansmen implement their programs to initiate and sustain relations with ancestors and affines. Insofar as both modes of social exchange are both oriented towards social reproduction they have the same final value, as the nar-rative continuity of the myth illustrates. Women provide the power of procreation in the double sense of birth and tillage, the ancestral spirits provide for the well-being and fecundity of man, land, and beast.

By virtue of its dramatic presentation, the myth also encodes a theory of social transformation, the process which makes changes in

well-being

man + woman $----\rightarrow$ lineality $----\rightarrow$ social reproduction

fertility

Figure 5 Male/female complementarity

clan identity a cultural possibility with precedent in the genesis of the clan itself. Note that migration, the *sine qua non* of reaffiliation, initiates all the social fireworks, not the least of which is the advent of the gift. In fact, migration is a leitmotif in the mythology in origins, serving as device for ordering social relations especially between brothers. This ordering principle is projected onto a group level, subclans being differentiated as the eldest, middle, and youngest roots. From this standpoint, the myth is a play on time and space, clan and land. The transplantation of clan ancestors transmutes a geographical distance, covered in the journey from Hagen, into an historical time, expressed by ancestry itself, this being the hallmark of lineal continuity. By the same token, territorial occupation denotes the continuity of the clan, the succession of generations which claim certain land by birthright. The interconvertability of time and space, landedness and ancestry, is a premise lying behind the social dynamics of clan formation.

The origin myth also previews male/female relationships and the sociality of cooperation; it would be singularly incomplete without it. The distinction between men and women appears as a global subdivision of society into a line of men (*yu kongipo*) and a line of women (*ambra kongipo*). Speakers use these terms quite independently of reigning social amenities, kinship affinities, or the partitioning of society into exogamous clans. The storyline endows the male/female relationship with an historical primacy as it develops against the advance of culture itself. This primacy in the beginning reflects the compelling force of this generative scheme in the living practices and events of society. Women are conceived as born to the land in its primal state, when the rudiments of culture, such as exchange and domestication, were still undiscovered. The arrival of men of foreign origin (non-kinsmen) completes the dyad, their contribution turning stubborn land into a fertile garden. The following social equation (as shown in Figure 5) expresses this mythical relationship which culture inscribes in its practices.

The social relationship between men and women, especially as realized in the brother/sister and husband/wife dyads, is one of complementarity. Each makes distinctive although interdependent

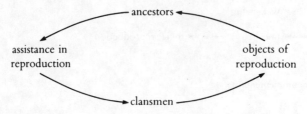

Figure 6 Ancestral exchange

contributions to reproduction. Life parallels myth in the sense that virtually all interactions between men and women take place during the
production, preparation, and exchange of food, or during sexual relations. So the exchange of food is a digest of social relations and the
machinery of their genesis and replication. It links the elements of production – the use and ownership of land, ancestor worship, labor, and
fertility – both together and to the generative schemes of organization
of everyday life. It defines that linkage as the road to social reproduction.

Modes of social exchange

Recollection of the ancestors reflects the lineal continuity of the clan.
Such continuity is mediated by, concretized through, and expressed
transitively in production. Clanspeople make a point of emphasizing
that an unbroken line of forebears have tilled and harvested the same
land on the understanding that to have a place is to have an identity.
And like the living community, ancestors live on and identify with
clan lands. Besides being rooted in one place, a clan's image rises with
the military, political, and other victories of its ancestors; and oral
history enshrines their more notable accomplishments. Beyond being
historical landmarks, the ancestors are in the thick of ongoing affairs
which bear on the immediate destiny of the clan and subclan. They are
instrumental in the workings of the political economy, and the fate of
social reproduction hinges on their assistance. Ancestors are sentient
beings who exercise power in their own interest, sometimes to the
mystification of their descendants, and demand social recognition.
Clansmen meet these demands mostly by making ritual sacrifices in
their honor. Neither simply benign nor malevolent their relations with
the living, like relations among the living, depend on the harmonies of
exchange, its express purpose being to coordinate the dispositions of
men and ancestors.

The ancestor spirits are the major supernatural force that affects the life of the clan. They are a locus of knowledge and power, influence and prestige, and the most telling statement of agnatic belief. Ancestors are a category of social persons and people patronize, ignore, and otherwise respond to them with this in mind. They are distinct from the living community only in the sense that they are its representation and extension into another zone of existence. The continuity of life and thus of the clan flows from the belief that people are composed of a corporeal and spiritual essence. Maring understand the spirit as the seat of man's social, linguistic, cognitive, and volitional faculties; accordingly, they define humanity in these terms. Features of a person's spirit, these faculties persist into the afterlife thus making the nature and sociality of ancestors an extension of the community's. Ancestors parallel the living in that they reside on clan land, exercise their own proprietary interests, and have a human social perception of behaviors and practices.

It is worth noting that Maring find Jesus Christ perfectly intelligible and have no problem incorporating him into their schema. The Christian claim that Christ was a man who died very long ago and is the ancestor of ancestors finds no contradiction in local cosmology. Maring focus on the recently dead and claim no special knowledge about the distant past. That the original ancestors may have had a common father is neither far-fetched in their eyes nor particularly noteworthy. Equally, that Jesus is a sentient being who lives everywhere, including in their sacred groves, has economic interests of his own (e.g., the trade stores run by the Church), and punishes those who do not propitiate him is wholly consistent with Maring beliefs about ancestor spirits. Thus, they have no conceptual problems in mounting Jesus Christ atop their own ancestor lineage, and receiving the Christian mass as the form of worship for the paramount ancestor. The various Christian missions are seen as reorienting ancestor worship away from near relatives to more distant ones. What Maring debate is the value and efficacy of reorientation – whether Christ demands more in exchange than he is willing to return.

Ancestors are part of the environment, taken in the Maring sense of the simultaneous social/physical world. Their involvement runs deep because its implications touch the roots of reproductive power. The spirits interact with the clan through seances which counsel members on strategies of action and belief. After the fact, clansmen read the political climate, the outcome of crucial exchanges, the productivity of gardens, the fertility of women, etc., as a barometer of their relations with the ancestors. They involve three species of knowledge besides descriptive: evaluative, normative, and prescriptive. Clansmen evaluate styles of action and practice in terms of the ancestors' reaction. Recently, many claimed that the conversion to Western medicine, and the shunning of traditional means, was responsible for a rash of deaths from pneumonia. One ready argument against any new policy (hence a common rhetorical device) is to note that it was never practiced by one's forebears, thus implying that the ancestors had already passed judgement on the policy. Normative knowledge decrees that certain categories of kin should perform some specified action on the appropriate occasion. For example, a man should sacrifice a pig to the ancestors when his brother or father becomes seriously ill, for they can stay the illness and speed recovery. Finally, this knowledge is prescriptive in that it often specifies what agents must do in order to accomplish their aims. These forms of knowledge are clearly interrelated and mutually supporting. They are also double-edged in that the clan's knowledge of ancestors is the ancestors' knowledge of how to meet the clan's social goals.

For Maring, apprehension of reality is as real as the current state of affairs, being by its very nature the processes whereby people acquire knowledge. The ultimate test of the truthfulness of knowledge is its conversion into the power that people need to overcome whatever obstacles stand in their way. Of first importance is the degree to which knowledge advances the practical and immediate ends of social reproduction. The abstract quality of this epistemology is never more evident than in ordinary action, from talk about the weather to whether to talk about a sensitive subject. In the Maring world, knowledge and interests, like all thought and action, are inseparable and interdependent. It is the way in which people interpret reality – that is, ascertain what is true, false, or unknowable about social relations. Maring expect that knowledge about the ancestors can and will be converted into power, meaning control over the processes of social reproduction. Shamans hold seances in which the ancestral spirits, through the mediary of the Smoke Woman who enters the shaman's body, divulge their opinions on clan policy and conduct. Social exchanges are especially critical. Ancestors may speak out on which marriages should be made to increase prestige and strength: exchanges that repay past debts (those incurred by the ancestors), obtain access to garden land, or cultivate allies. By faithfully observing the recommendations obtained through seance, clansmen expect to reap practical benefits. A failed exchange calls into question both the integrity of the living and the truthfulness of ancestral wisdom.

The harmonies between the clan and its ancestors are also embodied in herd and garden. The dead can assist the living in controlling what

Maring perceive as a natural cycle of fertility, growth, death, and decay. Because control is of utmost importance, clansmen formally petition their ancestors for aid. In the sacred grove where the spirits dwell, clansmen make ritual offerings of roasted taro and pig – as in the myth of their beginning. Should the gift appease the spirits they will repay their descendants by promoting the growth and fertility of crops, animals, and people. The weather will hold true; there will be a dry spell when the gardens can be cut and burned, followed by a period of rain to spur rapid growth. The community will enjoy a long harvest of the more seasonal foods, particularly the pandanus nut and taro. Most of all the food will be rich in substance, the pandanus laden with oils, the taro dry and sweet when roasted in the fire, the sweet potato strong and filling. Not only will the gardens fruit well, but the pig herd will be healthy, fertile, and will not invade gardens, an ever-present problem. Good pigs follow good gardens is common knowledge as people recognize the interdependence of these two aspects of production. But most of all, the ancestors will use their powers to look directly after their descendants. Women will be strong and fertile, men potent and influential, and all will be able to fend off attacks by demons and sorcerers. In this world view, sickness and death, the failure of crops or social exchange, decreases in power and prestige, mean either that clansmen have not propitiated their ancestors properly or that the knowledge of the ancestors (or of a particular ancestor) is false.

In this sense, ritual exchange is always precarious in that no sanctions can be levied against ancestors. The only recourse a clansman has is to sever the exchange cycle which is inevitably self-defeating and an open admission of failure. Lowman (1974) cites several cases of men who refused to sacrifice pigs to their ancestors. This negation of the exchange cycle, besides jeopardizing these men's futures, underlines the uncertainty of ancestor exchange, the only litmus of propriety and perfection being the pragmatic test of whether the exchange is successful so that the land is productive and the clan strong in materials and numbers. Jesus is subject to the same standards, and the extent to which he figures in religious ceremony varies among clan clusters, clans, and within clans along generational lines (see LiPuma 1986).

The value of this point extends beyond the Maring case. A feature of Highland ethnography is that it reports two seemingly contradictory views of the interrelationship between religion and society. On one hand, the writings document that the spiritual world and its being are important in things as varied as the construction of the cosmos and protection against sorcery to garden production and successful festivals. On the other, the writings also document that Highlanders easily jettison their own forms of worship and adopt those of Christianity. Why should Highlanders put their faith and practices aside so readily if their religion is so critical? For the Maring at least, religion is not a body of knowledge and thought which exists independent of action and praxis. This cultural view means that ancestors as a category of people will always be ambiguous. So the failure of ancestors to intervene on behalf of their descendants during the first twenty years after pacification (1955–75) was interpreted, specially by up and coming big-men, as questioning the existence of ancestors as powerful, sentient beings. The truth of their existence was not partible from their actions in the world. Accordingly, there was no reason to worship ancestors and some clans turned to Jesus as an alternative form of practical ideology, orienting production around his teachings and seeing the Mass as a Western version of sacrificial exchange. Maring belief is a category of action and Jesus can no more escape the social logic of evaluation than any other ancestor. So many clans, feeling that Jesus has been only a moderate success, and uncertain about the changes of modernity, have reinstated ritual sacrifice, often propitiating both Jesus and ancestors, while still attending Church services. In effect, Maring cultural epistemology dictates that ancestors will remain ambiguous and largely anonymous because their existence is always mediated by action, just as all actions (e.g., being ill or making a successful exchange) are always mediated by spiritual concepts (e.g., sorcery or power).

Ritual sacrifice is a true social communion simultaneously bonding clansmen and segregating clans. In the sacred grove where the bones of the dead are buried, the clan gathers to dedicate their offering both to the entire corps of ancestors and to those whom they have known personally. The living consume the flesh of the slaughtered pig, the ancestors partake of its spirit. Each clan has its own sacred grove(s) which are its centers of power; and outsiders are not permitted to view the ceremony or trespass on this ground. The ritual's express goal is to entice the ancestors to cooperate, by creating a situation in which the morality of exchange compels them to give unstintingly. Offering of pork and taro is charged with significance, epitomizing the two cycles of cultural continuity, natural and social, cultivation and exchange, where the clan desires and weighs the ancestral assistance. Pork and taro represent the two exemplary means, meat and vegetables, by which people renew their bodily substances. The quality and magnitude of the gift index success or failure of past exchanges.

Transactions with ancestors cannot stand by themselves but must be coupled to marriage exchange. The goodwill and advice of the

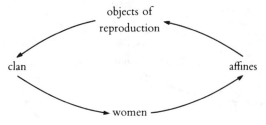

Figure 7 Marriage exchange

ancestors can bear fruit only when the clan exchanges women under advantageous circumstances. Men and women know the importance of inter-clan prestations – both to their personal well-being and that of the clan – and devote time calculating gifts and preparing feasts to honor in-laws. They understand that the clan depends on such transactions, and that having a stable of reliable allies is politically and economically essential. The idea is to cultivate and control exchange partners by developing matching interests, interdependencies, and an embedded kinship by constant intermingling of bloodlines. In this way, the clan always maintains a full set of options so that it can successfully maneuver social reproduction. Intermarriage triggers a series of payments which keeps objects of reproduction flowing between intermarried groups, as each exchange provides leverage in social relations and suggests future transactions. This mode of exchange can be diagramed following the earlier treatment (see Figure 7).

For the Maring, marriage is of overriding interest precisely because women play such an important part in exchange. The natural cycle involving the regeneration of land and people is the domain of women; it expresses fertility, growth, death, and decay, the processes of reproduction over which women preside. The fertility of women, their ability to bear sons and daughters for the patriline, endows it with life and permits it to flourish against the tides of war, disease, and death. The reproductive role of women transcends procreation as they are the major force of production. Both dimensions of cultivation, the making of gardens and raising of livestock, are women's responsibility. Without production from women, a clan could neither propitiate its ancestors nor present compensation payments to affines. Death, too, is the particular concern of women as they perform the vital tasks of treating the corpse, watching over its decay so that evil spirits or sorcerers do not harm the *min* of the dead.

Pork and land, the most important objects of reproduction, are crucial elements of social organization. They generate a forceful relation-

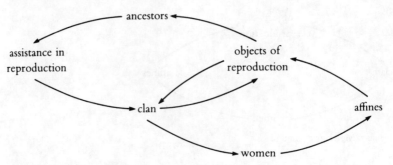

Figure 8 Relationships between modes of exchange

ship between the donor and the recipient of the gift, and are considered worthy compensation for a woman, because they are identified with the owners. Such gifts inspire confidence being evidence of success, a commitment to further exchange of goods and services, and a sign of mutual interests. Beyond this, pork and land are sources of substance and thus of kinship. They replenish the bodily substances of one clan with those of another. In this sense, the blood that women bring and contribute to procreation is always repaid in food which in turn produces blood and semen. For Maring, the truth of the exchange is the degree to which a woman produces children, gardens, and pigs, and the extent to which the gifts of pork and land further the purchase of women.

Social reproduction so intertwines these modes of exchange that in practice they often become unified. The defining concept of co-substance transitively relates the two cycles of exchange; for both forms of substance, blood and grease, flow within the clan and between clans. Organically and functionally, neither mode of exchange works in the absence of its counterpart. Clansmen must obtain wives in exchange for their sisters to lead productive lives for their line, make good gardens, and produce pigs for ancestors and affines. Equally, ancestor spirits must cooperate with men in production and exchange in order to attract women. Male and female substances are continually circulated; a woman uses her blood to create agnatic heirs, just as men use pigs and land, sources of agnatic substance, to create affines. The key point to develop is that the interlocking of exchange cycles permits the Maring to convert affinal relationships into agnatic ones and vice versa. A model of this integration is represented as in Figure 8.

The modes of exchange contain a system of objects which accord the highest values to men and women; they are not only the objects but the subjects and beneficiaries of exchanges. Second in value are the transactable signs of men and women: land, pigs, money, and other species of wealth. In third place are subsistence goods such as taro and yams which are themselves transactable signs of land, pigs, and money and so indirectly of men and women. The internal ordering, valuation, and efficacy of these objects in exchange defines the system of objects as a manifest dimension of social organization. What is crucial here is a three part relationship: the cultural utility of objects such as land, pigs, or taro to meet social goals and obligations; the relations between objects which shape the strategies and tactics of exchange; and finally, the relations between kinsmen and of kinship embodied in material flow.

Social ideology and culture

Ideology is a culture's own view of its practices and institutions, a self-representation or ethnotheory, in this case of the social system. The Maring, like other Highlands societies, have befuddled analysts by the absence of a well-articulated ideology of residence, exchange, or descent – an ideology that compares with the ethnographer's own native awareness of the West or at least that of some African societies. Immediately coming to mind are American views about kinship (Schneider 1968), the Tallensi ideology which permeates the *Web of Kinship* (Fortes 1949), or the elegance of the Ndembu in laying out the relationship between social organization and ritual (Turner 1957; 1967).

But the ideology of social organization gleaned from Highland groups, especially when systematized, always seems forced. The ethnographic fact is that some individuals, including those in positions of power and authority, hold no expressible view on the substance of social organization. Others may express a piecemeal ethnotheory rift with logical inconsistencies; while still others may furnish different and contradictory views. No Maring, for example, could provide a verbal account of concepts of substance which was systematic, consistent with those given by others, or socially recognized as statements of fact. Accounts of ideology are, in a word, schematic.

As if to compensate for this ethnographic impasse, ethnographers have taken several tacks. They have ignored local ideology as much as possible and with it the conceptual structure of the social system. The famous writings on Highland social structure, those of Meggitt (1965), Brown and Brookfield (1959), Kelly (1977) and Glasse (1968) focus heavily on institutions and behavior and away from anything having to do with the cultural level. Wagner (1967) and Strathern (1972), persuaded that a cultural account has merit, have aimed to comprehend social organization in terms of its ideology. They have rung as much ideology as possible out of the system. But when their informants explained their ideology of procreation, residence, exchange, and so forth, the outcome is too disjointed, fragmentary, and contradictory to understand social organization. Thus, Strathern compromises and devotes the first half of his analysis to recounting Melpa ideology and the second half to an institutional and behavioral study, but never joins the two halves. Wagner more clearly follows this line of analysis to its logic climax. If Daribi ideology organizes and defines social groups, and if the ideology is schematic and variable, then there are no social groups – only cultural distinctions (e.g., those who share meat versus those who do not) which generate temporary and highly situational boundaries (Wagner 1974).

I have sought to argue and illustrate that the structure of cultural categories of social organization is not to be found in any single practice, such as residence or exchange, and even less in ideological statements. True, Maring concepts of substance can be found in each and every practice involving kinship, but only in partial form. Only certain elements from the totality appear in any particular event or practice, and hence they resist immediate interpretation. Neither native nor anthropologist can formulate a theory of substance based on discussions about practices. This is especially hopeless in the decontextualized environment of the ethnographic interview which allows mostly ideological material to seep through.

My argument about the relationship between system and practice can be crystalized in four points. First, the ethnotheory of social organization will reveal only a fragment of the indigenous social system. In particular, it will disclose high referential aspects of the social order, such as rule-like statements about marriage exchange which serve the function of allowing the clan to present itself as an immutable unit whose structure is timeless (LiPuma 1983). Second, lacking a well-articulated ideology is no handicap because the basic structure of the social system is found on the level of practice. It is here that the cultural utility of human labor and objects, the pragmatic strategies of exchange, and the social relationships embodied in material flow join. Third, the conceptual structure of co-substance, or of the social system in general, will never be encapsulated in any single institution or practice. It is mistaken to think that underlying principles or generative schemes will be "mapped out" in residence patterns, mythology, ritual, kinship terminology, or especially the clan's self-representation or view of its own formation. I would argue that social systems like the Maring can be defined as "putatively patrilineal" only if the analysis of social organization mistakes ideology as a full disclosure of the cultural order. Fourth, the structure is only partly manifest in any one practice, although wholly manifest in all. Accordingly, social organization must be understood by analysis of the relations within practice and the connection between these relations and those appearing in other practices. As I will show for Maring, the nature of the burial system, food exchanges, food taboos, cooperation in the making of gardens, land tenure, and the model of vegetable growth make sense in terms of a sense of embodied substance, although none of them reveal it in more than a partial way.

3 The natural cycle: food, land, and substance

Where the previous chapter described the dimensions of social exchange, this chapter centers on the natural cycle. It sets out the interconnection of co-substance, land and food – their place in the cultural order and the practices built on their interrelationship. It is the key chapter in understanding the meaning and value of agnation and exchange, the ways that they harmonize in practice and furnish the cultural premises for action. The interconnection between food, land, and substance is the logic that interconnects practices from discrete domains: from burial procedures to exchange values, from the distribution of bridewealth to food taboos, from land tenure to the ceremony of the garden.

The term "natural cycle" is a gloss on a complex of Maring concepts and practices that can only be translated by way of an extended analysis. The term "natural," as used herein, does not refer to a materialist construction of nature, as the West would have it. It refers to the cultural logic which defines and links physical and physiological processes, and the corps of practices which follow from this construction of reality to reproduce the social world.

The principle of the natural cycle, first reported by Rappaport (1968), is that death and decay lead, in the Maring view, to fertility and rebirth. Substance flows from the bodies of clanspeople into clan lands, from there (mainly through use of female labor and male ritual) into taro, pigs, pandanus, and other foods, and then returns to clan members through their eating foods and is passed on in procreation.

Death and burial in the natural cycle

In the Maring world view, with its conception of a natural cycle of fertility, birth, growth, death, and decay, a person's death is as much a beginning as an end. The funeral service is in three parts, each of which manipulates notions of substance and spirit. When a man dies his body

62

lies in state for three days or more, depending on his prestige and the kinsmen and friends who will come from afar to pay respects. Within the closed quarters of the house, the body passes from the arms of one mourner to the next, all those gathered wail in his honor. They guard his *min* or life-force, so easily attacked and vulnerable between death and the grave, and watch over his spirit. His brothers, often standing atop the men's house, their faces smeared with mourning clay, sing out to the ancestors to announce his approaching spirit.

Before European health codes were enforced, a raised outdoor platform was built of timber and lined with *rumbim* (cordyline or tanket), the sacred plant symbolizing the clan's territoriality in which clansmen invest their collective life-spirit. The corpse was then laid on the platform and exposed to the elements until rotted away to bare bone. In the damp, tropic weather of the rain forest this rarely took more than six weeks. During the body's exposure women stand vigil because death, as a point of transition in the natural cycle, presents dangers to the living. Attention at the platform is essential, especially the night fires to protect the dead from evil spirits and sorcerers who may approach in the guise of dogs, pigs, or birds of prey.

The outdoor burial recaptured the conditions which prevailed before birth, the neutral state of being; it effected a reseparation of bodily essences. The platform stood several yards above ground because being raised above the earth confers social significance and because the construction of distance created the possibility of the sharing. As the corpse decayed its agnatic substances, those contributed by the father, slowly dripped back into the land that conceived and replenished them. The agnatic spirit departed and found shelter in the nearby trees and rocks, fully sentient to the attention of kinsmen and the truthfulness of their grief. The matrilineal bones, the essence of the mother's contribution, remained alone upon the platform when the processes of decomposition were over. Women came and carefully wrapped the bones in leaves and brought them back to the house of the man's wife or mother. Some of the smaller bones, those of the finger and sometimes of the lower arm, were kept by the widow, sister, mother, or other female relative of the dead, and either hung near the sleeping quarters or worn around the neck. The highest sign of womanly grief, reserved for those men who have unselfishly and faithfully helped their kinsmen, is the matching of bone for bone. The woman, taken by the "spirit of sorrow" lops off the joint of a small finger. Or, commonly, a small girl gives up a finger joint.

Finally, the mourners removed the larger bones and buried them in the sacred grove where the spirits of the ancestors reside. On this oc-

63

casion clansmen sacrificed a pig for the newly deceased, the sacrifice meant to celebrate his new status and to insure his cooperation in the future. After the grave has been dug about five feet deep, a niche is carved into one of its walls, and the carefully wrapped bones together with some of the man's possessions and gifts from relatives were inserted into the niche. Once the community sealed the grave they built a fence around it and lined the wooden stakes with *rumbim*.

Now that the government bans outdoor burials, the Maring have taken to consolidating steps two and three. The fresh corpse is wrapped in cloth, and sometimes, in imitation of Western custom, laid in a roughly hewn coffin. Mourners then place the body on an underground platform by inserting it into a niche they have carved in the wall of the grave. At this point, they build two fences, one within the grave itself and the other above ground after the grave has been sealed; generally, they proceed as in traditional ceremony on the view they have found the narrow path between traditional and modern ways. Occasionally and in great secret the mourners will dig up the bones some months later and rebury them in the sacred grove.

The key point is the return of bodily substances to the clan earth from which they originally sprang. Recycling is crucial to the fertility of the land, to the value attached to the origin of food, where it is grown being a concern to all, and to the relationship it generates between living and dead. The importance of burial place surfaces in the logic of compensation. For example, if a man or woman dies before having compensated their mother's agnates for her gift of blood, the mother's clansmen can then lay claim to a share of the body and the right to bury "their son or daughter." Their contention, shrouded in the language of emotion and solidarity, is that they gain the privilege of burial as fair compensation. Rarely does this occur, as the mother's agnates are compensated and goodwill prevails. It is not only solidarity with the deceased that seems to inspire such an emotional outpouring, but the fact that land and substance are at issue.

Soil and fertility in the natural cycle

Maring know from experience that revolutions of the natural cycle regenerate the land's capacity to produce fruitfully. Practical measures, particularly magic and careful cultivation, and the inevitability of death and decay drive the continuity. Taro, yams, sweet potatoes, bananas, and tobacco, symbolically and materially the truly important cultigens in the indigenous scheme, grow by absorbing the soil substance. People, comparing the function and reticulation of roots to the human circulatory systems, claim that the roots "eat" the "grease" of the land. A myth told to me by a senior clansman captures the interrelationship between substance, land, and fertility, not to mention the everpresent theme of the value of exchange.

Many generations ago when men always lived in the men's house a woman from his subclan made a garden alone. She cultivated taro, yams, sweet potatoes, leafy greens, and other vegetables. Each day she would work diligently in her garden but to little cause as the crops hardly grew at all. One day, discouraged by obvious failure, instead of working she built a small fire in the corner of her garden and prepared a meal, mostly of sweet potatoes fit only for the pigs. A young man, attracted by the swirling smoke and the smell of cooking food, came to investigate. She invited him into the garden, fed him some of the sweet potatoes, and then began to have intercourse with him. But the man became frightened because he was still young and pulled out of the woman suddenly. However, as he did so he could not control himself and spilled his semen all over the ground. The following day the woman enticed him again [he was again passing by] into intercourse; soon after, she became pregnant and the garden grew with new vigor.

A premise of this myth is that the conjunction of male and female powers is the basis of fertility and a principal dynamic of the natural cycle. Moreover, the story tells in no uncertain terms that labor alone will not win the harvest, for an essential catalyst of reproduction is the grease or substance of the clan. Just as repeated insemination feeds the developing embryo and spurs its growth, so in the myth the spilling of the young man's semen feeds the crops and produces a bountiful yield. The parallel is rather straightforward: in procreation men contribute grease to bind women's blood; in production the agnatic lands furnish grease to the crops planted by women. People say that the land fertilizes the *wump* or planting material that is of women. Not surprisingly, gardens are often settings for sexual meetings, and a woman who suspects her husband of an illicit affair will commonly stake out the garden she is not scheduled to be working that day.

As tubers absorb the soil's substance their internal structure changes, a smooth interior replaces one interlaced with fibrous canals. Plants differ in their capacity to absorb substance; the best taro, for example, has a smooth, homogeneous texture whereas the average manioc or sweet potato is somewhat fibrous and stringy. The intake of grease fertilizes the tuber which then gives issue to cormel, the planting material that women will use to create a new garden. Logically, the more grease available the larger and better the cultigens. A conscientious gardener will pack soil around the base of the taro stalks and periodically replace the old soil with new. The local account is that tubers continue to grow until they have depleted the earth of nutrients. The quality and dimensions of cultigens are a direct measure of the quality of the soil in which they were planted. This fact is charged with significance because the inclusion of cultigens in social exchange is meant and taken as an index of land quality.

In the course of common events, people talk earnestly about the nature and quality of soil. Whether in the language of substance or more often in terms of hardness, texture, and color, they seek to describe the fertility which is the quality of life. The very best soils are those that are fine and free of stones, rich and dark in color, and with a palpable moisture content. By the same standards, rocky red ground is no one's desire, being like "a body with no flesh" or "a man without children" to quote one informant. Those organisms which are of the land, and have in the past nourished on its substance, return this essence when they die and decay. Animals, men, and plants all add grease to the soil. This includes the secondary growth which is cut and then burnt during the construction of the garden, the first step sacrificing the trees and the second step burning away all the essential. The best ground should be planted with taro and yams – taro because they require grease, yams because they enjoy moisture. And where taro and yams prefer black, soft humus to other soils, sweet potatoes and strong bananas thrive well in hard. Color, texture, and hardness are indicators of the earth's quality, and people assume that crop failure in good soil must result from either sorcery or the wrath of ancestor spirits.

Complementary interaction between male and female elements applies to the garden in a total sense. Not only is male and female labor necessary, a point mentioned in the initial chapter, but an association of male and female crops promotes fertility. There is a key distinction between the objects and relations of production. It creates the opportunity continually to exchange food and labor between the sexes, the greater and more harmonious the complementarity, the more power can be generated.

In the context of gardening, taro, yams, and sweet potatoes, female objects produced by women, dominate cultivation. But there are also female plants and trees, most notably bananas, sugarcane, and pandanus, which men produce. It is significant that clansmen say that women are like banana trees – which in fact are not trees at all but easily transportable herbs with shallow root systems. Just as women move from their natal clan to the gardens of their husbands, so men move banana trees from one garden to another. And, as I shall explain in a moment, both sugarcane and pandanus are instrumental in renewing female substances. In the symbolism of the garden, men are not cultivated plants at all, but great trees of the primary forest, with their huge boles and entrenched root system. Tobacco, *rumbim*, and *amame* (a low, fragrant, greenish-leaved herbaceous plant) are the male plants which men cultivate and use to control the natural and social cycles. Shamans contact the ancestor spirits by rapidly inhaling strong native cigars, thus inducing a trance which opens lines of communication. Smoke is the only and proper ritual medium for the bridge between living and dead. Although *rumbim* and *amame* are not edible, they are merely one step removed from food in that they are the material symbol in the semiotics of fertility and landedness. In the ceremonies of the ritual planting of *rumbim* clansmen safeguard the social cycle; their individual *min* commingle and are infused into the ground, thus indexing the alliance between man and land. Moreover, the planted *rumbim* insures that men will grow fast and strong and be able to produce many children. Maring plant *amame* "for the benefit of women, domestic pigs, and gardens" (Rappaport 1979:111) because *amame*, being associated with ancestors of the natural cycle, promotes the fertility of this trinity. Both *rumbim* and *amame* are planted in the vicinity of graves, and traditionally close relatives of the deceased would plant them over the spot where the corpse had been left to decay. This was meant to insure the truthfulness (*wundok*) or fairness (*kopla*) of the death, that it would promote fertility. Finally, pigs are the primary male object which women raise. Pigs are, of course, featured in both modes of social exchange as the object of mediation between men, this possible because of the strong identification between the giver and the object given.

Much more than simply food, then, the garden produces a complex of complementary relations. Similarly, proper orchestration of these relations is essential for a good garden. One implication is that, in response to context, agents may identify an object as either male or female and react accordingly. In this sense, almost all objects have both a male and female aspect, the aim of practice to make smooth transitions between modalities as this augers well for the clan's social reproduction. For example, women give pigs to men so that men may give pigs to other clansmen in exchange for women. Note that complementarity extends not only to the objects and relations of production but to the spheres of use, whether the objects further cultivation and the making of female substance or exchange and the reproduction of male substance (see Table 6).

Predictably, people feel that association of male and female crops produces the best gardens. No garden should be an island of tubers alone, planted and harvested solely by women, and as a rule they

Table 6 *Sexual complementarity in the cultivation of food*

Objects	Relations	Sphere of use
Female		
Taro, yams, etc.	Female	Women → men
Female		
Sugarcane, bananas, pandanus, etc.	Male	Men → women
Male		
Tobacco, *amame, rumbim*	Male	Men → men
		Natural cycle
		Social cycle
Male		
Pigs	Female	Men → men

include sugarcane and bananas (pandanus is grown in special groves). To round out this program, a single tree, whose branches have been stripped to allow penetration of sunlight, stands in the garden's center. The association of crops is one rationale people give for the division of labor by sex, saying, for example, that "without women the garden would include only bananas and tobacco." Trees mature more slowly than bananas or sugarcane and these more slowly than taro and other tubers because the soil's substance has farther to travel. Maring see the difference in rates of growth as characteristic of a natural order in which women and all things female mature faster than men and things male. So female products grow more swiftly and women marry at an earlier age than men, the cycle of war and peace is slower than the gardening cycle.

Much can be said about the symbolic and material connections between clan members and their land. But within the circle of everyday activity and discussion and at more formal events such as trials, the most profound expression of this kinship lies in its psychological depth, the emotional electricity that flows whenever speakers bring up the issue of territory. Maring are passionate devotees of the history of land use and ownership; they speak with great intensity as if there are no trivial issues where land is concerned. I have heard it said that "a line without land is like a clansman without a penis," incomplete and with no possibility of becoming whole. When this line was said the small audience of men erupted with laughter, the humor all the more humorous because of the anxiety and fear surrounding both types of castration. Because all problems over land are crucial, nearly half of all court cases held at the local level – the only level for which I have full data – involve land disputes. Here is an excerpt from a recent trial over a disputed tract of land lying between two clans from rival clan clusters.

Litigant 1 (Kauwatyi) ... your claim to this land is a lie. My father and my father's father have made work upon this ground; they did not come for some other reason. The food from this land has been cooked by our wives and it has filled our hunger. We have bought the bones of our wives and planted them here... So this is our land because we are from the land.

Litigant 2 (Manamban) ... if this land was yours why don't your ancestors protect it. Why did they not fight for their land like men? Why do the crops we have planted come up on Kawai [the disputed tract] just as they do on all our land and make us strong? The reason behind this is that our ancestors worked this land, died here, and now we work this land in the same custom.

Historically, it appears that both clans did work the same tract of land, though at different points in time. The Manamban worked the land more than six generations ago; the Kauwatyi held the land from four to two generations ago; the Manamban have held the land since 1956 when an Australian kiap declared it theirs. The Kauwatyi are now trying to retrieve the land permanently on the legal argument – now decided by a local court made up of Jimi Valley leaders – that their use of the land for three generations provides legal title. This title was established by relations of substance and co-substance over time, as the flow of the narrative indicates.

The notion that clan boundaries are mapped according to legal referents is itself a new idea, one that codifies and concretizes practice. In the past there was no clear demarcation at the clan cluster border other than the pattern of land use. Cultivators would rotate among adjacent or nearly adjacent plots of land. As part of their occupation, land users would demarcate boundaries with plantings and stakes. The boundary marker is itself an index of the cultivation cycle. By nature, it fits the cultural concept that cultivation makes boundaries real, and that when land is deserted, the boundaries fade. Hence, one clan might use the garden land, then switch to some other sector of the clan territory, and after the secondary growth is established another clan might begin gardening. Territorial borders were thus part of the structure of land tenure and patterns of cultivation – the relationship between man and land being reproduced substantively.

The plant designated to demarcate clan boundaries and signify the relationship between clansmen, ancestors, and land is *rumbim*. Rappaport (1968:170) describes its significance with respect to the recreation of clan boundaries after war:

If the enemy was not driven off its territory in the last fight, but remained to plant *rumbim*, or if, having been driven out, the enemy has returned and planted *rumbim*, the stakes are placed at the boundary that existed before the fight.

If, however, the enemy was driven out of its territory and never returned to plant *rumbim*, the procession does not stop at the old border. It proceeds into the territory of the former enemies and the stakes are planted at a new location. A new boundary is thus established, incorporating into the territory [i.e., clan cluster] land previously held by the enemy.

The Tsembaga and most other Marings say that fights do not take place over land and that land occupied by other groups cannot be annexed. To signify its occupation, however, a group must plant *rumbim* upon its land. Areas annexed in stake-planting rituals are areas upon which no *rumbim* is planted; they are, therefore, no lands belonging to the enemy, but lands the enemy has presumably abandoned – they are vacant.

More, Maring believe that when a clan abandons its land its clan ancestors are also displaced. Severing the reproductive cycle and thus the flow of substance means that the ancestors of the defeated have been severed from the land too. The victorious group – and victories may be *de facto* as well as *de jure* – may now begin to cultivate the land and initiate its own reproductive cycle.

Consistently, deforestation and uprooting of crops, especially those that are both great symbols and means of producing substance, are chosen indexes of land dispute or warfare. When a clan cluster overruns its enemy, special pains are taken to lay waste the pig herd and pandanus groves. When stakes are planted after the war, the victors and their allies fell large trees, one for each of the enemy killed, so that they fall across the enemy border. Again, in the present litigation, the Kauwatyi to underline their land claim uprooted the coffee plants that the Manamban, knowing full well the implications of the act, had grown on the disputed soil.

The trial is a show of how clansmen modify tradition through cultural conceptualization of modernity. Not only do Kauwatyi wish to displace current tenants, but to do so permanently regardless of land use. The indexical marker gives way to abstract legal code, the new boundary registered at the district office. Thus, modern institutions make available new strategies for waging war, promoting the reproduction of the clan, and investing emotionally as well as productively in land.

In the course of the trial, the Manamban spokesman claimed that his clan had used the land for many generations, though fear of Kauwatyi attack compelled them to concentrate their settlements far from the borderlands. Land use had accordingly lapsed though "we worried about our ancestors who had used the ground" – implied reference to a broken reproductive cycle. Kauwatyi then moved in and cultivated the land until the war of 1955, a war in which the Manamban were routed from their territory. When the Australian administration, in the person and personality of the kiap, restored peace the Manamban returned to their land. The kiaps also turned the disputed land over to the Manamban mainly because the Kauwatyi, still in the flush of victory, were less disposed to pacification and would have less truck with the Australian administrators. The Manamban used the kiap to exact some revenge against the Kauwatyi, and the kiap used the land dispute to establish his authority.

The modernization of land title

After the trial had been winding along for some months, with the usual starts and stops, the councilor/big-man hearing the case summed up its progress when he adjourned court in August 1980:

The Manamban worked the land many generations ago, but we have no record of this. It was a time when we were rather primitive and nobody remembers. Now it is true that the Kauwatyi line has cultivated this land. They harvested taro, yams, bananas, sugarcane, cabbage ... from this land. Their pigs have also grown from this ground. I know, for I have eaten with the Kauwatyi who worked this land. This land is named Waiwa [a Kauwatyi given name]. But times have changed and warfare is a practice of the past. Now we grow coffee, use money, and have law – law is number one today [said in English with exaggerated hand gestures]. My belief is that if the Manamban want the land they must pay compensation. The Kauwatyi must be paid for their labor in working the land. I say that since the Manamban are presently growing coffee on the land, they should not be forced to leave. The Manamban should pay Kauwatyi 20 pigs and 5,000 kina [$US 7,000]. I have nothing more to say.

The logic and emotion of this discourse derives from its reference to the reproductive cycle. Listing foods is a common rhetorical device aimed at underscoring affinity, here the relationship between the Kauwatyi and the land in question. Naming the land has the same effect. It implies baptism, new tracts of land invariably being named, typically on the basis of an iconic relationship. ·(*Waiwa*, a type of vine prevalent near this plot of land, suggests any number of possibilities.) The premise behind the legal argument is that in the traditional system perdurance establishes legal title and that the basis of perdurance is the actions, deaths, and labors of the ancestors. The appeal is to transformations of substance: production, commensality, burial. Transformational cycles are not interchangeable. They are part of the clan's identity and thus belong to a specific clan. The notion that the land

71

could be worked cooperatively, both clans sharing the profits gleaned from the coffee production – a not uncommon arrangement among subclans – was not worth considering. Nor was it a possibility that the feuding clans divide the land. At no point in the trial was a joint venture mentioned.

The councilor punctuated his speech with a phrase in English although neither he nor his audience spoke English. The sentence was as intuitive as it was masterful. Reference was achieved by the tenor of the previous sentences and by analogy to Pidgin English, a language that many Maring, especially those coming of political age, can understand. (So compare "law is number one today" with Pidgin's "lo em i numba wan tude.") Invoking English, or in other cases Pidgin, spells out the social gravitation towards modernity. Here, the use of English is doubly indicative, change being reported through the language and office of change.

Maring perceive a sharp and transforming social break from warfare to legality. Their ethnotheory is that they have crossed a social divide with the coming of Western customs. This break is a cornerstone of the ideology of modern Maring culture and the withering away of a less viable tradition, one that exhibited military and later economic weakness in the face of the Australian and missionary might. Like the councilor's hand gestures, the ideology of social change exaggerates. Compensation payments, for example, antedate the advent of the Australian legal system; they have long been a mainstay of dispute settlement. The character of the proposed compensation (20 pigs and 5,000 kina) derives from local concepts of restitution, even when the community legitimizes the settlement by reference to modern law. As a coda, note that the relative unfamiliarity of English also indexes the difficulties and ambiguities involved in shifting from war to law.

The orientation of the councilor's speech foreshadowed its conclusion, weaving a fine line between tradition and modernity, mixing elements from both in considered proportions. There is a crucial disparity between the indigenous view of land rights and that borrowed from European law. In the former, legal title is based on continuity of use; possession is more than nine-tenths of the law. In the modern system, land rights reside in ownership which, in turn, depends on the continuity of the original title. This implies the cultural premise that land, once owned, cannot be legally alienated without due process – a contract between the two parties. This changeover has incited a wild and increasing scramble in the land courts, through the Jimi Valley and the entire Highlands. The Kauwatyi clans, for example, are chasing land claims throughout the Jimi and Simbai, based on an abundant oral

72

history of migration. Working on the modern standard, the councilor suggested that the alienation of the Kauwatyi tract, as ordained by the colonial administration, should be duly accepted. Nonetheless, his suggestion's force rested not only on an appeal to modern values, but the traditional wisdom that contemporary owners, the Manamban at this point in time, had developed a consubstantial relationship to the land. For this reason, their land claim held despite inconclusive evidence of first ownership. Neutral informants felt that Manamban cluster had the better land claim because "they were growing coffee" – again the theory of land title stated pragmatically as a description of gardening. On the other hand, the Manamban had circumstantially recognized the Kauwatyi title by waiting nearly twenty years after acquiring the land to initiate planting. The proposed compensation of pigs and money recognized the Kauwatyi's loss of reproductive power, and that the Manamban should make restitution in like terms. When the councilor ended his speech, murmurs of agreement swept through the audience.

Social reproduction is the clan's dominant perspective. From this vantage point, the clan losing land is in the same relative position as the clan which gives a wife or suffers a homicide. The loss falls in-between the wife-giver, who expects another woman in return, and the homicide victim, who sustains a permanent loss of procreative and productive power. Hence, the recommended land compensation was greater than brideprice and less than homicide payment. The councilor, of course, pointed all this out when he likened the loss of land to war casualty, and then proposed his settlement in the next breath.

For Maring, homicide is an expression of individual emotion and a crime against society at large; but the salient social fact of murder is that it depletes the reproductive potential of the victim's clan. This view of homicide surfaces in the relationship between an individual's punishment and clan compensation. Justice never centers on misdeeds, rather on the transfer of pigs, money, and women needed to return the victim to its previous level of reproductive power. A homicide in 1978 drew a compensation of 50 pigs, 20,000 kina, and a woman. However, time has no compensatory value, not being an object of reproduction, and murderers usually serve minimal jail sentences. A murderer is jailed only until the compensation payments begin. The man imprisoned in the 1978 killing was released in 1981 once his clan paid the first installment of the compensation – 30 pigs and 10,000 kina. Following the same logic, if a clan receives a woman as part of wergild, and she does not bear any children, the clan may legitimately ask for further compensation. Given the logic in force, it is easy to see why the

73

only alternative to compensation is payback murder, and why any male member of the perpetrator's clan may be killed: for what is at issue is a corresponding reduction of substance and reproductive power. Indeed, widespread presence in Highland societies of the payback formula would seem a concrete expression of the substance theory of clanship.

Food and substance

Maring say that "the land feeds the garden crops:" and that "the taro and yams eat the ground." Such statements capture, in a broad ideological stroke, everything from the physical properties and location of a garden to the origin of its planting materials and the common labor that has gone into cultivation. Gardeners space tubers, especially taro and yams, so that each has its own patch of ground. "Plants are like children at their mother's breasts; if more than one child sucks at the same breast they will both die." Human reproduction and garden growth share a common vocabulary. Speakers use lexemes like *kangi* to refer to nursing a baby and to growing a plant, the force of the verb being the metaphorical equivalence of women to land. Both are conductors of substance at different points in the natural cycle. The timing of fertility is as important as the spacing, for if plants remain too long in the ground and thus absorb too much fertility, they will begin to rot and decay. This reflects the cultural premise that the apex of fertility is also the beginning of descent into decay, death, and ultimately renewal. Accordingly, garden magic focuses less on controlling the weather or keeping away garden pests (e.g., rats), than on encouraging plants to grow and to show themselves so that they may be found and harvested before they rot.

People's words about the properties of plants and animals, their preparation, and bodily effects express the relationship between food and substance. Reasons for ordinary actions, such as returning food to the fire for further cooking, focus on the food's attributes and the effects of cooking upon them. Freshly harvested yams, for example, are especially moist and should, I was told repeatedly, be roasted until they are soft and bone dry. To cultural agents, the logic interlinking attributes, preparations, and effects, and this trio to the generation of substance, is opaque. Agents typically focus on single dyads (e.g., attribute and cooking method) which are the most meaningful units for achieving interpersonal goals (e.g., explaining how to cook taro).

Cooked foods fall into distinct categories and, separately or in combination, have different effects on the human body. Maring make a

Table 7 *Categorization of cooked foods*

Attributes of cooked foods	Vegetable	Animal
Grease	Marita	Pork, cassowary, eels
Soft/dry	Taro, yams rice	
Hard/strong	Sweet potatoes, hard bananas	
Wet/watery	Sugarcane, soft bananas, cucumber, leafy greens	
Hot	Tobacco	

distinction between vegetables (*tap aingundo*: literally that which grows from the ground) and animal (*tap wandundo*: literally that which moves of its own volition) foods. Five gastronomic categories cross cut this distinction: grease (*ananga* or *imbana*), softness/dryness (*ainyom*), hardness/strength (*anginai*), moistness/wateriness (*kinim*), and hotness/fieriness (*rombanda*). Table 7 systematizes these intersecting lines of categorization. The table is less a classification of foods, in the discursive sense of classification, than a description of foods from the perspective of consumption. The content of the categories are their most significant constituents; pork, for example, is an exemplar of grease and taro an exemplar of a soft/dry vegetable.

The value of consuming certain types of foods connects with the local theory of procreation, specifically with the conception that men contribute semen and women blood. In the culture's conception of nature, the intrinsic processes of sexual intercourse drain a man's store of semen. Bachelors fear that sexual indulgence will precipitate physical dissolution. They seek both to attract women and to avoid them: to prove their manhood and also preserve it. Older, married men, have paid the price of wrinkled, loose-hanging skin for their years of sex with their wives and the production of children. The active fathering of a child, requiring repeated inseminations, is particularly draining; and "when a man's family is carrying a child it is good for him to eat meat." On the train of the natural cycle, of course, sexuality and reproduction are one step closer to decay and death. "Men who marry and have children are no longer young saplings; they are a fully realized hardness although soon they will be old. Some men never become hard before they get old. We feel sorry for them; it is the shame that must live on their skins."

To replace male semen and to feed the *imbana* system, men eat the meats and fats of animals. I have described elsewhere in some detail how fat content determines the valuation of the pig and the relative ranking of the parts (LiPuma 1981). The concept of grease encompasses a variety of substances which are organically related, and ultimately united through the medium of the human body. It includes semen, fats of local plants and animals, especially pigs, and certain oils and mucuses that the body secretes. Consumers, for example, consider the brains of the animal the most delectable and nutritious substance.

In effect, pork and other types of meat embody the continuity of male substance and people see the maintenance of an adequate supply of meat, and gardens capable of sustaining pigs, as necessary to their own reproduction. The state of an individual's skin publicly reveals his success in maintaining his body, and more pointedly the frequency with which he has eaten meat. This is one step removed from the cultural inference that such persons have been the beneficiaries of good judgement, good gardens, and gifts of pork. There is a continual cycle unto death to renew the grease dissipated by the emission of semen, destructive powers of sorcery, and illness. Death and burial ultimately terminate this cycle as part of a larger one. As one informant remarked: "All of us eventually get old and die. You can see that the skins of old men wither on the bone. But powerful clansmen [names several] take more than one wife and produce many children and store strength. All of us die, but some die more gradually than others."

The remarks convey the idea that powerful men remain fertile longer and that their wives and children are index of their power, especially in the art of exchange which revolves on presentation of self and flow of gifts of pork. This is similarly a commentary on the social self and its expression – that is, the pragmatic representation of reproduction.

One of the first things a Maring surveys when "sizing up" another person is the quality of their skin and height. The smoothness, color, and gloss of the skin provide a measure of physical vitality and strength. More than anything else, the Kauwatyi were first impressed by the color and quality of the European's skin and hair, as well as their height. The premise is that the body, especially the skin, showcases a man's substance, substance being the measure of men. Many types of illness, particularly malaria, sap a person's substance, and those seeking medicine complain of "slack" or "weak" skin. Conversely, people rub pandanus oil, pig fat, and nowadays imported tinned drippings, into their skins prior to public appearances, such as a dance, to improve their image. In other words, grease, as the highest food value, exemplifies the link between personal reproductive power and that of the clan.

This logic rests on a more general series of mediations. In it, food, a primary category of value in the natural cycle, appears publicly as power and strength, and therefore a value of the social cycle. There is a chain of implication by which people adduce prior states of affairs as they evaluate the evidence of everyday action:

prosperity of the natural cycle $\rightarrow$ food $\rightarrow$ substance $\rightarrow$ power and strength of the gift, body, or action

By this set of mediations, the human body manifests the reproductive power of the clan. Note the legendary capacity of Highland body decoration to evoke strong emotions, publicize a clansman's fertility, and index capacities of clans (e.g., to wage war). For the ethnographer, as for any hearer, this implies that reports about the embodiment of substance are told in terms of power or strength. In statements such as "X dances powerfully" or "Y has given a very strong gift," power and strength point to much more than qualities of individuals or objects; they index a sequence of reproductive relationships based on the transformations of substance. The ethnographic truism that "prestations of pork denote the strength of the clan" is the usual gloss for this.

One added detail rounds out this account, or more precisely, explains the connection between public events, nearly all of which involve the use of food, and social reproduction. Maring make an epistemological distinction between the inside and outside of persons, objects, and relationships. The epistemology applies to all categories of value, not solely food but people, land, military assistance, and movables. The interior of a gift, action, or word is its truth whereas the surface or public presentation allows for illusion and dishonesty. Careful men are alert to the possibility, perhaps probability, of some misrepresentation. To determine the truth is to reconcile the value of inside to outside, to discern their relative unity or distance. To say that something "lies on the skin of a man" is to say that something of importance has not been fully revealed: that any determination is pending further revelation. The judgement that a certain person is powerful or, what amounts to the same thing, that he gives powerful gifts is a commentary on the truth value of events – truth, here, defined as the convergence of public display and reproductive achievement.[1]

Marita (*komba*), the nut of the pandanus tree, is the female correlate of animal fat and the complement of taro. Pandanus flourishes in the low altitudes, the ground which Maring call the *wora* and explicitly associate with the ancestors of fertility and the natural cycle. The tree bears a waxy cylinder-shaped red or yellow fruit which, when prepared with water, produces a rich greasy sauce. Lowman (1980:59) observes that Maring identify over fifty varieties of marita and create an oily sauce from its syncarp, "an oblong aggregate of hundreds of waxy, bright red or yellow drupes." Men should harvest marita: "It is the help men extend to women who are busy harvesting taro and yams." Women cook marita in earth ovens, always with other vegetables. They line hot stones along the sides and bottom of the pit, cover the stones with banana leaves, and then lay the taro and yams on top. The tubers are then covered with a layer of greens such as ambiam because "it is our custom to eat the marita [sauce] with greens." On top of the greens are laid the pandanus nuts, usually 2 to 3 feet long and split lengthwise. Women cover the oven with banana leaves and hot stones and then pour on water to steam the contents. Organization of the oven, with the tubers on the bottom, the various greens in between, and pandanus on top, replicates the vertical plane or stratification of the garden.

Once the mix of vegetables are done, the "bones of the *komba*" (men or seeds) are removed into a broad leaf or other container. A senior man blends the greasy seeds with water poured on slowly by an assistant. He then squeezes the marita in his hands, the red, blood-colored, juices seeping out between his fingers and onto the greens. Maring believe that eating marita stimulates the blood, and may provide additional blood especially for women, and thus strength to make children. The local view is that under normal circumstances blood is stationary, flowing only when the body's skin is breached or stinging nettles agitate it. People generally measure the seriousness of injury by the loss of blood; thus local curers treat nosebleeds much more seriously than Europeans at the health station.

Men do not bleed naturally, only due to the intentional acts of other men. Injuries which lead to bleeding are the result of sorcery or fighting. As one informant explained, "when a man's axe cuts him he

[1]This, incidentally, explains the seeming contradiction that pigs are both a measure of personal and clan wealth and status, and a social secret. People have deep reservations about discussing their pigs in front of others, and, if asked to do so, perhaps by an inquiring patrol officer, will usually underestimate the number and size of the pigs.

knows that someone is to blame." Recall also that the ancestor spirits of the social cycle, the Red Spirits, are so called because they have spilt their blood in the acts of war. By contrast, women lose blood not only in social interaction but because they are women. They bleed because of injury or during menstruation and childbirth. Trying to capture the naturalness, one person drew a direct parallel between nocturnal emissions by men and menses by women.

For men, eating marita stimulates by adding blood to a relatively closed circulatory system. Men say they feel a rush or a sensation of strength when they consume pandanus, especially red varieties which dominate yellow in number, value, and efficacy. Maring produce an extract (nearly 100% oil) from the drupes of the yellow pandanus. People rub this oil on their skin to give it a glistening, golden tone. Needless to say, there is a brisk trade in this oil as few things are more valuable than the presentation of self. For women, eating marita encourages menstruation and childbearing by making the blood flow (presumably to the womb and vaginal orifice), and replaces the blood lost during childbirth and menses. Recall that the role of semen in procreation is to bind the blood in the initial stages of pregnancy. A corollary of this belief is that a woman stops menstruating during her pregnancy because her blood has been diverted to the child. Blood thus mediates a connection between cultivation and procreation. Within the scope of the natural cycle, the reproduction of gardens and clansmen are directly tied through women.

It is significant that marita is made from a combination of water and vegetable fat. Water is the characteristic female element, just as fire, and even more so smoke, is the male counterpart. The effects of women on men is compared with the effects of water on men. *Kinim*, for example, may refer to cold, wet, and vaginal secretions, invocation of one meaning playing off against the others. More, speakers use *kinim* to express states of being, conditions of actions, and attitudes. Driven to preserve their strength, men traditionally washed "only when it rained," fearing that running mountain waters would turn their skins cold and wet and lead to physical dissolution. Some men avoid eating fish and eels on the same rationale, things associated with water the polar opposite of hard, dry, and hot, the characteristic male qualities.

Blood itself, because it flows and clots, is thought to be an admixture of water and female grease (*ambra amanga*) – that is, the grease derived from vegetables. A curing rite to halt the loss of blood involves placing water in a bamboo tube and then inserting a mixture of leaves, including pandanus leaf. The curer passes a spell over the tube which instructs the blood to still itself, the action of leaves and spell to "control" the water. The flow of blood is thus controlled by magical intervention in the relationship between vegetable matter and water. By the same token, the speed with which an injured person's blood clots is a measure of strength. Informants would account for clotting in terms of overall physical prowess, sometimes citing such factors as height.

In Maring eyes, pandanus nuts, like bananas, resemble women's breasts and not the phallus, the symbolic image of the West. Or, less graphic and more ethnographic, the pandanus embodies both male and female qualities and thus its value changes with practice. It is male from the standpoint of the harvest, female as substance, male because it rises above the ground, female because it is a vegetable food, and more. It articulates the complementarity of male and female production and reproductive roles. This reintroduces the notion that the attributes of food as eaten, exchanged, or prohibited on a given occasion are the content of generative schemes and so always belong to a larger universe of possibilities.

Maring wartime ritual condenses, displaces, and energizes the relationships between blood, marita, and the natural cycle. The pandanus has a significant part in the uprooting of the *rumbim* and the ritual cycle that culminates in the mass slaughter of pigs. The ceremony centers on pigs, marita, and taro – the elementary forms of substance in the Maring schema. On the day prior to the uprooting of the *rumbim* clansmen harvest two large, red-skinned pandanus fruits from the *wora*, or low ground. They harvest only fruits planted by persons now deceased and grown where the bones of the dead are buried because the substance derived from these pandanus must be the recycled substance of the ancestors. Then, a procession of men and women forms; they are led by two men who raise and lower the two pandanus as the body circles the fire chanting. The men's skins become hot and some take on the persona of their ancestors, breaking into sobs. "People's blood flows very fast." The chant directs the pandanus to ascend to the abode of the Smoke Woman – the spirit who mediates the relationship between shamans and ancestors – and then return. After the chanters have "called out many names" – locations in the iconography of the high ground – the procession halts. Men grab hold of one pandanus and women the other. As the chanting subsides, a son or other blood relative of the individual who made the marita garden seizes the pandanus off the men and leaps onto a bed of hot oven stones. "Dancing" over the stones he stabs the fruit with a cassowary bone dagger. Leaping off, he snatches the pandanus of the women and repeats the sacrifice: letting the "blood" of the pandanus.

Since pandanus creates female blood and possesses the qualities of water, men index their male practices – such as becoming shaman or hunting for game – by placing a food taboo on marita. But during the stabbing ceremony, they abrogate these taboos on marita by spitting out a mouthful of the pandanus seeds in the forest. Once the participating clansmen have eliminated the taboos, they rub pandanus oil on their thighs, genitals, buttocks, and legs – the lower portion of the body being the region of fertility guarded by the spirits of the low ground. They smooth oil especially onto the bellies of the women so that they may "bear children and plant gardens." The cassowary bone dagger which shed the blood of the pandanus now serves as spoon. Each person eats a share of the pandanus as the leaf is passed. Thus, the ceremony distributes the substance of their ancestors to all the clansmen who have, in turn, planted pandanus for the future. The only explanation Maring give for the practice is that eating marita is to consume the spirit of the ancestors of the natural cycle.

Taro and yams are the highest achievements of women's cultivation of the land. Taro especially is a material sign of women's gardening contribution and appears in all celebrations of fertility and reproduction, from ancestor worship to marriage exchange. Taro is the complement of marita's gift of blood as it builds the bone and muscle/flesh that individuals also inherit from their mothers. Where the child suckles mother's milk, adults eat taro. By virtue of transformation, taro and milk are organically related. When women are pregnant they call for sugarcane and taro because "this swells their breasts" – implying that a combination of taro and water is the source of breast milk. Similarly, taro mashed with water is fed to young children as a substitute for breast milk. Maring mothers generally aim to breast feed their children for as long as possible "so that they grow quickly." Older siblings sometimes suckle at their mother's breast when she becomes pregnant again. In effect, foods which are soft, white, and dry like taro strengthen the bone, muscle, and body in general. Types of taro are ranked on these qualities; and thus *watachi* and *alome* species, being soft, homogeneous in texture, and white, are thought best.

The female body creates milk by virtue of eating taro although Maring neither offer an explicit axiom of relationship nor conceive that one would be useful. Nonetheless, there is a link between a woman who is a good gardener and one who is fertile. Asked why a particular woman has many children, people will likely point to how hard she works in the garden, often taking the rhetorical tack of listing the vegetables she harvests and with which she feeds her family. There is a cultural logic in which the presence of children (of either sex)

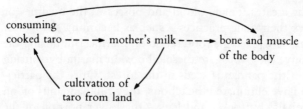

Figure 9 The transformation of taro

allows the inference of a good garden brought about by skill and sympathetic fertility. Thus there is a cultural transformation implicit in the logic of taro consumption (see Figure 9).

Note that taro is similar to marita in that both female substances are created from a water base. The cold moist taro becomes hot and dry when roasted only to be transformed again by addition of sugarcane or water. Taro is served at every important meal. It is usual during a formal presentation of vegetables for the gift-receiver to denigrate the size and species of the taro given, pointing out how few taro were proffered in comparison to the less valued sweet potato: "We are not domesticated pigs," the speaker harangues, "why have you given us so many sweet potatoes when we will only feel satisfied and equal/ balanced (kopla) when we eat taro?" Like other highly substance-producing foods, local wisdom implies that the human body almost instantaneously absorbs taro. Hence, people think it possible to consume large amounts of taro, pork, and marita in comparison to other foods.

In the Maring view, refined white rice resembles cooked taro in color, consistency, and texture, and they regard rice as taro's modern equivalent. People habitually "overcook" rice, boiling it for at least half an hour, until it has lost its bite and taken on the qualities of good taro. Like most New Guineans, the Kauwatyi are avid consumers of white rice and believe that Europeans are as fond of rice as they are of taro. In 1980 New Guineans consumed so much rice that imports threatened to disrupt the national import/export policy; and, for a short period in 1980, the government placed an embargo on overseas rice, so as to maintain an import ceiling until domestic rice production could develop. Public outcry was deafening and the administration quickly back-peddled. When the government announced the ban on rice the Kauwatyi called a public meeting at which the main spokesmen denounced the "stopping of rice" as a symbolic of a much wider social relationship:

Each year the government officers come and collect taxes. We ask them when will the government give us a road [there is a proposed road from the district office at Tabibuga to Koinambe Mission station which would cut through Kauwatyi territory]. The men we elect get drunk and raise their own name, but do little else. The government is cutting off the rice because it does not want business [e.g., coffee growing and tradestores] to flower. It is cutting off the rice because it has no real intention of building the road. It is cutting off the rice because it wants to think only about itself. But things are different than they were when we did not have law. Now we must eat and give rice.

The tenor of the speech takes the relationship between the government and Kauwatyi to be one of the social exchange, taxes given for roads received. Food, in this case rice, indexes the state of the relationship from the local perspective. Thus the "cutting off" of rice is the government's denial of the relationship in its totality. Not merely an analogy on competence – those who falter in one area are likely to stumble somewhere else – but a way of telling that the road would never be built. Whenever the national government intervenes, whether by limiting rice or initiating a poultry project, it makes a social statement it never intended.

Local consumption of rice escalates during the six rainy months when taro is not in season. During the government embargo period brown rice remained available, but there was no demand. It stayed on the shelves at the Koinambe mission store while people clamoured for white. Inspecting a pot of brown rice I had cooked, a friend explained that "brown rice is not rice at all. It is truly an error to name it rice, for it is like eating hardish sweet potatoes, something a man may do when his belly is empty, or when he does not have a good wife or sister, but which he would usually throw to the pigs." The Maring, needless to say, are willing to pay dearly for white rice, over $1 per pound retail. It sells briskly despite the absence of a well-developed cash economy and the travail of lugging the 25 kg sacks up a mountainside. The wholesale acceptance of rice into the system of food prestation, its value in relations to other foods, and the significance of its use turns on its perceived attributes: that it is an imported version of taro.

In contrast to taro, pork, eel, marita, or cassowary, foods which contribute to the production of bodily substance, sweet potatoes, manioc, plantains, breadfruit, and corn, are hard/strong foods which only fill a person's stomach. They have no nutritive value, given the indigenous assumptions about nutrition, but are much needed to alleviate hunger. Although taro is "superior to sweet potato, when a man eats taro he is soon hungry again." I quickly learned that on gardening days (I "owned" a garden with my housemates) it was more sensitive and appropriate to serve sweet potatoes that morning. Here one sees an

83

inverse relationship between food's nutritive value and its ability to relieve hunger. Common opinion is that excrement is composed primarily of sweet potatoes and like foods, which, by direct inference, is why pigs are so fond of gobbling up human feces.

A large class of foods are water foods, meaning that they are mainly composed of water bound with vegetable matter. While they may be tasty, they contribute virtually nothing to the human constitution. "They are eaten one moment and pissed out the next." Therefore, papaya, sugarcane, cucumber, pitpit (a tall grass-like vegetable), and greens are all rather valueless, being neither a source of strength nor nutrition. "We eat them because they taste good and go well with other foods."

Starting in the late 1970s, the Kauwatyi instituted a weekly market where clanspeople (almost all from within the clan cluster) gather to buy and sell mostly vegetables, though an occasional pig or bush egg may be sold. Marketers place a monetary equivalence on the different kinds of food offered. A public meeting in January 1980, involving men and women discussants, officially moved prices higher. The denominator of value is the 10 *toea* piece (which people construe as their own New Guinea replacement for the Australian shilling). Here are the prices quoted at the January 1980 meeting:

1 red pandanus (large)	1 kina (100 *toea*)
1 large taro	10 *toea*
2 medium taro	10 *toea*
3 smallish taro	10 *toea*
3 German taro	10 *toea*
2 yams	10 *toea*
5–7 sweet potatoes	10 *toea*
7 stalks of pitpit	10 *toea*
1 large papaya (about the size of a soccer ball)	10 *toea*
1 hand of bananas	10 *toea*
2 stalks of sugarcane	10 *toea*
any bunch of greens	10 *toea*
5 ears of corn	10 *toea*
1 package of tobacco (5–7 leaves)	20 *toea*

These prices codify perceived values: they reflect the relationship of value between goods more than market operations which invariably take into account other social factors. The pricing of pandanus and taro and the degree of differentiation written into the system (i.e., distinctions in size) indicate relative value. (I say written because I was asked to write down the prices and then type out a list that marketers could consult).

Today, Maring see fish (canned mackerel) and rice as Western versions of pork and taro. The combination has become standard, middle-range feasting fare because it is readily available in stores while taro is seasonal and pork scarce. Most ceremonies, such as payments for a wife, a child's blood, or a wife's bones, include pots of rice and tins of fish in addition to pork and taro. People say that fish and rice "are part of the new era and enlarge a clan's capacity to give" so that nowadays prestations are larger than ever before, a commonsense sign that the standard of living is on the rise.

The power of ancestors, affines, or sorcerers lives in their ability to disrupt the eating of food. Whether they intervene in production, exchange, or digestion, the results are parallel from the consumer's standpoint. In line with the view that a shortfall in rice supply has wider implications, the disruption of food is taken as an index of the overall status of the relationship. For example, men who are disenchanted with the performance of their ancestor spirits, usually because bad times have befallen them in spite of conscientious sacrifices, may suspend offerings to show their displeasure. Sometimes they will warn a certain ancestor that no pigs will be forthcoming until the relationship improves. Given the belief that ancestors consume the spirit of the pig and clansmen the flesh, the logic of the dispute is: ancestors have cut off the food supply to demonstrate their anger; but clansmen, feeling that the ancestors have made an unfair assessment, register their dissatisfaction by refusing food also. Clanspeople cancel food exchanges with affines to announce publicly that the relationship has deteriorated.

The market exchange

Each Saturday, rain or shine, the Kauwatyi hold a market as part of their self-styled conversion to the modern economy of cash cropping, store-bought food, and iron technology. For the Kauwatyi and other Maring, the market is the essence of modernity, in part because it imitates the markets which have grown up around urban centers such as Mt Hagen. As important, the flow of transactions disperses social ties by widening the distribution of food which creates and maintains these ties. People characterize the markets as "now many sell/buy from many." The entire community of clans can legitimately trade goods and services, each person executing his modern social right to buy and sell from whom he pleases. So the market provides a forum which the community has decreed to be more open than traditional food exchanges, usually more restricted and conducted under the critical eye of senior clansmen. Freedom of the market is a totem of modern ideology and explicitly couched as a new found capacity to exercise individual preferences.

Ideology notwithstanding, the market's founding principles lie in the indigenous food exchange system; for the idea that traffic in food is a means of pulling the community together and advancing individual's rights derives straightforwardly from clan and subclan organization. Ironically, from a utilitarian viewpoint, the modern market is quite irrational since everyone produces nearly the same crops. Rarely does anyone buy something they could not get elsewhere at lower cost. In fact, women borrow crops from other women to sell and sometimes the husband or brother of the very woman who lent the foodstuffs buys them back. Less a commercial market, the movement to a modern idiom purifies traditional circulation. The exchange of food has become more diversified at the expense of clan differentiation but to the benefit of clan cluster unification. The rise of individual freedom, meaning the right to trade food more broadly, in particular integrates the young men. The market helps create a Kauwatyi identity, sharpening its focus by widening the political arena – such as election of representatives to local, provincial, and national office.

The one market convention, appropriately stated as a personal value, is that people should not purchase foods from their own clansmen, and certainly not from their own subclansmen. Buyers say, "we feel a bit uneasy when we buy from a sister or mother. If we ask them they will give it to us for nothing." Buying from a clansman confuses the essential distinction between sharing within the clan and exchanging between clans. As a result, people see a fellow clansman's request to buy their goods as a request to share, making the offering of money a new means of registering a desire. Inversely, between clansmen it is also a way of dramatizing anger or dissatisfaction. Several fights broke out over one clansman forcing another to accept money for produce. Cash payment was chastisement: "you don't share food like a clansman so I'll treat you like an outsider who knows only exchange." Buying and selling, nonetheless, are open to several levels of pragmatic manipulation. Hence, a member from the Baigai clan can give another Baigai money for a particular good by saying that he is sharing his money just as the seller is sharing his goods. Because a single Maring verb denotes both buying and selling, the linguistic convention is to use Pidgin to index exchange and Maring to index sharing.

The market, like Maring meetings in general, solidifies slowly as

Table 8 *Market food exchanges for three families*

Family	Raw food bought	Raw food sold	Cooked food given	Cooked food received
Kaiya[a]	Sugarcane[c]	Pitpit[e,f]	1/2 taro[b]	1/2 sugarcane[f]
	Bananas[c]	7 taro[b]	1/2 taro[b]	2 cigarettes[e]
	10 taro[b]	1 marita[d]	Tabacco[c]	1/2 yam[b]
	2 German taro[e]	Plantains[b]	1 sugarcane[d]	
	Tabacco[c]	Tabacco[c]	1/2 sweet potato	
	2 marita[e]	10 corn[c,f]		
	15 sweet potato[b]	Greens[e]		
Punga[b]	20 sweet potato[a]	10 sweet potato[d]	1/2 taro[c]	1 banana[f]
	30 corn[a,e,f]	4 corn[a]	1/2 yam[c]	1 taro[e]
	Tabacco[c]	Bananas[d]	Tabacco[c]	
	Greens[d]			
Mina[c]	10 German taro[a]	5 German taro[e]	1/2 taro[b]	1/2 yam[a]
	3 taro[e]	7 yams[c]	1 sugarcane[a]	1/2 sugarcane[b]
	Pitpit[b]	Greens[b]	Tabacco[a]	Tabacco[a]
	20 corn[a,d,e]	10 corn[a,d]		
	2 marita[a]	1 marita[b]		
	3 cucumber[a]			

a Kamjepakai clan
b Kakupogai clan
c Kambant'igai clan
d Angengbogai clan
e Baigai
f Other

people drift in from dispersed settlements, some more than 10 miles away. When enough buyers and sellers have accumulated, the market begins. Women, their children who assist, and an occasional man form a circle on the dance ground. There is a formal presentation of lining the food up for inspection. After the buyers, all men as a rule, have looked over the foods the village Committee (a political post) gives the word and the market commences. Buying carries on until the market is sold out. Kauwatyi, who may hold the largest market, have 300–500 participants, plus an assortment of unfettered pigs and dogs swarming about, sometimes stealing a sweet potato from someone's pile amid the orchestrated pandemonium.

Prior to and during the market a considerable trade occurs in various cooked foods. Men arrive at the market eating roasted taro, sweet potatoes, corn, yams, and smoking tobacco. They circulate among the pockets of clansmen, shaking hands, doling out small amounts of food. Men distribute whole taros or ears of corn which, in turn, are broken and further distributed. Food-giving inaugurates all public gatherings and Maring dismiss as curious the European practice of calling a meeting without a hint of food. During the market, raw foods flow from women to men and back to women again, husbands buying and then piling their purchases next to their wives' string bags. The market circulates cooked foods from women to men and then to other men; or, alternatively, from women to women. The distribution realized in the market surpasses local, less organized, exchanges of food, at least this is what people believe. Table 8 provides a basic idea of the dimensions of the market exchange. The data confirms that people buy what they sell from a broad range of people and that cooked foods travel widely.

Food as social and psychological control

In the domain of worship, ancestors exert their hand on the living by controlling the prosperity of gardens and livestock. The ability of ancestors, or of the Christian god for that matter, to affect the abundance of food resonates in Maring psychology. A modern result is that people believe that the foremost deed of the Anglican god has been to send the mission trade store, thereby providing a new food source. Mission influence is inextricably tied to its control over food, a fact so palpable that the missionaries worry about "rice Christians" – meaning "natives who honor Christ only in order to gain access to Western cargo." But from the Maring perspective, the essence of being a Christian, indeed the power and authority of Jesus Christ, is his worshippers' access to rice and fish. The food distributed by the Church is not an added benefit of Christianity but its heart and soul. As one pundit put it: "without the trade store there would be no Anglican god." Local mission power has waned in recent years, in part because of the coming of clan-owned trade stores which undercut its power as a food source. This seems to be occurring throughout the Highlands as New Guineans have become more sophisticated in Western business ways.

Closer to tradition, food is the index and instrument of personal control in two senses. First, a gardening pair show control in planting of food by working long hours, and by making more and larger gardens than they strictly need. Second, a person modulates food intake, especially in tough situations. When a man turns away a gift of food because the food is taboo, he is exhibiting strength and self-control, particularly if he has no definite proof. Those who demonstrate such restraint – that is, those who have so mastered their appetite that they need take no unnecessary risks – win social approval. One of the attributes of leaders is that they have the power to accept or reject even the most desirable kinds of foods, such as pork, without blinking. Maring see a direct correlation between the man who can control his desires about food and the man who is worthy of controlling others. Not surprisingly, many fears, anxieties, and possibility of pollution are bound up with eating. People silently condemn themselves for a lack of self-control over food, aware that revelation would be embarrassing. In consequence, there is much secret eating, with all the attendant guilt and fears of discovery. People disdainfully mark others who allegedly have eaten pig alone or failed to share some marita or taro. The strong man taps his garden resources slowly: eating in public, giving food away, consuming moderately in relation to guests. Maring perform magic, and nowadays some say Christian prayers, to help them exercise control over food.

Due to foods' relationship to the ebb and tide of bodily substances, it figures prominently in the execution of sorcery and is the favorite medium of *koimps* (witches). They attack food "because they know that that is where we are vulnerable." In keeping with the theme of self-control, the community often considers the attack to be partly the victim's fault, a result of his/her weakness in dealing with food. The destruction of substance is the inverse of its generation. Meat, particularly pig, and taro, yams, sugarcane, and marita are especially receptive vehicles for sorcery because they are involved in producing human substances. Sorcery usually does its damage by creating blockages, mainly in the liver. The most frequent kind of damage causes the liver to move, shutting off one or more of the human orifices. Fluids, for example, restricted from one orifice will be channeled into other inappropriate ones, causing such symptoms as spitting up of blood, flow of mucus, and vomiting. Inasmuch as liver movement is responsible for illness, kinsmen treat sickness by sacrificing a pig to the ancestors and feeding its liver to the victim.

A sorcerer's control over food epitomizes his control over people and events. Clansmen attempt to regulate their relationship with ancestors by modulating food sacrifices; ancestors, in turn, withhold the rewards of the garden to spur the living. Overall, the emotional investments in food make it a volatile material. Maring rationalize the causes of warfare in three ways, all of which have the same final significance from the perspective of social reproduction; the theft of a woman, and thus female blood and garden labor; sorcery, leading to the disruption of the liver and food canals; and the theft or destruction of a garden or food. Hence, the culture thrice motivates the leitmotif that such and such a fight broke out over a theft of marita or pig: by the logic of substance, by the affective power of food, and by desecration of garden food to signify the ultimate in hostility and contempt.

Food taboos

The link between food and social organization is nowhere more evident than in the form and function of food taboos. Maring labor under large sets of prohibitions that specify a range of variables, from the species of food to where it was grown and who cooked it. People adopt and abandon taboos for reasons ranging from personal squabbles to full-scale war. Each individual possesses a roster of food taboos which bear a personal as well as a social stamp. The ancestors supernaturally sanction and enforce these prohibitions, infidelities eventually punished by illness, accident, or death. As an example, informants pointed to a man disfigured by fire, explaining that some years ago he had eaten pig alone in the bush and later been punished by the ancestors for his greed. Today, the one Anglican rite adopted enthusiastically is Lenten renouncement of certain foods, and much to the chagrin of the local priests it overshadows even the resurrection on Easter Sunday.

I am arguing that commensality, due to its depth and subtlety of expression, allows clansmen delicately to map a wide spectrum of social relationships. Food taboos are powerful means for indexing the state of current affairs or the desire to negotiate a new one. Further, food taboos speak of the past as much as the present since they perpetuate social distance arising from the wars and conflicts of ancestors. In Maring words, "men who do not eat together cannot be brothers, they share nothing in common but anger."

There are three categories of food taboos, each of which has a different social trajectory.

1. *Relya* Absolute prohibitions against eating certain kinds of animal and vegetable foods which are identified with certain clans and subclans. Their origin is the mythical and autochthonous circumstances under which the earliest ancestors moved into the Jimi and transformed the natural universe into the social one. Within the envelope of ideology, *relya* are thought to remain in force forever. In reality, however, these taboos differentiate clans, and the present pattern of prohibitions is the sedimentation of social history, the dynamics of fusion and fission in which new clan status is accompanied by the transference, adoption, and extinction of food taboos.

2. *Moi* Temporary prohibitions circumscribing the nucleus of individuals who are related to the recently deceased. They apply especially to the surviving spouse and those women who are charged with pre-

paring the body and watching over it during funerary services. During the period prior to burial, the *moi* prohibits the spouse from cooking with people who are not in mourning; a woman will also assume the taboos suffered by her husband. Widowers are supposed to renounce eating pork during the mourning period and a ban is levied on sexual intercourse and remarriage. The deceased's agnates also abstain from certain foods to express not only a personal loss but a social relationship. By assuming a taboo they commit themselves to sacrificing pigs to this new ancestor sometime in the future. The length of time these prohibitions are endured is taken as a sign of the affinity which existed and should continue to prevail.

3. *Acek* Prohibitions defining the ongoing state of affairs between specific people or clans by establishing dietary rules. Across time and context, application varies as does membership. The history of clan events (e.g., war), the developmental cycle of the person, and the social persona of the clansmen (e.g., caretaker of the fight stone), are important. A taboo either terminates automatically if pegged to the natural calendar (e.g., period when taro is planted), or else ritually if pegged to the social one (e.g., the planting of *rumbim* to indicate truce). *Acek* may apply to all foods raised in a particular precinct, to eating with a specified set of people, and to certain foods and mixtures of food for periods varying from several days to a lifetime.

Structurally, the taboo categories mediate the oppositions orienting many Maring practices: social growth/natural fertility, ancestor spirits/living community, and war/peace. The culture relates the categories by using them in concert and in the same practice. Only issues of land and war elicit a greater emotional response than food taboos. Commenting on what they see as the disintegration of the social order, older men rail loudly at the propensity of the young to disregard food taboos. They rightly perceive the force of the taboo, though they overlook half of current reality; for members of the new generation reshape their social universe not only by abandoning their parents' taboos but by adopting new ones. For example, some young men held that it was prohibited for them to smoke the locally-grown tobacco, only the storebought variety was acceptable. Where food is concerned, the young men swing between indigenous and modern moods, testing the waters in each. So, for instance, one of my housemates ate forbidden pork (from the Cenda clan cluster), noting diffidently while he ate that such taboos no longer mattered; however, when he took ill a week later he had little doubt of the cause and confessed to a shaman.

The use and manipulation of food taboos

On a day to day basis, *relya* taboos are relatively passé since people neither cultivate nor serve forbidden foods. *Relya* focuses on certain, very specific foods, such as a sub-species of banana, species of snake, or dog (though nobody recalled having eaten dog, taboo or no taboo). Because *relya* get scant social play, clansmen can invoke them on specific occasions especially to delineate clan affiliation. A non-agnate assumes the *relya* if he intends to stay for the forseeable future. A person may adopt a friend's taboos out of sympathy on a specific occasion because "it is not polite to eat a tabooed food in front of a friend." Such situational adoption announces the closeness of the friendship; it shows that the two are brothers insofar as they share the same clan taboos. For non-agnates, the *relya* becomes a play on social identity. A first generation non-agnate can never become a *bona fide* agnate because he has not been born of the clan soil: he was born of clan grease of another group, and nothing can reverse this inalienable fact. His sons and daughters, however, can fully assimilate because they are born of substance derived from the land of his new clan. By adopting the clan taboos the non-agnate signals a desire for his offspring to remain permanently in the new clan. He assumes the *relya* not just situationally, but out of true attachment (like an umbilical cord) to his new clan. Alternatively, "true" agnates can cast a vote against his inclusion by offering him prohibited food – that is, by treating him like a non-agnate.

Example of taboo use

Kam is a Kwima man from the eastern Jimi who is living with his wife's clansmen, Kakupogai of the Kauwatyi cluster. After the Saturday market has finished and the court cases which follow have been adjudicated, some twenty Kakupogai prepare an afternoon meal, which includes snake. About a dozen non-clansmen join the party. Soon after the meal is ready, a senior Kakupogai offers Kam snake, a prohibited food. A dialogue ensues to negotiate the meaning of the offering.

Kam: "I do now want to eat snake." His voice is stage firmness as he clearly views the proffered snake as an indication that the senior man still considers him an outsider and is not willing to accept him.

Senior Man I: "Kam and the other guests [he glances my way as if to say the meat was prepared for my benefit] are lucky to be able to eat snake; it is meat, but we cannot eat it." The "we" very specifically excludes addressees.

Kam: He nervously pokes the snake the senior Kakupogai put on his plate. Then he intones: "Since I came I have helped Punt build a garden. We cut trees, rolled logs, burned the garden so that the crops would come up strong. I have joined with Tumj in planting coffee, picking the beans, shelling them at Kompiai [a place name], putting the coffee in the sun to dry, and carrying it to Koinambe to get money. I have given money with my brothers [referring to other Kakupogai] for the bride wealth of my namesake, Kam, and to other young men who wish to marry." He continues for several minutes more naming new deeds and reiterating the ones mentioned. Kam then turns and passes his plate of snake to me saying, "if I eat snake I am afraid I will become ill." The mention of illness points to Kakupogai ancestors who would be angry if their descendant ate snake. Thus, by inference, he is Kakupogai.

Senior Man II: (chuckling) "I have seen Kam eat rat at Kwima." The particular kind of rat named, which is quite edible, feeds on this tabooed snake. Note the theory of substance that the rat's body derives from the snake through consumption and thus eating the rat is equivalent to eating the snake. Although playing on a cultural theme, this inference was sufficiently far-fetched that Kakupogai supporters of Kam mocked the suggestion. One man pretended to question a pig about where it had been feeding and what it ate. His mockery sent waves of laughter through the audience, and released the building tension.

Senior Man III: "Kam should not eat the snake; Runga cooked the snake." Far from a supportive statement, this introduced a new set of variables to explain Kam's reluctance to eat the snake. Runga's natal clan fought on the side of the Irimban against Kam's natal clan and thus Kam should not eat what she has cooked according to the fire taboos associated with warfare. Strictly speaking, a fire taboo was in force and Kam should refuse the snake for that reason. Thus, the community could see his refusal as no more than respect for custom. In effect, the remark deflected the trajectory of the index, since the fire taboos had the same final result though altogether different meaning.

The Kakupogai involved in the incident seized upon this latter alternative as a compromise solution, and the matter was dropped at least for the time being. However, shortly afterward Kam signed up for a two year stint on the plantations near Port Moresby.

Moi and *acek*

Moi are death taboos assumed by the surviving spouse(s) and those women who attend the corpse during its ritual decomposition. Parents and close kinsmen of the dead also renounce eating certain foods, such as pork, to commemorate the deceased, and to convince the new ancestor that they are not about to forget him. In addition, they will sometimes assume a taboo against eating a food associated with the dead person. Husbands will place a ban on a species of taro their wives cultivated; wives often renounce their husbands' favorite food, or, at least in two cases, the last food they ate before they died. As social statements, *moi* announce publicly the willingness of the clan and clan cluster to honor an individual from a particular subclan. Thus, clansmen frequently air their grievances through funerary behavior in general, as feelings run high and the opportunities for significance are great. Those who participate in *moi* transitively mark their affinity to each other in terms of their relationship to the dead. From the vantage of exchange, affines gauge their relations by the taboos they assume. So when a married woman dies, her natal clan watches the funeral to determine whether her husband's clan wishes to continue the affinal tie or begins to dissolve it. A man assumes *moi*, sacrifices pig(s) for his wife, and announces his intention of "paying for her bones" anywhere from six months to two years later to reconfirm the tie. Eating of *moi* foods thus becomes a means of launching insults at an affine, perhaps as a rebuke for not having lived up to his obligations on an occasion. By the same token, people who suffer illness sometimes attribute its cause to ancestors seeking revenge for breaking of *moi*. During the funeral and once the taboos are assumed, manifold possibilities open up for use and manipulation of food.

Here is another example from the Kakupogai clan. When Tuj, an elder clansman with two daughters, two sons, and a host of grandchildren, died, affines came from nearby Kauwatyi clans and from distant Kwima and Tuguma clans. Relations between the various sets of affines had not been sanguine and hence the funerary proceedings walked a knife's edge. Tuj's eldest son, Bunt, took the initiative and warned that it was wrong for affines to honor the bones of his father with lingering bitterness. To indicate that he was taking his father's place in the upcoming Jimi Valley elections, Bunt had seized the occasion to make peace. It was an instance of the wise use of power and a means of consolidating a nucleus of supporters. Bunt then killed a sacrificial pig, offering it to the spirits of the low ground and distributing it to all those who came for the burial. He carved up the pig and had all those present eat a morsel in his father's name. Then Bunt, breaking out into deep sobs, declared he was overcome with grief, and pushing the pork before him away immediately renounced the eating of pork. He also said that he could no longer eat *golup*, a type of banana, or *acquia*, a type of pandanus. The audience was visibly moved as he urged it to follow suit and rally around his father's "name."

Although *moi* and less so *relya* do come into play, *acek* is the most dynamic category of taboo, playing a conspicuous role in the cycle of war and peace, and in day to day creation or differentiation of consubstantiality. Maring use these taboos to mark sacred or profane relationships from ordinary ones. For example, it is taboo for non-clansmen to eat pig sacrificed to the ancestors of Fight or Red Spirits. Disputing clans can signal their enmity by establishing *acek* on each other's foods. Such action widens the breach between clans by outlawing commensality. Members of the same clan sometimes willfully assume such taboos to underscore the seriousness of the internal conflict – that is, they adopt taboos intended for outsiders to demonstrate the gravity of the slight and to elicit neutral mediation. Another reason *acek* is serious is that once assumed, it can be abrogated only by the sacrifice of pig. Fight-magic men and other ritual leaders mark themselves as extraordinary by suffering a great number of taboos, entailing avoidance of foods associated with women (i.e., wet and moist). Fight-magic men are referred to as *acek yu* or taboo men.

Warfare is the momentous occasion for declaration of *acek*. When a clan cluster uproots the *rumbim*, war is formally declared, and numerous taboos take effect. The clan cluster moves into the social cycle of war and peace, the cycle dominated by men, the Fight Ancestors, and all things male, just as the natural cycle revolves on women, spirits of fertility, and all things female. In this light, the clan cluster prohibits eating marita of many species, eels which are cold and wet and thus debilitating to the hotness of the warrior, and marsupials which may not be trapped or eaten together with marita of any kind. No cultivated food grown on enemy land, harvested elsewhere by enemy hands, or by an ally of the enemy may now be consumed. At each stage of ritual progression into war, central combatants adopt new taboos; and on battle days all contact with women and female foods is banned. In essence, the war taboos separate the social from the natural cycle, particularly fight leaders from all pollution, and separate the warring groups by prohibiting a common renewal of bodily substances.

Food taboos arising from hostility are of two general types: ground or cultivation *acek* and interdining *acek*. Ground taboos forbid the eating of food from a land which is also providing food to the enemy. No one may consume any domesticated food, animal or vegetable, grown on the land of the enemy clan cluster. The taboo is based on the circulation of clan substances and the resulting identification of man, crops, and cultivated land. Such statements as "if we ate the food of our enemy there would be no difference between us" or "the food of an enemy belongs to their spirits not ours" embodies this conception. The taboo logically extends not only to land but to planting material also. So no one may consume domesticated foods, animal or vegetable, grown by a person (1) who is a member of a hostile group even when his garden is on friendly territory; (2) who served as an ally of the enemy cluster; and (3) who has killed a member of one's own group, whether or not war has been formally declared (Rappaport 1968:126, 134–6). The issue is separation of substance; it never applies to storebought foods. The Manamban, for example, regularly buy rice and fish from the Kauwatyi trade store although they may not eat from Kauwatyi land.

Interdining taboos prohibit clansmen from eating food cooked over the same fire, food harvested from the same plant, or cut from the same animal as an enemy. Fire taboos apply to anyone already separated by a ground taboo, the descendants of a former enemy, or any clansmen having a ground taboo on someone who shares one's cooking fires.

Prohibitions arising from enmity are not eternal. With the advent of truce and the passage of peacetime they progressively dissolve. Return to the coexistence of prewar days requires at least four generations, although progress is rarely that rapid, since warfare often erupts again. Ground *acek* melt away sooner than interdining taboos as warring clan clusters begin to stabilize their relationship. For example, children of combatants will retain the ground taboos assumed by their fathers at the outset of war but lift the ban on any form of interaction. In subsequent generation only fire taboos will be retained and eventually this last vestige of war will slip away. The progressive dissolution of taboos is a trace of political conflicts and the state of relationships between groups after the battles. Mutual decisions to lift or perpetuate taboos are a sensitive indicator of intergroup attitudes at any historical point. The Kauwatyi have taken steps, for example, to eliminate taboos with Cenda but not with Manamban. Especially Kauwatyi employed by the Anglican mission at Koinambe, a site purchased from the Cenda, no longer observe any taboos. They aver that Koinambe is Jesus' land and that, anyway, the Church has lifted the taboos. Ironically, the abrogation of the taboos under "God's law" has allowed the aggressive Kauwatyi to infiltrate Koinambe and seize most of the business post (e.g., coffee buyer, station manager, trade store manager). To no one's surprise, trouble is brewing over this monopoly.

The ethnotheory of growth and development

As cultivation drives clan reproduction, it is fitting, almost necessary, that Maring should represent the development of the clan in terms of vegetative propagation. As noted when discussing the association of crops, the relationship leans in the other direction also: people speak of garden productivity in terms of clan propagation. An organic and instrumental link exists between garden and clan florescence, not only because success in one breeds success in the other, but because the same principle of fertility and growth operates in each. The ethnotheory locates the dynamics of growth and development in the exchange of female substance against the backdrop of fixed male assets (i.e., land, semen, and ancestors). This ethnotheory appears in the belief that men and all things male are permanent while women and things female are transient. Also in the understanding that the fertility of exchange is the exchange of fertility.

From the clan's perspective, its growth and development rides squarely on marriage exchange, the acquisition of female labor and substance. Men transplant women from their natal clan and thereby import the fertility to enrich their clan substance. In terms of cultivation, growth depends on the marriage of female crops and labor to male lands. This entails transplanting cultigens from one garden to the next. The explicit link is that just as the transfer of women fertilizes the clan over generations, so transplanting of cultigens fertilizes the land over seasons. Human ingenuity consists in bringing the principle of exchange to bear successfully. This is further reason why people evaluate the measure of a clan in terms of its gardens, seizing on garden size, composition, health, and dozens of other factors.

Speakers exploit the links between clan and garden development in vocabulary, inference, and explanation. A man sums up his dissatisfaction with his wife by claiming she is a poor gardener. In a sample of nearly thirty divorces, men universally cited their wife's gardening as a major reason for the breakup. People attribute a clan's poor gardens to its failure to make fruitful marriages. Or, more metaphorically, men compare a breakdown in affinal relations to a dying garden. That clan and garden growth share a common principle and are linked reproductively allows Maring to blend statements of fact and principle.

Clansmen refer to their affines and uterine kin as *indok wump* (people/planting material). It translates both as clans who are sources of women and as human planting material, the latter a specific reference to the inmarrying woman. The entwining bloodlines of marriage generate the affinal networks of *indok wump*; the birth of sons and daughters and their subsequent marriages sustain it. Maring believe that the propagation of taro parallels the social process. It embodies as symbol and index the same principle of exchange. I paraphrase from Lowman (1980:129) who has eloquently described (Figure 10) the indigenous model.

Taro (*Colocasia esculenta*)

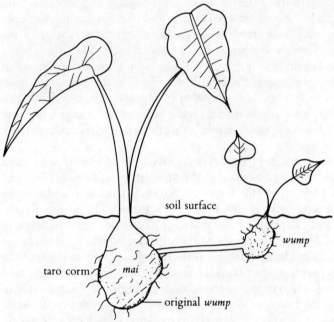

Figure 10 Vegetative propagation as a model of clan growth

In terms of cultivation, the mature taro plant has two main components – the corm and cormels. The corm, or edible portion, was originally a cormel harvested in another swidden and transplanted to a new
one. As the cormel matures, it develops subsidiary dwarf cormels that
encircle its periphery. Maring describe the taro corm as *mai* and harvest
it for consumption. Speakers use *mai* to mean a mature entity, such as
an older person, a mother (especially one who is breast feeding), a
source of progeny, or the final point of growth. The taro cormels are
called *wump* and speakers use it to denote an immature entity, a progeny, the basic source of further propagation. Women harvest the
wump to transplant it to a new swidden in which they become *mai*, producing a new generation of *wump*. *Mai* and *wump* mark two distinct
points in a process of organic continuity, each *mai* produces a *wump*
which becomes a *mai, ad infinitum*. Although *mai* and *wump* constitute
an organic unity, both conceptual and natural, they are always separated by time and space. People can perpetuate the cycle only if they
transplant the *wump* to new swiddens. The method of propagation differentiates taro from other cultigens.

Local ideology characterizes men as the giant trees of the primary forest, with thick boles and deeply entrenched roots nourished by clan lands. The leitmotif is the connection between permanence, landedness, and clan growth. Such primary forest encircles the sacred grove (*raku*) where the bones of the ancestors are buried. The motif plays on many levels. The lifespan of the primary forest transcends that of the individual tree just as the clan outlives the man; historically, both trees and men are a part of the land which are recycled. In another breath, the ideology likens women to banana trees which men cut and transplant to new gardens. Women's image alternates from banana tree, to taro, to pandanus, each capturing an essential female characteristic from the perspective of the garden. In all these forms, practice equates gardeners with mothers and sources of food and substance. So, for example, *mai* refers to mother as well as taro corm. In the declension of kin terms, *ama* denotes my mother whereas *mai* denotes his/her/their mother. This lends the force of kin distance to *mai*; and indeed every *wump* which men plant on another clan's land will become a *mai*, mother and source of food for another clan's children. Men are responsible for planting a woman in a clan where she is likely to thrive and bear fertile children. She will produce the mother who will bear the female returned to the original clan – that is, in the second descending generation. Maring name this reciprocity "backing the *wump*" and failure to reverse the flow of exchange calls for a compensation payment of pork and money.

Both male and female children possess the blood of their mother yet were formed from their father's semen and nurtured from food raised on his lands. This intersection of co-substance relations means that children belong to the clans of both husband and wife. Lowman (1980: 131–2), though thrown slightly off course by a genealogical model, knows the relationship:

Compensatory gifts enable the husband's [clan/subclan] to regard the wife and her children as full members of their own territorial group. Failure to make these payments confers on the wife's kinsmen the right to reclaim her and her children. Sometimes wives actually threaten to or voluntarily return to their original territory. Remaining devoted to their own agnatic kinsmen, Maring women understand well the compensatory nature of gifts made on their behalf. This ideology, and the rules of social exchange it implies, reflect the statistical norm of patrivirilocal residence. However, in cases where uxorilocal or avunculocal residence are practiced, no connubial payments are expected since the wump are planted on the land of the wife's or mother's patri[clan/subclan].

land   – – – – – – – →   exchange of land use rights

garden – – – – – – – →   exchange of planting materials

food   – – – – – – →   exchange of food and food taboos

people – – – – – – – →   exchange of women

Figure 11 Main co-substance relations

This pattern reiterates the logic that substance must flow against substance, the wife–donor must receive tokens such as pork, planting
material, and land in return for the woman given. An implicit theme is
the great extent to which consumption of food from the clan's land is
the substance of agnation. More than "reflect[ing] the statistical norm
of patrivirilocal residence" the interplay between compensatory gifts
and living on clan lands defines an individual's agnatic identity. For the
Maring (and for other Highlanders), uxorilocal and avunculocal residence, in effect the replanting of men, parallels the exchange of
women. As the ethnotheory reveals, the shift in residence is not an
incidental part of clanship but one of its principal constituents. Ties between groups can arise as much from the movement of men as women,
though of course a clan which exported men and women would not
long survive. Historically, clans die in precisely this manner.

Within the compass of the natural cycle, clans conduct four levels of
exchange. There is (1) the continual flow of rights in land; (2) exchange
of planting material from one clan's gardens to gardens of another clan;
(3) commerce in food grown on the clan lands with planting materials;
and (4) the exchange of women who cultivate the crops, exchange the
planting materials, and provide the food to non-agnates. These interlocking levels of exchange, all involving substance in one form or
another; constantly generate co-substance relations between friendly
clans.

Figure 11 illustrates how the clan integrates its natural cycle with the
exchange system. Although, ideologically, the clan should be a master
of self-sufficiency, as exhibited in the oratory of clan strength, in fact
the propulsion of the natural cycle depends greatly on exchange. Each
of the critical points of the cycle is an opportunity to forge co-
substance bonds. For any intermarrying clans there are thus four co-
occurring registers of exchange. In its account of the natural cycle,
ethnotheory focuses on the transfer of planting material, particularly
taro, and by extending the parallel to marriage, creates a general
account of clan growth and development. Equally true, however, is

that the exchange of men and male assets is also at the center of clan development. It is an alternative of practice whose pragmatic form and
force is papered over by the agnatic ideology.

The cultivation of kinship

Because food produces and renews the substances which create kinship, the structure and development of kin ties is inseparable from the
management of production. For the Maring, the bonding of kinship to
cultivation is the nature of culture, the commonsense perspective of
people and gardens. Those who garden together or raise pigs cooperatively are both characteristically kinsmen and are generating kinship.
From the vantage of action and consciousness the open question is with
whom an individual will garden and under what circumstances. Much
conversational probing and interpretation centers on who helps whom
to cut a garden or pick coffee. Maring say that relationships made in
the garden make the person. As one woman put it: "Of course people
worry about their gardens; they worry most who will help them."

All married men, and many single men, oversee several gardens
while being less involved in as many as a dozen others. According to
my informal survey, the average married Kauwatyi makes three gardens "for himself" and participates in six others to varying degrees.
The spectrum of involvement has three benchmarks: (1) individuals
who participate directly in the making of the garden; (2) those who
assist the principal cultivators over the life of the garden; and (3) those
who render sporadic help, mainly during the garden's initial cutting or
planting. Degrees of social, material, labor, and emotional reciprocity
map the levels of participation and compensate those who have helped.

Food is its own measure as the exchange of produce summarizes the
modes of reciprocity. The food given in return for gardening assistance indexes the social, material, labor, and emotional values forthcoming. Those who participate directly share equally in the fruits of
the garden; those who assist heavily expect to enjoy a regular flow of
food gifts on an informal basis; and those who assist more sporadically
expect to receive small parcels of food and a meal following the day's
labor. The willingness to work and to give food is the most useful and
often-used gauge of the state of interpersonal relationships. Much
public grumbling at the Saturday market and compensation rituals
concerns who has helped or failed to help, who has reciprocated properly and who has not. Occasionally tempers flare and affairs of the
garden are frequently brought up at trials. Especially in recent years,
young men express their independence from senior clansmen by refus-

ing to assist in coffee, pandanus, and gardening tasks, or doing so half-heartedly.

The point is that in theory and ethnography the relationship between cultivation and kinship is a mediated one. Maring use exchange to comment on the kin ties developed from common production. Whereas gardening cooperatively invokes the structural possibility of kinship, reciprocity of labor, material, emotional support, and especially food specifies the scope, intensity, and future of the relationship.

Almost invariably, clansmen locate their different gardens in distinct ecological zones. This entails garden making at graduated altitudes along the mountain face as variations in altitudes of up to 4,000 feet with concomitant temperature changes allow different crops to flourish. Although clans strive to garden in lower as well as upper altitudes somewhat unequal access to land and ecological zones exist. There is thus a well-publicized material benefit to be gained from sharing garden land among clans or within a clan. Nonetheless, the ecological rationality of production is not its source of social dynamics, but rather a synopsis of the cultural practices which motivate action.

Maring are quite explicit that it is the social value of both low and high altitude products which inspires them to diversify. More, those clansmen who have access to both high and low zones are most likely to be engaged in the sharing of garden land. People typically respond to the question of why they are gardening on someone else's land by noting that the land-giver is helping them grow food. The issue is not that they need land – often they have no shortage – but that they help each other in cultivation. Maring utilize land as a trading vehicle, an institutionalized means of negotiating the social and political world. The member subclans of a clan disperse their gardens throughout clan territory, and the interdigitation of gardens across time and space is one of the basic cements of clan unity.

The Maring system of slash and burn agriculture opens up some interesting possibilities for the cultivation of social relations, almost all of which kinsmen exploit. The swidden regime calls for the perpetual rotation of garden sites, a particular expanse of hillside coming under cultivation about every ten years. The geography of garden land bears a cultural stamp, as Maring divide every foot of their territory into named sectors. The Kauwatyi, for example, partition their territory into some fifty-six named land units which vary in size and shape. Usually, designated natural landmarks, such as gullies, streams, and outcroppings, segregate the parcels of land. The units of land possess characteristics and a practical history connected to the clan. Each unit can hold multiple gardens, though rarely more than half a dozen at a given point in time. Its history is the collective memory of the association of gardens and gardeners, and sometimes significant agricultural events, such as the introduction of a new species of sweet potato.

Individuals who plant over the old gardens of previous kin recognize a continuity of tradition. Men are most inclined to use the gardens of their fathers, followed in order by those of subclan members, clansmen, and affines. Throughout, replanting establishes a meaningful bond between man and land which may be directed for social purposes. Individuals who have gardened the same plot at different times are close, "like two roots of a tree," and it is customary to give small gifts of food to those who have planted before. In many instances, previous gardeners will assist present tenants thereby exponentially increasing the strength of the tie. By the same token, feuding clansmen will occasionally use each other's plots without seeking consent. Maring construe this as a belligerent act. Thus, the pragmatic possibilities fall in both directions; the enrichment or demise of a relationship hinges on the intentionality and social demeanor of the action. In both cases, the determination of meaning begins in the linkage between man and land.

Another variation on this theme plays on who uses the adjacent gardens or ones inside the same unit of land. Maring aver that men plant next to one another "because they are brothers." But it is equally true that is why they are brothers (i.e., clansmen) in the double sense of consubstantiality and concerted action. Parallel gardening, and all that people associate with it, signals a closeness in a relationship, what Maring call "having your spirit in the same locale." Generally, those who make gardens in the same locale help each other in numerous ways on a day to day basis. It is impossible to isolate how much any one factor contributes to the relationship. What is clear is that the combined contribution of food sharing, joint labor, and common landedness enriches the sense and substance of kinship. What counts as garden proximity in space or time is a cultural construction which mirrors both the current human bonds and a deeper structural unity.

A variety of people participate in the making of a garden. The initial gardening pair should consist of a man and a woman; Maring perceive same-sex pairs as aberrant and excuse them only under unusual conditions such as a coastal plantation. The man cuts and clears the garden and constructs the fence while the woman plants and harvests the crops. The division of labor specifies this cross-sex relationship whose underpinning is the notion that men should not plant or harvest tubers. Both principals recruit a variety of same-sex helpers. So several men

Table 9 *Gardening pairs*

Gardening pair	Number	Percentage
Husband and wife	46	35
Married sister with brother	22	17
Wife and husband's father	12	9
Wife and husband's brother	16	12
Married daughter and father	11	8
Son and widowed mother	13	10
Wife and sister's husband	6	5
Wife and husband's sister's son	4	3

who may be related in every conceivable way work alongside the "garden's father" and several women assist alongside the "garden's mother." Thus four major sets of social relationships are directly developed in the making of a garden: (1) the gardening pair, (2) the same-sex bond between cooperating men, (3) the same-sex bond between cooperating men and women, and (4) the cross-sex bond between cooperating men and women. In the same season, an individual may be the principal in three or four gardening pairs plus a cooperative participant in the same number. It goes without saying that those who garden together also eat the same food and recognize a fertile developing kinship tie.

The most frequent gardening pair is a married couple. The following social combinations are also common and indicate the possible diversity (see Table 9).

I could enumerate almost a dozen other recorded combinations. But the key point is that practice encourages the diversification of gardening pairs and allows men and women to attract assistance along many kin lines. There is great potential for structuring kinship through cooperative production. The process not only further relates the principals, but the assistants to the "parents" of the garden and sometimes unrelated persons. For example, a man may receive help from an affine who will work alongside and share food with a woman's uterine kin. It is not uncommon for a man's brother's wife to garden together with his wife's sister.

The final dynamic of garden relationships is the exchange of planting materials. The flow of cultigens may involve almost any variety of kin. Maring believe that mutual concern and truth are key elements here because cultigens are open to sorcery. Thus mere acceptance of the cultigens is in some cases a sign of faith in the relationship. Traffic in planting materials is a favorite means of instituting a gardening tie when distance separates kin and makes joint gardening impractical. On such occasions, gift-givers say "we give them planting material because we want to help them though they live far away." Women usually exchange immature tubers, notably taro and yams, while men trade banana trees and sugarcane stalks.

The use of cultigens for social ends is deceptively simple and Maring carry it off with informality and great ease. Women may stroll up to a garden in the making and empty their net bags of an assortment of taros and yams, the "parents" of the garden casually sifting through the gift and typically sorting the species. There are many minor variations on this scene depending on its social persona and significance. What they all have in common is a careful evaluation of the merits of the gift of planting material. Between the gift and the production of social relationships is the system of food classification. That is, the use of cultigens for social ends imbues the food classification with pragmatic and practical value. As noted earlier, Maring rank all crops on a preference ladder. Taro, for example, possess a higher value than sweet potatoes which in turn have a higher status than manioc. With finer precision, the culture also internally ranks the numerous species of taro, yams, sweet potatoes, bananas, and sugarcane. For example, the *watchi* taro ranks higher than *alome* which outranks *pena*. The differentiation of cultigens, from generic through sub-species levels, has strong functional value with respect to the organization of social relationships. A gift of taro says something different than one of sweet potatoes, and a gift of *alome* taro carries more weight than one of *pena*. The cognitive salience of the food classification, as well as its formation and development, derives from its use as an instrument of social classification. The system is sufficient to allow groups or individuals to register the difference between persons or changes in the course of a relationship.

In overview, gardening practices shape cultivation and social organization by linking select kinsmen in food production. And, like food taboos and commensality, gardening practices concretize and enrich co-substance bonds. On one level, gardening is a particular set of instances of how people use kin connections for specific purposes. It is a small-group enterprise in which members aim to satisfy personal interests such as securing labor, credits, or repaying a debt. On a deeper level, group formation is not only based on kin ties but actively produces them. The cultural value ascribed to food imbues its production with significance for the production of social relations. Maring recognize this principle in views such as "gardening binds people," "endows them with common roots," thus "making relationships strong." Between husband and wife, it affirms the complementarity of sex roles in production and reproduction. Among agnates, cooperative gardening transforms an official clan relationship into a practical one with greater consequences for future concerted action. Among non-agnates, cultivation affords an opportunity to create co-substance bonds across clan lines. And these create and lubricate exchange routes along which women, goods, and sometimes entire subclans move. The power of gardening practices emerges most clearly in its role in the reaffiliation of people and groups to new clans.

The view expressed here takes issue with two current theories of the relationship between production and social organization in New Guinea. The first states that the social structure embodies a set of typi-cally patrilineal norms which specify who is to garden with whom and on what land. In many cases the realities of cultivation intervene and clansmen garden with the wrong people on the wrong land. Neverthe-less, the structure edits these wayward actions to preserve itself. The second theory believes that people work together on the basis of common material interests and from this spring bonds of solidarity which lead to kinship. Descent here is an ideology serving economic and ecological masters. The second theory has come to dominate the first as Highland ethnography brings to print case after case in which descent bows to material concerns. Analysts who began their careers favoring the structural or more "African model" have migrated towards a flexible or so-called "Melanesian model."

What both theories have in common, and what would appear from Maring evidence to be a misjudgement, is that they isolate production from the social system and then aim to detect the effect of one on the other. But what these theories perceive as errors in the system, or the winning hand of a material logic, are really cultural strategies working squarely within the framework of the social system and motivated by its principles. The social system is based on co-substance and thus encompasses production, exchange, and consumption from the start. There is a never ending cycle in which kinship/clanship gives birth to production and production cultivates kinship/clanship. Maring cannot help but maintain this perspective even in the teeth of modernization; and cash cropping, plantation labor, salaried employment at the Angli-can mission, and government service all construct "hard" social re-lationships.

The irony is that though New Guineans are characteristically frank and energetic in helping ethnographers understand their societies, they have managed a cultural deception. Against the background of West-ern ideology which sees all economics as driven by utilitarian interests, these societies are constructed on the sociality of exchange, production, and consumption. Accordingly, analysts have missed most of the action. They view gardening practices strictly in terms of making a living, focusing on such factors as utilization of land, labor, and resources. Meanwhile, the real play utilizes the distribution of land, labor, and other resources for the inspiration and management of social relations, only through the production of substance-bearing foods. To see production in utilitarian terms is to let the New Guinea solution as to how to be a social person slip through the cracks in our analytical categories.

4 The structures of clanship

Peng: giving and receiving is never innocent; sharing and exchanging less so.

Preceding chapters demonstrate that the structure of Maring social relationship lies in co-substance. Blood and semen are the two main forms of consubstantiality, just as *rawa* (spirit), *min* (life-force), and *nomane* (social wisdom) are their spiritual counterparts. Individuals transmit and receive blood and semen via the procreative process. Because men transmit only semen and women only blood, two descending lines of heredity coexist. For society, the natural cycle of production, managed principally by women and overseen by spirits of the low ground, circulates male substance; while the social cycle of marriage exchange, managed by men and overseen by spirits of the high ground, circulates female substance.

The structure of the natural cycle defines agnation in terms of the common sharing and transmission of male substance across generations and from one incarnation to another. Male substance passes from the human body to the land through burial procedures and from the land to clanspeople through the common consumption of food. Agnation thus has both a vertical and horizontal vector, and it is their interplay which defines clan identity. Ethnographers have described the vertical vector in their writings on exchange and material production. What is important is that (1) all of these institutions are part of an overarching structure and (2) that the literature tends to misinterpret them because it fails to see the nature of their unity.

This chapter develops the theory of Maring social organization by extending the analysis to the structure and function of clan and subclan. The formation of the clan cluster is the fruit of the marriage exchange system, and I will postpone its analysis to the following chapter on exchange. The emphasis here is on the differentiation, formation, and functionality of clan and subclan. This encompasses the elements of recruitment and lineality, the creation of clan boundaries and unit definition, and the use of kin terms to generate and maintain social identity. Siblingship particularly as expressed in brotherhood emerges as a fundamental principle in that it mediates the relationship between lineal and lateral structures, centrally the opposition between sharing and exchange.

A dominant thesis of my analysis is that there is no division between structure and social phenomena. Clanship is a principle, and the clan and subclan social units, insofar as they are one presentation, albeit privileged ones, of the structure of virtual relations of social reproduction. The clan and subclan are not simply social units of the world, an unalloyed result of a regime of production. They are a relation between a system of symbolic relations of reproduction and a certain people, who are already an empirical form of that system. The realization of clans/subclans as specific historical entities derive their forms and functions from the principles of social organization as these are set within the structure of reproduction. What is crucial about the system of reproduction is that it always puts the current organization of clans and subclans at the risk of the "intelligent subject and the intransigent world" (Sahlins 1985:156).

For theoretical reasons, the chapter focuses on agnation and clanship, saving analysis of local groups until after clanship and marriage exchange are in view. Agnation is built on co-substance; it partitions the kin universe by slicing a category of agnates out of the totality. Local groups arise from a larger, more inclusive set of principles (e.g., marriage, adoption, etc.), emerging at a lower level of social organisation. This distinction is important to theory and method. Highland analysts have often conflated the two with disastrous results. Even de Lepervanche (1973:5–9), after chiding colleagues for sliding back and forth between structural and functional criteria – i.e., between "descent" and local groups – further obscures their relationship by assuming that structural units (clans) have few functions and that functional or operative units (local groups) have little structure. The interrelationship between agnation and local groups will be analyzed in chapter 6 once the foundation is laid in this and the following chapter.

The clan cluster

Each Maring clan is a member of a clan cluster, with the possible exception of a few remnant clans inhabiting the fringe territory. Clusters, more so than individual clans, occupy bands of territory running from the mountain crest to the valley floor. There are twenty-one clan clusters in the Jimi and Simbai Valleys, and approximately a hundred constituent clans. Any estimate of clan number must take account of the inherent power of the system to transform. Some clans are currently being demoted to subclan status while certain subclans are emerging as full-fledged clans. Of the twenty-one clusters, nine are

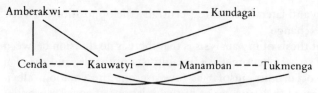

Figure 12 Patterns of alliance and enmity

comprised of four exogamous clans. The structure and practices of marriage exchange (LiPuma 1983) defines four as the optimal number of clans and there is incipient pressure for the cluster to move towards this configuration. On a larger scale, optimal arrangement is two inter-marrying clusters with a total of eight clans. For those clusters who do not have four clans, this bilevel pattern generates a number of hybrid arrangements, such as two subclusters of four clans each; or two separate but extensively intermarried clusters, one with three clans and the other with five. Clusters so aligned refer to one another as *aman yindok* (literally, inside people), meaning true or bonded people.

Due to the geography of the region and the social layout of the clan cluster territories, each cluster has two and occasionally three border-ing clusters. The clan cluster, unlike the clan, is not an agnatic unit, but a political and territorial enclave whose main function is to defend mutual lands. The name of the clan cluster is *yu nim* which denotes "many men." It implies an aggregation of discrete elements, as speakers use *nim* to refer to a assemblage of separate objects, persons, or groups. The alliance pattern, as defined by marriage exchange, inhi-bits any cluster from being bordered entirely by either friends (*yindok wumbi*) or enemies (*yindok ndemi*). The resulting pattern in the western end of the Jimi can be described as in Figure 12, the dotted lines indi-cating enmity and the solid lines alliance.

As will become transparent after the analysis of marriage exchange, it is the entwining of bloodlines which founds inter-cluster alliances. From the standpoint of political mobilization, this has two impli-cations. First, clansmen in cluster A recruit assistance – formerly in warfare and currently in elections – in cluster B on the basis of egocen-tric ties and the rights and obligations which follow from them. Second, cluster B whose member clans intermarry with two clusters, A and C, who are themselves enemies, may end up fighting or voting against one another. For example, during the war between the Kau-watyi and the Manamban, some Tsembaga clansmen fought with the Manamban and others with the Kauwatyi. More will be said about the structure of the clan cluster after the analysis of marriage exchange

living clansmen

living/dead
immediate ancestors

founding
ancestors

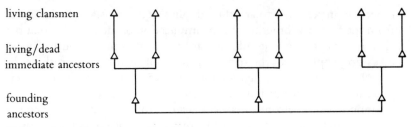

Figure 13 A model of ascent

since the unity and fissures within it reflect the network of ties through women.

The structure of clanship

That clansmen share a common substance inherited from their paternal ancestors forms the basis of descent. From the local perspective, "ascent" is a more appropriate description of how clanship works. Certainly local ideology and practice, indeed the entire world view and ethos, starts with this premise. Maring conceive the living community as the visible trunk and branches of a tree whose roots and base run deep into the land. People call the clan *ya kai*, meaning men's root/base. Speakers use *kai* and *gai* (an alternate form) to mean the fundamental hence non-negotiable portion of a brideprice, the underlying truth or basis of a reported action, or the base or foundation of a building. Note that the names of clans – Baigai, Merkai, Wendakai, Atigai – usually end in *kai* or *gai*. Male grease may be called *yu kai wunga*, which literally means "base that branches." Recall also that people symbolize men as the great trees of the primary forest and that such trees surround the sacred groves where clansmen sacrifice pigs to the ancestors.

Structurally, the clan ascends from a set of founding ancestors who are fatherless brothers ranked in birth order. That the most characteristic subclan names are Wendakai (first root), Amangai (second root), and Atigai (youngest root) exemplifies this principle. There are, for example, thirty-two subclans called Wendakai. Similarly, kin terminology uses the same roots to distinguish father's eldest brother, second, and third brother. Hence, all Maring clans have the form as in Figure 13.

The three brothers at the base of the tree are the putative founders of the clan. Some clans, randomly distributed throughout the Maring area, have myths which recount this original moment. Observe that there is no single founding ancestor, even if the astute informant,

111

especially in response to an ethnographer's questions, might infer one from the fact of brotherhood. The implication of the model is that the clan and its constituent subclans are initiated simultaneously. In no cases do people recall the names or deeds of the original brothers, or ritually resurrect their names on significant clan occasions. Their specific characteristics have faded from collective memory, thereby pushing to the forefront the salient fact of brotherhood. Clansmen believe that in the past the subclans were related as brothers and continue as brothers into the future. It follows that all male members of the constituent subclans are brothers. And, in some contexts, the term may refer to all clan members. The concept of ascent meshes with the understanding that a clan's growth and development parallels the model of vegetative propagation.

Genealogical knowledge

Given the concept of brotherhood by co-substance and the principles of its production, genealogy has no implications for clan formation. What genealogical reckoning does exist is the sole concern of the specific individual. Reckoning follows biological genealogy only to the extent that local ideas of parentage follow biology. Maring characteristically trace their origins to a territory rather than an individual, individuals being important only insofar as they gardened on the land in question. A reference to a named tract of land is a way of referring to a clan which owns, or more precisely, is that land. Asked about their ancestry, clanspeople associate themselves and their relatives with territory.

Not surprisingly, Maring, like Bena Bena (Langness 1971:300) and other Highland peoples, generally know very little about their forebears. Most of my informants could not name their maternal grandmothers or other kinsmen that they did not know personally. They were more likely to know what clan they came from and what land they gardened than ancestors' names and deeds. Yet, Maring genealogies are only shallow from a genealogical as opposed to a cultural perspective. In their conception of social time, current generations reproduce the same clan relations as their ancestors because they perpetuate the same natural and social cycles. The continuity of landedness is the local measure of clan continuity; it bespeaks the lineal transmission of clan substance from one generation to the next. So clan genealogies are unbranched at the base with an unfilled timeless gap between the founding brothers and the most immediate ancestors. In effect, though individuals may remember their ancestors for their own reasons, genealogy (as usually conceived by anthropologists) has no place in the social construction of relationships and thus no place in practice.

Recruitment

Procreation is the primary means of recruiting new clan members. As Maring note, both men and women are made from the substance of their father and bear an inalienable relationship to him. Because a new-born must embody the mingling of substances, blood and grease, from two separate lines, it possesses consubstantial links to both its father's and mother's clan. In terms of recruitment, these links are asymmetrical, there being a basic difference between male and female substances. All members of a father's clan share its clan grease. Any child born to the father thus shares a common identity and heritage with all his agnates. By contrast, a woman does share blood on a filial basis rather than with other members of the clan *per se*. It is this difference which constitutes the basis of Maring agnation.

Given that children are born from agnatic substance – the father's grease binding the mother's blood – they are automatically members of the father's clan. The key factor is the origin of the father's substance as culturally defined, not biological pedigree. If a man lives and renews his grease from the land of clan A, his children then belong to clan A no matter where his father may have come from. Since recruitment is generally overdetermined, it is the central and founding condition, although other criteria must also be met. The important facts are that there is no necessary link in clan identity (membership) between a child and its paternal grandfather. Clansmen see nothing unusual in this as long as the reaffiliation is done according to accepted practice.

That a clan's natural cycle – gardening, exchange, burial, sharing and prohibition of food – mediates the transmission of clan identity from father to children, places Maring social organization in a realm far removed from the simplicity of genealogy, where identity is built on natural facts of procreation and parturition. The theory of recruitment which follows from the genealogical model of descent only distracts the ethnographer from the real issues at hand. Perhaps some of the analytical uneasiness found in the New Guinea literature occurs because ethnologists employ a genealogical model even as they sense that something is amiss. As the Maring material shows, clanship centers not only on lineal relationships but on lateral ones, such as gardening, marriage exchange, and even the circulation of men, which interconnect the natural cycle of discrete clans.

The mother's natal clan has no agnatic claim on the child because the child possesses only the mother's blood, insufficient to create agnatic identity. Maring encode this fact in the understanding that a child, especially a son, is closer to its father than its mother. A child's attachment is not to his mother's natal clan *per se*, but to those male members who share blood with him. Nonetheless, members of the mother's bloodline, particularly the mother's brother, have a strong social and emotional stake in her children. They are one blood (*nukum rungai*), a concept that structures relationships, brings rights and obligations into force, and vibrates with strength. The mother's brother is the transitive link relating the sister's son to the mother's clansmen. For this reason, clansmen say that their mother's agnates are "like brothers and sisters" and that it would thus be wrong to marry them.

The subclan

The depiction of the subclan in terms of "ascent" captures the form and trajectory of the indigenous model. It defines clanship as consubstantial equivalence of brothers at the founding moment. So the myth of origin, recounted earlier, described a migration of brothers into a land inhabited by women. The model of democratic ascent has structural implications for the anthropology of clanship. In the frequent formula applied to New Guinea societies, an apical or founding ancestor is the point in the cultural horizon where all descent lines meet. Using this model, the impulse is to see the structure of the clan as familial kinship played out on a grander, jural-political scale. Africanists, such as Fortes (1945; 1949), take this tack when they understand the polygamous family as the model of lineage differentiation and identity. More, the difference between half-siblings, those having the same father but different mothers, parallels the difference between lineages.

Having no genealogical commitments and working on a principle of the ascent of brothers, the Maring model is entirely of another universe. The starting and determining point is a set of brothers separated into respective subclans. The clan does not fission into subclans as it descends from an original ancestor. Rather, it is the consubstantial relationships between subclans that unify them into a clan. Therefore, Maring clans, like those of so many New Guinea societies, are actually without founding ancestors. In one stroke, the model generates clans and subclans.

As lateral relationships tend to be the most creative ones, New Guineans are generally unconcerned with, and occasionally disinterested in, lineal relationships. While people know the subclan founders were (by definition) brothers, they do not know what kind of brothers they were (i.e., full siblings, half-siblings, etc.), nor do they care. The issue for founders, as well as for the living, is the binding force of consubstantiality, however derived. The determination of the founder's paternity is of no pragmatic interest to anyone save the anthropologist. Strathern (1972:44) writing on the Melpa, describes how members of the Kundmbo clan claimed to be brothers even though, in response to his questions, they could not agree on a common ancestor. Maring clansmen from the separate subclans are continually interchanging land, labor, and food, thus cementing the clan's components in the dimension of practice. So for the Maring, the clan is the union of subclans through the social principle of brotherhood.

The manner of the clan's composition explains why the subclan is the most visible and socially active unit. As one informant noted, "the clan is below the ground like the base and roots of a tree; the subclans are the branches above." Each set of subclansmen maintains its own sacred groves where it holds pig sacrifices to the clan's ancestors. The clan is also a silent partner to marriage exchange, as subclan members conduct the negotiations, organize the ceremonies of exchange, and collect or pass out bridewealth. For this reason, Maring can define subclansmen as those who distribute bridal pork, and clansmen as those who share in it. This is not merely a statement that all clan members have rights to a share, or that the practical logic of sharing fabricates clanship. It is an assertion of consubstantiality between subclans, for the sharing of pork both defines brotherhood and reproduces it.

People call the subclan *yu kai atemp*, literally a smaller or more narrow line of agnates. By the same token, however, speakers often characterize the subclan in terms of blood relations. Clansmen refer to agnatic kin not only as sharing grease, but as sharing blood and to segments of a clan as "one blood" people. In general, the term *nukum rungyi* (one blood) specifies any kinship rooted in bloodlines. It embraces a range of cognatic kin traced back to a female ancestor or set of sisters. More often than not, agents can name the linking female only if she was no more distant than the grandparental generation. The terminology for blood kin parallels that for agnatic kin, as members of the same generation use brother and sister terms. An informant explained the relationship between blood and grease in this way:

We call the subclan *yu kai atemp* because we all live on the same clan lands used by our fathers. We also say that they are "one blood" when we talk in a more specific way. The reason is that we have pig-woman roads with other subclans; we exchange sisters with them. The female line has many branches which make more branches [via marriage] in affinal lines. When the women's blood is finished [in a given subclan] we exchange women again. This is why we prefer to marry our sisters, though of course they are not our clan sisters, just the children of the blood stock.

This statement condenses the local understanding of the relationship between blood and marriage in the context of subclan formation. The text indicates that subclans desire to exchange women and thus inter-mingle the bloodlines. Intermarrying subclans will exchange women on a long-range basis (the "pig-woman road"), seeking the female descendants of brides they gave away. The mandate to "return the planting material" specifies the subclan or origin, thus codifying and reinforcing exchange between subclans. To expand on the text, sub-clans engaging in exchange are of one blood in the subsequent gener-ation and hence cannot intermarry, but they renew the exchange in the second descending generation. It is no accident that Maring call the payment a man presents to his mother's brother *nukum poka* (blood payment), meaning both blood compensation and blood intersection. For example, *ambra poka* refers to a bride payment and *ambra kon't nukmai poka* refers to the intersection or joining of two pig-woman roads. The concentration of marriages and the manipulation of blood relations occurs at the subclan level, and thus becomes its distinctive feature. In this sense, *nukum rungyi* (one blood) becomes a creative index of subclan identity when used in a sociocentric context (such as a ritual sacrifice) which presupposes the subclan (referent) in question. The significant point is that clansmen use bloodlines both as a locus of differentiation between constituent subclans and as a locus of simi-larity between non-constituent subclans.

The family

The only unit less inclusive than the subclan is the family, though groups of families often occupy a common clearing. By virtue of shar-ing food, labor, and sleeping quarters on a regular basis, they form a compound. The overwhelming majority of Maring marriages are monogamous, although the ideal is to have more than one wife. Among the Kauwatyi, there were between eleven and fourteen men practicing polygamy during my period of fieldwork. Representing about 14% of all marriages, this is higher than most other clan clusters, especially those in the Simbai (Rappaport 1969). Given that more men than women are born (Buchbinder 1973), polygamy is hard to attain, especially as Maring believe that all adult men should be married. As in other Highland societies, the Maring circumvent this constraint by marrying off women younger than men. That polygamy is valued but difficult to attain defines it as an index of male/clan wealth and power, and thus a key instrument of social differentiation. In the western Jimi, fifteen of twenty-one big-men have more than one wife, and of these, four have more than two wives. A clan may promote a gifted individual by "buying him another wife." This often entails overriding the interests of a younger, less well-positioned, man. The rising big-man will characteristically show his leadership by taking the younger man under his wing, lest (as one big-man put it) "he learns to dislike me and causes bitterness."

Kauwatyi classify their houses as either "modern" or "custom." Prior to contact, husbands and wives resided in separate houses. Today about 50% of mostly older couples maintain this arrangement. Speaking only for Kauwatyi, 57% of men live with their wives, with the figure approaching 100% for those living on mission stations at Koinambe or Togban. Before, men's and women's houses were often set considerable distances apart; but today, they are usually located in the same compound. Traditionalists, even as they maintain a separation, have compromised within customary limits.

The woman's house is built downhill from the men's house. In the traditional dwelling, each married woman lives with all her unmarried female children, her male children below the age of initiation (there is an informal initiation around the age of eight), and her pigs. Needy grandmothers, sisters, and other female relatives also come to stay for indefinite periods of time. Exceptions are the bride whose husband has not yet built her house, and the widow who is too old to live alone or cannot find a man to rebuild or repair her house.

Modern houses are built in the Papuan style, though rarely on stilts (and only then for effect). Under the one roof, Maring replicate their traditional arrangement of separate housing. The house is divided into two segments by a common area used for cooking and socializing. The women occupy the cells to the left of the center hearth, and the men the cells to the right. Again, if the house is built on a slight incline, an inevitability in the steep terrain, the women reside in the lower half. This conforms to a general set of distinctions; for example, male ancestors occupy the high ground and female ancestors the low.

No lexeme for "family" exists in the Maring language, the way it does for clan or subclan. Nonetheless, people can identify the family with a phrase "a man and his wife," or they can append the suffix for line (*po*) on the end of a man's name. Informants claim that such terms were in use long before they made contact with the Christian notion of family, "family" being a favorite homily of local evangelists. The critical point is that Maring understand "family" as an objectification of the complementary relationship between husband and wife, and, more globally, as an embodiment of the relationship between agnatic units. The institution of marriage creates rights, obligations, and duties – as expressed in the sharing of foods, labors, and goods – which in their fulfillment lead to the family. Bluntly put by informants: "if the man and woman do not live up to their responsibilities, there is no marriage and thus no family."

Clan boundaries

Although agnates recognize a common identity based on co-substance, imbuing the clan with external boundaries, agnation itself is incapable of creating or sustaining those boundaries. Agnation would be sufficient only in a system that neither segmented clans nor assimilated outsiders. What is ethnographically critical is that every social system undergoes some fission and some assimilation. The African systems seem to emphasize segmentation which generates a unit hierarchy; Highland societies appear to emphasize assimilation or the flow of individuals across clan boundaries. Along both African and Highland lines, unit formation depends on lateral structures (i.e., the practices which serve to incorporate non-agnates) working in concert with agnation.

For Maring, principles of co-substance, embodied in sibling terms, link individuals but do not specify when a relationship is close enough to count as an agnatic one. An example taken from war migrations will clarify the point. A man from clan B establishes a garden and lives with his wife's natal clan A because an enemy routed his clan cluster from its homeland. The son has a matrilateral claim to land and residence on his mother's clan and could legitimately pursue agnatic status because, in addition to his mother's blood, he now possesses the clan substance from eating off her natal clan lands. Alternatively, he might return to his father's homeland in the event of peace and retain his father's agnatic affiliation. This case occurred among the dozen or so Tsembaga who fled to Kauwatyi shelter in 1955; two have remained and their sons identify themselves as fully Kauwatyi.

The issue of clan boundaries concerns the flow and transformation of agnatic substance over time. There are two dimensions to this process – though, of course, participants are more aware of results than structure and do not consciously make the division. First, procreation, by virtue of the father's substance, creates an individual bearing a definite clan identity. Paternity in this respect is relatively mechanical and feeds the ideology of clan continuity and endurance. Problems arise only in rare instances of multiple paternity. Second, the father's pro-creative grease derives from the land and food: the ongoing process of replenishing the bodily substances. Ultimately, the child belongs to the clan from which his father acquired grease. This dimension impli-cates the practices of land tenure, gardening, food taboos, commensa-lity, and other means of cycling substance. This is the point at which the kinship system and the formation of the clan articulate with the general structure of social reproduction. Economic, political, and social forces all have a bearing on the practice of kinship. From the per-spective of practice, the acquisition of the father's substance, and clari-fication as to its origin, is prior to paternity. And, in most cases, a child's paternity and affiliation is never in question. The regeneration of substance is the real-time process of kinship in that it culturally endorses socially creative action to resolve ongoing problems.

The sharing of substance is thus overdetermined and particularly evident in the context of exchange. Those who are consubstantial by virtue of sharing stand in opposition to another group of the same qual-ity. In this respect, every gift simultaneously establishes similarity and difference. A gift of pork, to take an example, creates continuity be-tween exchanging clans even as the presupposition of separateness necessary to motivate the exchange indexes their separate identities. This is inscribed in the fact that a clan does not marry its own women or eat its own pigs: to do so would be to confuse exchange and sharing and thus to topple one of the cultural distinctions which define social organization. Set in this context, paying or receiving bridewealth does more than demarcate clan membership, it creates consubstantial bonds through the sharing of pork. Bridewealth is imbued with formative powers precisely because of its dual nature.

Clan members define their identity on a sociocentric plane – that is, in opposition to other clans' members – through marriage exchange. The criterion is that clan members share exchange functions, giving and receiving together as a unit. Exchange in the "name of the clan" represents the sharing relationship in full social regalia. Giving and receiving are the discursive terms in which people phrase social inden-tity – from the level of the clan cluster all the way down to the indi-vidual. Hence, the concept of a unit is inseparable from that of sharing. For this reason, descriptions of a unit characteristically take the form of "we fight together" or "we eat together" or "we sacrifice pig in one *raku*." At the clan level, the equation reads that those who share sub-stance share bridewealth; those who exchange substance – women's blood – exchange bridewealth. The categories are explicit and in complementary distribution.

In terms of marriage itself, clansmen phrase this as the prohibition on a man marrying the sister or daughter of someone with whom he shares meat. From the local perspective, such a marriage is entirely irrational because it would instigate an internal transfer of wealth. Put plainly, "only a pig would eat his own pig," insinuating not so much that the person is greedy, although this would certainly be true and punishable, but that he is cannibalistic to consume his own social production. The action is irrational precisely because it neutralizes the dual functions of bridewealth to generate the social order.

The sharing of meat with ancestors and agnates in the context of exchange indexes clan membership. It is a declaration of clan membership of "standing with the clan," to paraphrase one big-man. A non-agnate who wishes to retain his foreign status does not contribute the same type of bride payment as an agnate; he provides some money and other valuables for the brideprice, but never pork. Conversely, the son of a non-agnate who wishes to join his newfound clan contributes pork, often more than is strictly necessary. In some circumstances, the son's father will give pork on his behalf, especially when the son is young and, having no wife, has few pigs of his own. The father is giving pork "in the name of the son" or because "he is a good father" (i.e., he knows what loyal affiliation entails). By the same token, agnates can refuse admittance to a non-agnate's son by refusing to accept his pork donation. This opens a small universe of pragmatic strategies aimed either at rejection or total assimilation. It follows also that non-agnates and their sons are even more preoccupied than most with the distribution of bridewealth.

The next example will clarify this point and give some color to the intricate possibilities which may arise in the ebb and flow of bridewealth.

Kam's case

Kama is living matrilocally in Kompiai with his brother and his mother, a Kakupogai. His father is from the Kandambiamp clan cluster's Wendakai line. Kama is extremely industrious and is highly regarded in the community. However, his brother is a "rubbish man" who is lazy, greedy, and above all dishonest. Both brothers desire to stay with the Kauwatyi cluster, although most Kauwatyi, notably from the Kakupogai clan, would just as soon retain Kama and discard his brother. Accordingly, clansmen do not want to accept pig from Kama's brother, nor do they want to give him any. In short, they want the brother to return to Kandambiamp and have said so loudly and publicly. But they willingly accept Kama's brideprice contributions and grant him a favorable share in pork distributions. Kama feels that he cannot desert his brother – by Maring standards this would be morally wrong – yet he does not want to return to Kandambiamp. As a compromise, Kama acts as an intermediary for his brother, generally mediating the relationship between his brother and other Kakupogai clansmen. His brother gives him the gift of pig and he in turn contributes it; conversely, when pig is distributed to him he offers a portion to this brother.

Essentially, marriage exchange forces all clan residents to declare where they stand in relation to co-residents. For most clansmen, this is not critical since their membership is not in question. But it is for non-agnates or the sons of non-agnates. Their actions define the value of commensality, co-gardening, and other practices with respect to agnation. From a pragmatic standpoint, there are few marginal characters and people are rarely in doubt as to another individual's affiliation.

Lateral structuring

Procreation is only one moment in the generation of co-substance ties. A father replenishes his procreative grease through gardening and other practices, while the child grows and develops by eating clan foods. Both are agents and results of the natural cycle. It is eating the same food – food being the final result of co-gardening, labor exchange, land transfer, and traffic in planting material – which renews and furthers agnatic bonding. Hence, the newborn enters the world formed from clan grease, and then builds upon this by consuming clan foods.

For this reason, meaning and purpose impregnate even the informal flow of food. It is typical for a pregnant woman to receive food gifts, especially sugarcane and taro, both from her own and her husband's agnates. Both clans wish, through the gift, to have an active part in the development of the child. The Maring concept of "helping" covers a multitude of intentions, and such gifts of food are conventionally phrased as a desire "to help the women " due to the strength of the kin tie, not to mention social credits which accrue to those who live the kinship ideal of generosity. The presentation of food to the pregnant woman, though done very informally, may take on social overtones if she rejects or denigrates the gift from one of the parties. She knows, as does every Maring, that (short of violence) there is no more powerful index of personal dissatisfaction than the voluntary rejection of food. So a woman may indicate that she is disenchanted with the treatment she is receiving at the hands of her husband's agnates by accepting gifts of food only from her own. The example illustrates that here a co-substance tie is in the making and thus the flow of food can take on great significance.

Insofar as a person's physical growth and development takes place in the social world and is integrated into a clan's natural cycle, transformations of agnatic identity are possible. Such practices as adoption institutionalize the transformation. Here, from an early age the adopted child is raised on food produced on the land of his adopted parents. From the standpoint of behavior, Maring say that an adopted son or daughter should act like a true member of his/her new clan; they should appear to cross over and become an agnate of the adopting clan. Such conventions aimed at aligning behavior with the clan of residence recognize that nothing can reverse the original endowment of substance. The compensation paid by the adopting clan to the "clan of the father" exemplifies this. The compensation is for the "child's body," signifying that adoption alienates clan substance. The children of the male adoptee will be the first members of the adopting clan. A clan admits a male non-agnate with knowledge that by eating and living on clan lands, the non-agnate will produce agnates in the next generation. Smaller clans, especially those whose numbers have fallen due to warfare, explicitly take advantage of this mechanism for recruiting new members.

Within the clan cluster and between proximate friendly clans, an entire complex of co-substance relations are in process. The force of these relations is potential, and clansmen activate them as economic, political, or social conditions dictate. The distinction Maring make between the value of proximate and distant marriages rests on the possibilities of creating consubstantial linkages and all that this entails. Affines are not only related through the reticulation of bloodlines but through the exchange of land, food, taboos, planting material, and other male/agnatic resources. For this very reason, clansmen focus on how and to what degree affines exchange clan resources with them. Two clans who exchange intensively will become antigamous for several generations or more. Two Kauwatyi clans, the Kumbant'igai and Kakupogai, define themselves as brother clans who are beginning to intermarry again after a period of avoidance. Between any nearby, intermarrying clans, the following interrelations exist to a greater or less degree.

The recruitment of individuals from one clan to the next is generally organized along bloodlines. Reaffiliation based on the exchange and sharing of blood is well-recognized, constituting what might be called a second channel of recruitment. Historical events in concert with practices map the specific forces of reaffiliation. It is usual for a child to

clan A   clan B

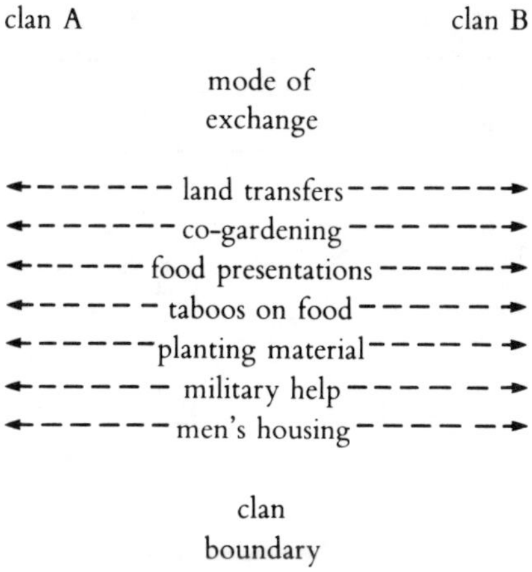

                    mode of
                    exchange

◄ — — — — — land transfers — — — — — ►
◄ — — — — — co-gardening — — — — — ►
◄ — — — — food presentations — — — — ►
◄ — — — — — taboos on food — — — — ►
◄ — — — — —planting material — — — — ►
◄ — — — — — military help — — — — ►
◄ — — — — men's housing — — — — ►

                    clan
                    boundary

Figure 14 Lateral relationships

join his mother's natal clan, especially in the event of his father's death or remarriage. Clansmen whose cluster has been overrun by enemy forces and expelled from native lands will go, sometimes permanently, to the land of their affines. Young men frequently help their mother's brother, nowadays joining them on economic ventures such as opening a trade store or marketing coffee (See Maclean 1984:316–68). The termination of war has probably decreased the necessity for reaffiliation but increased the opportunity.

Given the structure of clanship, there are two outstanding possibilities for any child. Either the child can become a member of his father's clan on the basis of inherited substance and the supplementary events of living off clan lands; or, the child can utilize blood ties to live and garden on the land of matrilateral kin and thus establish a consubstantial relationship of male substance which will accrue to his own children. Table 10 compares the frequency of select forms of reaffiliation.

The major line of reaffiliation is to the mother's natal clan, the flow of clansmen along this axis overdetermined. There is (1) the exchange of agnatic resources between father and mother's brother; (2) an intermediary link of shared blood between sister's son and mother's brother; and (3) the social right of the sister's son to garden on the land of the mother's brother's clan.

Maring recognize that blood is a powerful tie and rationalize reaffiliation in terms of the strength of the link. Thus it is not uncommon to hear that so-and-so is living with his mother's brother because they are one blood. More commonly, the speaker will simply name the kin

Table 10 *The frequency of forms of recruitment*

Clan	Father	Mother's brother	Sister's husband	Other
Kamjepakai	238	22	6	8
Kakupogai	222	23	5	9
Baigai	61	13	5	7
Kumbant'igai	53	9	3	4
Angengbogai	49	8	5	6
Totals	623	75	24	34

Note: the only individuals not included in this survey are temporary residents and in-marrying women who by definition are members of other clans.

term which signifies this relationship, the sharing of blood taken as a presupposed value in the speech event. A second major avenue of re-affiliation is to the clan of the maternal grandmother. This follows from the form of marriage system where clansmen attempt to retie bloodlines in alternate generations. In effect, some men go to live with their sister's husbands and their sons eventually become members of his clan. (Note that the brother has had a part in determining his sister's marriage choice.)

On the surface, the category "other" encompasses a variety of possible relationships (e.g., ego and FZH). But more importantly, it represents a chain reaction sparked by recruitment to MB and ZH clans. Those who reaffiliate serve as a conduit for the reaffiliation of other individuals, who transfer allegiance by virtue of a mix of agnatic, blood, and affinal ties. For example, if a man's children become agnates of his wife's natal clan, his agnates may reaffiliate through their kin connection with the children. This arrangement capitalizes on the fact that a reaffiliated person is a quasi-agnate and cognate with respect to his father's clansmen. To cite one case: Wani is a man from the Gai clan cluster (Kanmb clan) who is living matrilocally with a Kakupogai wife. His son, Kam, is a true Kakupogai, being born and bred on Kakupogai land. Several other men from Gai, including two cross-cousins, have now taken up semi-permanent residence on Kakupogai land by virtue of their tie to Kam. And, it is likely, especially in the case of the cross-cousin who has married a Kauwatyi wife from another clan, that his sons will become full-fledged agnates.

The cultural concept of clan reproduction, based on a union of lineal and lateral relations, merges agnates and non-agnates at the level of practice. This is particularly true for blood relatives. The sister's son has rights in land, labor, and food on a par with official agnates. Recall that gifts of women generate the clan's network of *indok wump*, or sources of planting material. Implicit in the model of vegetative growth where *wump* and *mai* stand in organic continuity is the conception that intermarrying clans constitute a common domain of land, labor, and resources. So men have full privileges on their mother's natal soil to hunt in the forest, call on labor, use the land and its planting material, and participate in food distributions. The ancestor spirits of the mother's clan will look after them. By contrast, non-agnates not linked by blood have a much more circumscribed set of privileges and must act more cautiously. Their access to hunting forest, land, and labor is more susceptible to the political intrigues of the clan. Lowman (1980:137–8) captures the essence of blood relations in a passage, like many inhabiting the literature on the Highlands, whose structural significance reveals itself only in the light of a theory of clan reproduction:

Relationships among first cross-cousins can be as close as those of classificatory siblings ... Young unmarried men may reside a year or more with their maternal uncles and cross-cousins (*mbapa* and *wambe*). Cross-cousins frequently participate in the same kinds of activities they share with siblings and parallel cousins ["brothers and sisters"] – hunting, feasting, fighting ... As one informant put it: "our fathers and brothers live together in these houses and our uncles and cross-cousins live in other houses on their own land. But we perceive them to be good and if they come to live with us, we live happily together. When people seeking new residence ... are our *wambe*, we give them planting material. We give them ground. We say, 'let us stay together.'"

The bilateral equivalence of *wump* in the first descending generation is expressed in the right of individuals to exercise the same privileges on their mothers' territories as on their fathers'. These privileges can be manipulated in terms of hardship to alter residence and group membership ... The rights to membership of persons moving to the territory of his/her matrilateral kinsmen is undisputed, even on territory where resources are relatively scarce. Interviewing a Kauwatyi resident about his agnatic status, I questioned whether he really could consider himself a Kauwatyi since he was born on a different territory, his father's. His mother was a Kauwatyi. He responded with annoyance. "I'm a real Kauwatyi; I'm their *wump*."

The local view of the equivalence of the triangle relating sister's son, mother's brother, and cross-cousins conceals the presence of bloodlines behind economic practices of production and exchange. Likewise, it conceals the overlap between levels of clanship and kinship, as exhibited in terms such as "brother." From the standpoint of the clan, a reaffiliated person calls his new clanmates "brother" and in so doing contrasts them with members of all other clans. He shares agnatic substance and exchange functions with them. From the standpoint of kinship, however, where calculation hinges on the actual procreative transmission of male grease, all of a person's father's brothers are his father and their sons his brothers. A person who is officially a member of clan A, although their father is a member of clan B, has "brothers" in both clans, but in different senses of the term. This allows for considerable play between agnatic (sociocentric) and cognatic categories. Members of the father's original clan will naturally cooperate with him as a matter of policy, exchanging land, labor, and so forth. They transfer agnatic resources on the basis of a "brotherly" relationship. This may lead to their reaffiliation as we have seen; or, more rarely, reaffiliation flows back in the other direction and a grandchild rejoins the clan of the father.

For the Maring, reaffiliated persons constitute a bridge or structural link which integrates the two clans and organizes the passage of individuals, services, and material between them. In this sense, it is analogue of marriage exchange. Certainly it is usual to use the reaffiliated individual as an intermediary when making a request for land, labor, or political help. It is my reading that Highland analysts, given their preoccupation with the powers and failures of descent as an organizing principle, have too often considered non-agnates as defects in the clan's structure, rather than as mediators in the structure of exchange between clans. The negative characterization of non-agnates, a residue of descent theory, has hindered an appreciation of their positive part in social reproduction.

Lateral relationships also involved the transfer of agnatic substance. Clan substance crosses clan boundaries not only via co-gardening, food exchange, and other transfer, but in the body of persons. One way is the assimilation of non-agnates. Equally significant is the exchange of women. Women embody agnatic substance even if they are incapable of transmitting it to their children. When a wife in good standing dies, it is customary to bury her on the land of her husband. Because this is a transfer of substance, it necessitates a payment to the wife's natal clan. The husband's clan offers several pigs and several hundred kina to "buy the bones for planting." The clan then places the body on an underground palate to decay and later retrieves the bones to bury them in the sacred groves. This recruits the wife to the clan's corps of ancestor spirits. In a sense, it posthumously finalizes the assimilation of the wife, completing the transition initiated by years of common gardening, labor, and consumption. Ultimately, marriage results not only in the entwining of bloodlines but the transfer of agnatic substance. Characteristically, Maring frame the practice in terms of the result of the exchange, burying the bones of the wife because she has worked well in the interests of the clan: helping clansmen with exchanges, making good gardens, rearing many pigs, and bearing fine children.

A fluid process of ancestral revision accompanies the incorporation of non-agnates into the clan. In theory, this parallels genealogical revision prevalent in other societies. In practice, it is more straightforward and in harmony with the principles of clanship because it is based on the production of co-substance ties. A non-agnate's children are full-fledged agnates because – like every other clan member – they were created and reared from substances gleaned from clan lands. They are fully integrated into the clan's natural cycle. When their father dies and is buried on the land of his new clan, he enters its corps of ancestor spirits which the entire clan will propitiate. Moreover, he also "calls" his own ancestors by co-planting his *min* into the clan's sacred *rumbim* plant. The merging built into the kin terminology erases the last vestiges of foreign origin. All members of the second ascending generation upward, including all ancestors, are either *koka* (male) or *apo* (female), obliterating any exogamous origins.

The ritual of integration

The sacrifice of pigs for the ancestors unites the elements of social identity through the synthesizing powers of ritual. The ritual offers pig to the *rawa mugi*, the red spirits of warfare who haunt the high ground, and the *rawa mai*, the cool spirits of fertility and the garden. (For more detailed discussion of ritual sacrifice and the status of pigs see LiPuma 1981 and Rappaport 1968: chapter 5). When sacrificing ritual pig, clansmen address the spirits in an arrhythmic, high-pitched, screaming style, complemented by stylized gestures. This is explicitly the voice of possession and spirit mediation, having no parallel in ordinary discourse. When "calling" the spirits' attention, rather than referring to them by name, clansmen use such poetic forms as orchid-cassowary, sunfire, and smoke-rising, which unleash a set of association. Clan elders address the *rawa mugi* as "hearth/cooking fire" and other allusions and tell them that there is an offering of "taro" – really pig. Maring call the *rawa mugi* by land names of the high ground, or by certain creatures and tree species which inhabit their domain. Concomitantly, *rawa mai* may be called by land names of the low ground, or by those creatures or vegetation associated with growth and fertility. Allusion to eels, sometimes called the pigs of the *rawa mai*, is the most common trope.

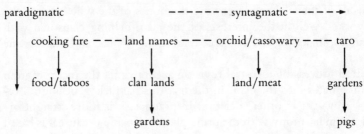

Figure 15 Semiotic structure of ritual

The poetic structure of the ritual centers around both the linear flow of speech and the associations triggered by a given reference. Taro, for example, is the exemplar of garden productivity which, in turn, permits a clan to increase its numbers of pigs. The poetic forms create the domain and sphere of influence of the ancestor spirits. They forge a linkage between ancestors and the main elements of clan reproduction: land, food, gardens, grease. In so doing, they internally connect and weld the elements of the ritual into a statement of social relations. The concatenation of terms binds ancestors to an entire complex of relationships: to commensality and food taboos; to the coordination between gardening and pig husbandry; the regenerative cycle of clan lands; and ultimately to the founding divisions between men and women.

The pig sacrifice takes place in the *raku*, or sacred grove, located in the midst of primary forest. Large trees shelter the *raku* and custom forbids outsiders to trespass on the grounds, let alone watch a ritual performance. Once the ancestors have been called and the congregation assembled, clan elders dedicate and sacrifice pig(s) to the spirits. They single out some ancestors by name, though they address the ancestors as a body through the kin terms *koka* and *apo*. Clansmen then club the pig and divide it, cooking the head in a raised oven and the remainder in an earth oven. In the naming process, participants acknowledge and recognize their relationship to this set of clan ancestors. A ritual communion follows the dedication and cooking. All participants share in the flesh of the animal. Such sharing invokes lateral mechanisms of building co-substance, as the participants renew their bodily substances with meat from the same pig, recreating and reinforcing their clanship in death as much as in life. In this way, non-agnates are recruited to the clan by virtue of their death and burial on clan lands, and the subsequent participation as ancestors in the ritual sacrifice.

The ritual collapses the diverse presentations of the social order by linking them through the same practice and sign vehicles. Informants

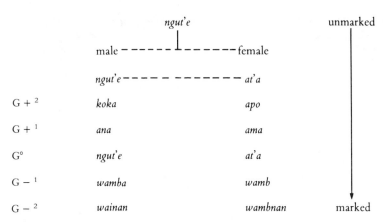

Figure 16 Sociocentric terms

are aware of the individual contexts in which substance motivates relationship, but not of the relationship between contexts. The cohesive power of the ritual lies in the fact that linguistically and virtually it unites pigs, gardens, ancestors, land, food: all indexes and symbolic sources of clanship.

Speaking of kinship

As illustrated in earlier descriptions, kin terms and their use play a significant part in the construction of agnatic identity and the structured passage from non-agnate to agnate. In Maring culture, kin terms are an organized semantic field of reference involving categories which emanate from, and reflect, the lines of co-substance. At any point in time there are two principal levels of terminology in play. The first is agnatic terminology, those terms which operate on a sociocentric or clan level to define relations of clanship or alliance. The second is cognatic terminology, those terms which operate on the level of social persons, taking ego as the point of reference to construct a network of relations.

At the agnatic or sociocentric level, Maring kin terms fall into the pattern as shown in Figure 16.

This configuration of terms is possible because the sociocentric level reckons kinship from the standpoint of the clan. It defines the clan as a type so that any individual member of the clan is equivalent to any other, subject to marking conditions. *Ngut'e* (brother) is the unmarked category which speakers use for all members of the clan wholly irrespective of sex. The unmarked status of *ngut'e* follows from the principle of clan brotherhood: all members of the constituent subclans

Table 11 *Distribution of* ngut'e *and* at'a *on the cognatic level*

Kin type	Co-substance relation	Kin term
B	Grease and blood	*Ngut'e*
Z	Grease and blood	*At'a*
FBS	Grease	*Ngut'e*
FBD	Grease	*At'a*
MZS	Blood	*Ngut'e*
MZD	Blood	*At'a*
MMBSS	None	*Ngut'e*
MMBSZ	None	*At'a*

co-share substance and its source of reproduction in precisely the same way. Relatively marked are the categories which differentiate male and female clansmen irrespective of generation, *ngut'e* (brother) and *at'a* (sister). Implicitly, this is a distinction between grease and blood, and dual lines of heredity which flow from them. Maring use *ngut'e* and *at'a* most frequently to refer to the complementary activities of production and exchange which characterize male and female roles. The most marked sociocentric terms are those which incorporate generational distinctions. A speaker, for example, may use *wamba* to refer to the son of any of his clan brothers or to all males in the first descending generation (i.e., that generation of clansmen below his own). This generational format harmonizes with the structure of interclan alliances, marriage always being between individuals of the same generation. From the perspective of the marriage exchange cycle and the calculation of bloodlines, generation is a salient category. Insofar as sociocentric kinship defines the clan as a concrete unified entity, the terms ignore systematically differences which exist at the cognatic level. It treats the clan as an individual body by not parsing the membership into the possible kin type egos.

The sociocentric level generates classes of classes. Each of its slots are filled with a variety of kin classes from the cognatic level, though at no point are the two levels fully aligned. Terms such as *at'a* and *ngut'e* possess both broader and narrower scope on the sociocentric level than on the cognatic one. Every agnatic term – *koka, apo, ngut'e, at'a, ana, ama*, etc. – figures in the semantics of cognatic terminology and reference to non-clansmen as well. At the cognatic level, ego is a structural type at the center of the kinship universe. Taking any person in the society as ego, a speaker can classify every other member of the society within a certain range. Thus, there need be no more than twenty basic terms which the Maring apply cyclically to the entire range of consub-

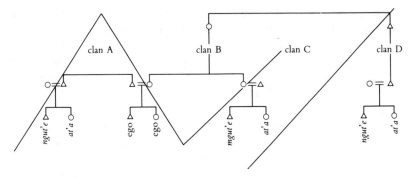

Figure 17 Brother and sister terms on the cognatic level

stantial kin. In essence, the cognatic system organizes all possible kin into terminological classes.

An instructive way to enter the cognatic level is via the terms *ngut'e* and *at'a*, without doubt the most frequently used kin terms with the greatest expanse of meaning in Maring vocabulary. That they should be the dominant terms on both the cognatic and sociocentric level reflects the Maring reality that siblingship, especially brotherhood, is the dominant principle of organization. Sibling terms are same-sex reciprocals. Illustration of their form and function is a paradigm of how the system works as a whole.

Clearly, there are several senses of the terms *ngut'e* and *at'a*. From a Maring standpoint, the terms may refer to persons related by either or both blood and grease, or to those who are defined as bearing no co-substance relation. Note from Figure 17 that any person will have "brothers and sisters" in four separate clans (and possibly more). Given the high rate of clan cluster endogamy (in the neighborhood of 70%), almost all Kauwatyi have "brothers and sisters" in most of the constituent clans.

The most salient usages of *ngut'e* and *at'a* are those which denote fully consubstantial individuals. The Maring gloss these as *ngut'e wundok* and *at'a wundok* or true brother and sister. *Wundok* connotes truth not only in the existential sense, but that which is internally the same. It contrasts not so much with falsity, but with superficial simi-larity or similarity only in some limited contexts. In interview situ-ations, Maring who are asked to provide a definition of brother begin either with "one father, one blood" in reference to fully consubstantial brothers, or they specify the entire set of clansmen. Because people never pose decontextualized questions of "siblingship" to one another, the informant always has to interpolate as to which level, cognatic or sociocentric, the ethnographer has pitched the question. In other words, every request for information about a kin term activates a virtual set of presuppositions which constitutes the basis and conditions for successful reference. The ethnographer who asks decontextualized questions is in a particularly bad position to discover these presuppositions because (1) knowledge of them is non-conscious and (2) they are revealed only in contextualized, socially recognized speech situations (e.g., requesting land or accusing a sorcerer). Failure to understand this has led to a variety of misinterpretations of Maring kin terms (for example, MacLean 1984:55–6; Healey 1979).

A different sense of *ngut'e* and *at'a* is for the children of father's brothers. They are, of course, direct recipients of clan substance in a single unbroken line of transmission which has an identifiable starting point (i.e., grandfather). Informants, in describing patrilateral parallel cousins, use the metaphor that they are practically "true brothers and sisters." This seems to mean that such *ngut'e* and *at'a* share the same activities. And discussion quickly turns to the common practical interests which underlie relationships between "cousin-brothers" – the Melanesian Pidgin idiom for such links. Such usages are more marked than the fully consubstantial sense of *ngut'e* and *at'a*. Their specification in discourse depends heavily on co-reference, previous mention of the individual in question, and other indices.

An equally circumscribed usage of *ngut'e* and *at'a* is for mother's sister's children. The Maring concept is that both share one blood with ego and are thus bound in some special way. The mutual assistance which usually characterizes this relationship reinforces this conception. Use of brother and sister terms in this sense almost invariably appears in the context of exchange, particularly where commerce centers on regionally traded objects such as bird plumes. People see mother's sister's son as a trade resource insofar as he constitutes a vital link between ego and members of other clans. Healey (1979:104–5) notes that Maring have a "penchant for identifying, even creating, classificatory kinsmen, especially mother's sister's son, in other communities for the purpose of trade and hospitality while on the road." Essentially, the local pragmatic strategy is first to identify the blood relative on the egocentric plane and then step up to the sociocentric level. In this manner, all of mother's sister's son's agnates can stand as *ngut'e* to ego. What is particularly interesting is that negotiation of this relationship is itself a negotiation of the willingness to exchange. If an agnate of MZS accepts his designation *ngut'e*, this means that he is interested in building an exchange relation. This movement between levels can be diagrammed as in Figure 18.

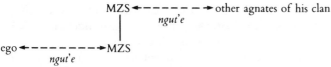

Figure 18 Linguistic negotiation of exchange

Maring informants sometimes tell ethnographers that any man and woman who call each other *ngut'e* and *at'a* respectively may not marry. This phrasing uses a relatively context-free, yet still bound, concept of brother and sister. As Cook (1970) has noted for the Manga (an eastern Jimi clan cluster which occasionally intermarries with Maring), marriageable persons do use sibling terms. Indeed, the most marked usage of *ngut'e* and *at'a* refers to patrilateral second cross-cousins who are surely marriageable. They are the preferential marriage partners as specified by the practice that women should marry into their grand-mother's natal subclan. As marriageable, they are diametrically opposed to other brothers and sisters in that they can bear no substance relationship. A reason for the marriage is to retie blood links which have lapsed by the second descending generation. Clear reference is confined to explicit marriage contexts, such as bridewealth nego-tiations. In normal discourse, speakers usually revert to more definite descriptions, calling second cross-cousins *wamba mamia* (children of *mamia*). *Mamia* is a semantically distinct class which encompasses only ego's father's cross-cousins; speakers use this as the reference point for calculating which brothers and sisters are marriageable.

The two sets of terms, cognatic and sociocentric, overlap to a sig-nificant degree. Nevertheless, it is not possible to derive one level from the other as they do not match up perfectly. The reason is that the two levels are based on distinct principles, which are manifest in distinct points of reference. Accordingly, there is no way to reduce *ngut'e* (clan brother) to *ngut'e* (male sibling) without serious ethnographic distor-tion. There are two vectors of meaning in play here. The first is that *ngut'e* and *at'a* have a multitude of senses; they can be deployed to refer to several distinct classes of people. Speakers can use *ngut'e* and *at'a* as definite descriptions for several different relationships. The second is that these relationships are distributed on two distinct planes. The two levels represent separate approaches to the social use of language. For Maring, *ngut'e* and *at'a* are open to a wide set of uses and interpret-ations, all of which devolve on context. At the semantic level, the referent of the kin term is underdetermined. Hence, although the eth-nographer may know the senses of the local terms, it takes much additional pragmatic knowledge to be able to identify the referent. More than anything else, terms like *ngut'e* and *at'a* are a linguistic resource through which people construct a social relationship.

In terms of form and function, sociocentric and cognatic terminologies represent different aspects of the social system. Recall that the clan has two images. One image is context-free and generalized, telling that the clan has roots which extend far back in time. It is a perduring unit which neither seeks nor admits outsiders, having a single, unbroken continuity since its founding. Myth, orations, and the laws of land tenure inscribe this clan ideology. The second image is context-specific and local, taking into account that people flow continuously from one clan to another. Clan members have only to look around them at any given point in time, while collecting brideprice for example, to be impressed with the influx of new members. This is a pragmatic or how-to ideology which specifies how people transform affiliation and how clans assimilate outsiders. This ideology abstracts from various concrete situations – thereby implicitly distinguishing the salient from the peripheral aspects – to produce a picture of what clan reaffiliation is about. This ideology, insofar as its reference point is how individuals infiltrate a clan by virtue of their personal networks, is pitched to the cognatic level. It specifies, for example, under what conditions sister's son may legitimately take up residence with her brother, rather than how clans absorb outsiders or reproduce themselves by virtue of omnivorous recruitment. Hence, two perceptions of the clan co-exist: the clan as perduring and fixed since the beginning of time and clansmen as able to shift affiliation and more fluidly from one clan to the next if kinship and circumstances are right.

These two images of the clan correspond to terminological levels. Sociocentric terms are most often used in situations where at least part of the intent is to depict the integrity of the clan, and from the fact that such terms take the clan as a social type. Big-men when making public oration in brideprice ceremonies or political debate refer to their clansmen using kin terms or the clan name interchangeably. Frequently, such orations explicitly harangue on the continuity of the clan because this is a shared source of strength and power. Clansmen say, "brothers who have lived off the same ground form a truly powerful unit." Overall, terms of the sociocentric level are linked to land and the other elements of clanship. By contrast, speakers generally aim cognatic uses of *ngut'e* and *at'a* to those outside the clan. Their use for collateral kin is mainly in the context of exchange. Whether this exchange is formal or informal, the underlying value is the construction of lateral relationships. Maring sometimes make a distinction between *ngut'e wundok*

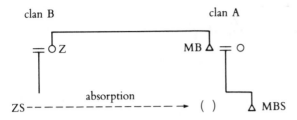

Figure 19 Reaffiliation: stage I

(here, meaning members of the same clan or sharing brother) and *ngut'e awi* (literally, brothers with whom I give/take).

A very common mode of reaffiliation will illustrate how this relation between language and agnation motivates and smooths the transition from one clan to the next. A sister's son begins to live and associate with his MB (*mbapa*) and eventually decides to take up permanent residence there. The ZS is recruited on the basis of cognatic ties manifest in substance; namely, he shares blood with his MB. Informants noted that whereas the tie between father and son is grease, between MB and ZS there is blood. In their phrasing, the MB is "like" a father because he shares one substance and takes on a roster of rights and responsibilities, especially in helping the ZS gather a brideprice payment. (The same holds true for the FZ as she is "like" a mother although linked by grease as opposed to blood). On the basis of his blood tie, the ZS has rights in clan lands, distribution of pork, and clan reproduction in general. By virtue of such sharing the ZS produces sons who are fully consubstantial with other clansmen of the MB's clan. As anticipated, the category of clan brother includes ZS's sons and daughters. The assimilation process becomes finalized by the second descending generation when revision takes place on the cognatic level. The revision attaches the incoming line of descendants to that of the MB. Essentially, then, there are three stages in the process of reaffiliation. This process weathers potential contradictions by systematically manipulating the levels of terminology. It smooths the reaffiliation by capitalizing on the overlap between levels of terminology, reading from one level onto the next and then back again. In the first step, recruitment, the blood tie between ZS and MB provides the terms of entrance. He is his *wump* or planting material.

Figure 19 simply depicts the reaffiliation of ZS and the fact that he is not a member of MB's clan, however much he may participate in its life and thus assume the behavior of a clansman.

In the following generation, the clan incorporates the sons of the ZS

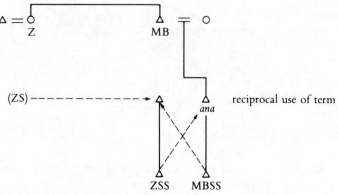

Figure 20 Reaffiliation: stage II

as full-fledged agnates. They possess and transmit grease of clan A. Reciprocal terminology develops between the sons of the MB and the sons of the ZS. This reciprocity manipulates the fact that such terms may be used from a purely sociocentric standpoint. All men of the first ascending generation may be called *ana* (father in the clan sense). That ZSS calls MBS *ana went*, meaning "father's eldest brother," a term reserved for cognatic links, indicates that something more is going on. Reciprocally, MBSS calls ZS *ana at'i*, meaning "father's youngest brother," also a part of cognatic terminology. This relationship between older and younger brother holds irrespective of the actual age of the fathers in question. The MBS is invariably *ana went* and the ZS is *ana at'i*. In essence, the system invents a birth order on the basis of immigration. Observe that this ordering replicates the ordering of subclans which are ranked from Wendakai (oldest root) through Atigai (youngest root).

Two generations beyond the original recruitment, the kin terminology fully merges and the "cognatic" revision becomes complete. All traces of non-agnatic origins are exterminated as descendants of ZS are linked to those of MB. The process edits the provenance of ZS and MBS so that, looking upward through the generations, they appear as younger and older brother respectively. The issue is not how genealogical amnesia expunges anomalies of agnatic derivation, but how the interplay between levels of kinship systematically alters relationships so that they become relationships of another type (see Cook 1970:195). Areas of overlap between cognatic and sociocentric terminology become points of salient indeterminancy from which practice can remap relationships. What is structurally indeterminate from the

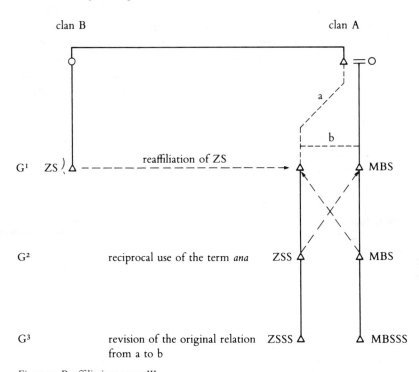

Figure 21 Reaffiliation: stage III

standpoint of kinship may be determined by the structure of practices which reproduce the clan. When ZSS lives off MB's clan lands, assists in brideprice and the sharing of pork, co-gardens with other clansmen, observes the proper food taboos, etc., revision of the kinship relation becomes inevitable. So Maring believe that foreign origin is practically irrelevant after the first generation because it has no practical effect.

The reaffiliation of individuals already called *ngut'e* is even more straightforward; the process simply transforms the sense of the kin term with each additional generation. In generation O, *ngut'e* designates a first cousin, in G+1 a clan brother, and in G+2 a brother in the fully consubstantial sense. As indicated, people are more likely to be recruited to the clan of the MB than the FZH, although this says more about the power and authority vested in men than about types of re-affiliation *per se*.

How reaffiliation works has troubled Highland ethnologists, and some like Strathern (1973) have turned to the Maring material for further clarification. After noting the importance of food, Lowman

(1971) writes that Maring non-agnates disappear by the second generation because of the merging in the kin terminology. As all members of the grandparental generation are called either *koka* or *apo*, "members of non-agnatic origin would be addressed by the same terms as clan members" (1971:323). Healey (1979) has responded that two refractory aspects of Maring social organization cast doubt on the value of this explanation: (1) persons outside the clan are called by terms for male and female sibling (i.e., *ngut'e* and *at'a*) and (2) newcomers are long assimilated by the second generation. As an alternative, Healey points to the "importance of exchange in effecting the assimilation of non-agnates" (p. 114).

But as the discussion of stages illustrates, there are by no means incompatible interpretations. They are simply different and partial views about how reaffiliation works. Every step of the journey from nonagnate to agnate links a way of using kin terms to the evolution of a cosubstance relation. What results is an ordered process of reaffiliation, exhibiting systemic creativity based on the context-sensitive, situationally dependent interplay between food, exchange, and the meaningfulness of kinship terms as used. Healey's analysis seizes on the dimensions of stage I in which the non-agnate acquires substance and identifies with his newfound clan through sharing food and participating in exchange. Everything said so far would support this understanding, even if Healey exaggerates its importance because he has misread the kin terminologies. By contrast, Lowman (and also Rappaport 1968 and 1969) focuses on the final stage of reaffiliation in which practice revises the original linkage. This analysis is also accurate and to the point, though it must be understood as the culmination of a structural process. The main problem with all of the partial interpretations – for the Maring and for other societies as well – is that they make reaffiliation appear arbitrary and discordant, rather than a structural process rooted in the social history of the clan or subclan.

One cardinal reason why New Guinea theorists have had so much trouble with reaffiliation is that they have misconstrued kinship terminologies in two related ways. First, there is the habit of conflating sociocentric and cognatic kin terms by defining ego as the sole point of reference for kin term use. This is tenable if and only if both levels (1) are constructed on the same principles and (2) they match up perfectly. As it turns out, the principal feature of Highland kinship terminologies is that the principles are different and that the levels only partially overlap (see Shaw 1974 and Cook and O'Brien 1980 for numerous examples). Unaware or unwilling to take the ethnography as its own value, analysts have continually erred by reducing sociocentric terms (e.g., brother as clansman) to cognatic terms (e.g., brother as male sibling), and then have sought to account for the cognatic level by appealing to the facts of paternity (and thus implicitly discounting indigenous concepts of kinship). So the literature on Highland societies is littered with statements such as "non-agnatic kin are terminologically *treated* as agnates" or "the term brother is *extended* to all clanspeople," and so forth.

The first misconception leads naturally to a second. Analysts have assumed that it is possible for speakers to discriminate kin term usages purely in light of their descriptive or semantic function. But this is never true because the distributional properties of kin terms demand that assumptions be made about the context of utterance. As the varied uses or distribution of *ngut'e* and *at'a* illustrate, reference is impossible on the basis of semantic criteria alone. That much Highland analysis confuses denotation (or types) with meaning (or tokens) aids and abets this misconstrued view of how people do things with words. Many analysts seem not to realize that if the kinship terminology was really based only on the principles they reported, speakers would find it impossible to refer and predicate successfully. It is no exaggeration to say that most descriptions of kinship terms rest on a faulty theory of language and its use pragmatically. The irony is that theorists have insisted on the pragmatic basis of reaffiliation even as they have excluded the pragmatics of speech from analysis, one thing that would show them the way between "concepts of identity through locality and identity through descent (as a special case of kinship)" (Strathern 1973:33).

The status of non-agnates

Like the Mae Enga (Meggitt 1965:25), the Maring place a high value on agnation as the primary basis for recruiting male members of groups. This is revealed in a clear patrilineal ideology and in the fact that most individuals are recruited to the clan of their father. Men who are agnates should live together, share land and food, and cooperate in important activities, especially exchanges. But there are also lateral structures which encourage the flow of men and women between clans and make it inevitable that every clan, no matter how large or small, landpoor or rich, will have a contingent of non-agnates in its midst. The Kamjepakai clan, most densely populated of all Maring clans, counts one in every fifteen clansmen a non-agnate. The implication is that clans continually rotate their membership, and that the incorporation of non-agnates is a condition of Maring society as constituted.[1] That is, practices and processes which make clanship possible make reaffiliation inevitable. The reproduction of the clan depends on the transmission of substance in its various forms across clan boundaries.

Maring non-agnates do not as a rule suffer a loss of status. Most have equal access to garden land, cooperative labor, hunting grounds, planting material, and other agnatic resources. For the incoming non-agnate, there is a rather fine line between sharing and exchanging, though they seem to operate successfully in this transitional zone where the distinction need not cause practical problems. One of the current Kauwatyi big-men is the grandson of a non-agnate, a fact he makes no effort to conceal, partly because his ascendancy from non-agnate to leader indexes the power of his personal line. How a clan initially treats an immigrant depends on the kin tie. Those who do reside with their MB or FZ incur no loss of status whatsoever. Individuals naturally affiliate with those cognates with whom they have a strong personal relationship. Thus, in most instances, there exists a strong practical as well as structural connection. Non-agnates, especially those with less solid kin links, are more cautious about exercising their rights. They are more likely to test the waters of clan opinion before undertaking any major action. A problem for non-agnates is that they sometimes become pawns in intra-clan power tussles. For example, one faction of the Ambiape subclan refused to support a MZS of another faction, not because they harbored any ill-feeling towards him, but because they felt that the opposing faction was not being sufficiently diligent in rounding up bridewealth for one of their sons. Hence, though non-agnates do not suffer a customary loss of status, they are more prone to encounter unforeseen obstacles that could make life a bit more complicated. At such times, I have heard non-agnates rue the loss of their natal lands and freedoms.

The growth and decline of clan and subclan

Local ideology, as inscribed in oral history, depicts clan formation in historical but undynamic terms, allowing minor room for structural

[1] This seems to be a condition of Highland societies irrespective of their agnatic ideologies and the status they accord non-agantes. Though Meggitt (1965:45–8) reports that Mae Enga are fiercely commited to the clan as a corporate group and only very grudgingly extend land to non-agnates, his statistics indicate that Mae Enga clans admit as many non-agnates as do Maring clans. Thus, in ego's generation he shows that there were 16.5% non-agnates and 7.9% quasi-agnates. The spread between 16.5% and the Maring figure of 17.6% is not statistically significant. Indeed, the main difference between the Maring and Enga systems seems not to be in the number of non-agnates assimilated, but the speed with which they are assimilated.

revision. Ideology omits the possibility of fusion, fission, and segmentation in the interest of defining the clan in lucid, crystal terms. Clans' oral histories tell that the current array of clans represent original migrations of brothers who put down roots in foreign lands. Kamjepakai clanspeople, for example, relate that their founding brothers come from the vicinity of Mt Hagen, and the clan is now actually pressing a legal claim to land on the outskirts of Mt Hagen, nearly three days' walk from their present settlement.

Ideology notwithstanding, people know some clans and subclans have changed their status historically. Warfare, in particular, always induces change since segments of the defeated clan cluster resettle with relatives in other locales. Moreover, there are pragmatic accounts of how changes in group affiliation and group status occur. Maring know, for example, that the interdigitation of gardens tends to draw two clans closer together, leading to the amalgamation of territories in some cases.

Context separates ideological and pragmatic accounts; people do not perceive them as contradicting, but as two perspectives on the clan's reproduction. Again, the metaphor of vegetative propagation comes into play. People say that the clan parallels a garden: it is planted, matures, withers, and is reborn, all with the assistance of infusions of planting material from cognatic kinsmen. The implication is that just as the clan must rotate its gardens to maintain itself, so sometimes it must rotate clansmen also. As one man put it: "men must occasionally move to grow and garden the same, and though we think this is not a good thing it is not really bad."

The Pan Maring survey conducted in 1963 made an effort to catalogue the name, size, and structural position of the agnatic units in the Jimi and Simbai Valleys. Some of the units named in the survey no longer existed in 1979, while other new ones seemed to have emerged or changed their status in the social structure. Most strikingly, some subclans have been promoted to clan status. Rappaport (1968) reports an instance of fusion among the Tsembaga where three formerly autonomous clans were in the process of merging. There is thus historical evidence that Maring subclans and clans have been fusing and uncoupling in a regular way over time, although historical revision now blurs the details.

Agnatic units fuse when their economic and political wherewithal is insufficient to meet the demands of exchange. Clan and subclan are each responsible for specific social functions, such as assembling bridewealth, holding ritual sacrifices, furnishing political support for allies, etc. To fulfill these responsibilities, clan membership must reach a critical mass, the necessary numbers depending on prevailing economic and political conditions. In the Maring's relatively undifferentiated economy, there is a close correlation between wealth and population. Maring often discuss clan size, their notion of size summing up variables in the social economy. The issue is not number *per se*, for Maring clans vary in size from less than 50 to more than 300, but the capacity to exchange.

Maring believe that the only good exchange relationships are those in which the participants maintain balance and reciprocity (*kopla*). In exchange, there must be relative parity between the groups. Hence, exchange regiments the options which are open to smaller groups. First, smaller clans may trade with one another, forming narrow localized circuits of exchange. Second, smaller clans may band together in order to meet payments to larger clan groups. Third, since smaller clans often have access to more land absolutely and relatively they may include land rights in brideprice compensation, thus reducing the amount of money and pigs they must raise. Fourth, smaller clans may act as wife-givers but not wife-takers to the larger clans. Many smaller clans exercise all four options, doing what is best according to circumstance. For example, not only are some Tsembaga clans fusing, but the relatively rich Kauwatyi are acting as wife-takers to the Tsembaga, paying 700 kina and 5 pigs, a very handsome brideprice by Simbai standards, and certainly a strong inducement for Tsembaga brothers to encourage their sisters to marry Kauwatyi men. Note also that in options three and four, smaller clans are substituting land and women respectively, for pigs and money, again showing the extent to which land, pigs, women, and money are interchangeable in marriage exchange.

The reorganization brought about by fusion emerges from the ordinary ways of social reproduction. On the basis of common interests, merging units begin to pool resources more closely. They look first to one another for help in accumulating the pigs, plumes, and other wealth needed to exchange successfully. The existing exchange of garden land escalates, and clansmen cooperate so as to coordinate their schedules – in making brideprice payments for example. Sharing land implies that the memberships of the two units will work together in the gardens, men lending each other a hand felling trees and fence-building, women helping with planting and harvesting. When people garden, work, and live close by, they are disposed to share an evening meal and perpetually to give and receive food. Interdependence grows, evolving into friendships, common projects, and mutual commitments to third parties. In the words of one man, the merging clans are "like two taro whose *wump* has been planted in the same garden." Merging units interdigitate gardens, co-garden regularly, share labor and planting material, pool their valuables, defend a common territory, and share food. All of these lead to economic integration and joint reproduction. Members of the two clans become increasingly related by shared substance. Those who share substance and act as a unit unite in exchanges, thereby defining themselves further by sharing exchange functions. This cycle feeds on itself; every step towards unity invites another step.

From separateness to unity is thus a logical and practical progression. No special or extraordinary steps need be taken, just the initiative of a few clansmen and the willingness of others to follow suit. Ideology phrases the transformation in terms of the obvious benefits of cooperation, informants explaining that they garden with non-agnates because "it is right that we should help our friends nearby, for they will help us with our gardens."

In the initial generation the fusing clans still appear to maintain their own identity, much the same as non-agnates would. The merging precipitates a ban on intermarriage, giving rise to "territorial units" which are exogamous. The local view is that men and women from the two clans should not marry because they "resemble brothers and sisters." People see such marriages as foolish and pointless because the existing connection is already close, and thus the marriage offers no possibilities for real gain. When such marriages do occur, they either retard fusion or reverse the process altogether. Whatever the outcome, bitter feelings always arise because someone's authority has been stepped on. Fusion seems to involve an intricate struggle for authority and power on two levels: (1) between rival factions of a given clan, often along subclan lines and (2) between the merging clans. On both levels there is an oscillation and interplay between collaboration and competition. Collaboration is essential for unification, competition for establishing rank and leadership.

In the second generation, the members of the merging clans slip into sociocentric kin terminology. Recall that because sociocentric terms take the clan as a social type, the use of such terms reinforces the idea that the two units are now one. In this sense, the gradual switch to more sociocentric usages helps create fusion.

When merging units reconstitute themselves, they appear as the constituent subclans of the new clan. Meanwhile, subclans of each merging clan are consolidating their functions so that the clan may assume the role of subclan in the new formation. For example, the subclans will jointly sacrifice pigs to the ancestors, a ceremony in which the subclan is the operative unit. Also, participants reorganize the collection of brideprice so that the former clan provides the pigs, a subclan function, while the other newly formed subclans contribute the money. This reorganization of function is a central reason for the fusion and thus visibly signals progress in that direction.

There is another interesting linguistic feature to fusion. The new clan is left unnamed through the second generation. People will refer to it by using some hybrid of subclan names. The Pan Maring Survey thus describes some clans as having two names and others as having none. This explains the existence of unnamed clans in a culture which defines clanship as important and naming as socially significant.

My survey of clan histories for the Kauwatyi, Tuguma, Cenda and Tukmenga indicates that the final stage of fusion occurs in the third generation. Informants recall (mostly from stories they have heard) that the fused subclans once lived apart and were separate entities. They conceptualize the fusion in terms of migration or remapping of a clan's territorial lines. Merging clans reappear as subclans of a larger and more powerful clan, a point not lost on friends or foe. The subclans avowedly stand in a brother relation to one another, though few people are willing to declare that the founding members were brothers. As noted earlier, being able to specify ancestors is not critical to agnation, co-substance links being reproduced on a constant basis. Thus, most clans say they have common forefathers, others say they do not know. It may well be the case that those clans who are unsure of their ancestors have recently undergone reorganization (though I have no direct evidence that this is true).

By the third generation, merging clans have assumed all the functions of subclans, while formerly separate clans are now treated as a single unit. They take on the rights, responsibilities, and obligations that accrue to one clan, such as collective responsibility for the actions of each member. Homicide compensation or retribution would fall on the clan as a body.

In the fusion process, former subclans lose their functions but not their names. Structurally, they are demoted to subsubclans (I use the terminology coined by Vayda and Cook 1964). Maring are adamant that a named unit never dies until all its members are dead. The salience of having a named unit, in conjunction with the historical processes of fusion, suggest why the composition of the agnatic hierarchy should vary so drastically from one clan to the next. So all clans have subclans (with the possible exception of remnant clans), some have subsubclans, and fewer have subsubsubclans (sometimes composed of only one member). The local concept that names last for as long as there are people to bear the name appears accurate; once a unit assumes a name, that name is never discarded. This makes sense of what would otherwise be an anomaly: that there is a positive correlation between the smallness of a clan and the elaboration of its agnatic hierarchy. Clans that are contracting in size tend to fuse more often, and, preserving their name, generate further cuts in the agnatic hierarchy.

Structurally, fission is the opposite of fusion in that a clan divides along subclan lines. This occurs when each subclan is (1) capable of upholding its end of compensation payments and (2) the subclans can garden on separate territories. To Maring, the idea that subclans who garden together and share food could divide runs contrary to all logic and experience. The fragmentation of clans is primarily a result of warfare and the fact that alliances are strongest at a subclan level. Subclans who are evicted from their homeland and take refuge in different locales may be absorbed into different clans. The principles of land tenure particularly act as a barrier to fission. Because the clan as a body owns the land, it is next to impossible for members of one subclan to garden totally separately from members of other subclans. Informants aver that a clan will only divide under special circumstances such as warfare or intra-clan homicide. Some subclans have more people than entire clan clusters, yet show no signs of splitting.

This section tries to illustrate two things. First, fusion is similar to reaffiliation; it is rooted in concepts of substance and relies on the same mechanisms. Indeed, without a notion of agnatic substance and reproduction, the connection between residence and kinship remains a mystery, leading to the supposition that "residence can create 'kinship' only in a metaphorical sense" (Strathern 1973:33). This goes against the grain of what Highlanders do and say, especially when analysis unravels the implications and meaning of local notions of size, wealth, strength, and other seemingly simple descriptions of the world. Second, a diachronic view accounts for what would otherwise be three peculiar properties of Maring clans: (1) clans vary widely in size and seem to grow very large without dividing; (2) below the subclan level the composition of agnatic hierarchy varies greatly and smaller units appear to possess more elaborate hierarchies than larger units; and (3) some clans do not possess a name though naming is socially significant.

Practice and principles of clanship

In the description of substance and exchange laid out, four sets of relationships are in motion:

1. the sharing of grease by clan members
2. the sharing of blood with a variety of matrilateral kin
3. the exchange of grease across clan lines
4. the exchange of blood across clan lines

These relationships move on lineal and lateral axes and interrelate clans across time and space. Agnation emerges at the crossroads of the practices and principle of sharing and exchange. The reproduction of agnation hinges on their interaction in the social field, leading to the conclusion that analysis cannot talk about clanship apart from exchange. The ethnography reveals how co-substance relates clan members because they share the same food, taboos, gardens, land, rituals, labor, ancestors, and affines. In general, they are co-participants in the same natural and social cycles. As visible social units, clans intermarry and thus intermingle their bloodlines. But for Maring, marriage is more than the exchange of female blood and labor, although these are certainly important. As noted, the woman herself embodies clan substance and her burial on the land of her husband necessitates compensation to her natal clan. Marriage involves several channels of exchange of clan substance, beginning with the original proffering of roasted pork and followed by land, labor, and all else. Management of this interflow determines the degree of relationship and cooperation between affines.

For clanship, sharing grease is necessary but not sufficient for determination of clan identity. The unrestricted exchange of clan substance would effectively dissolve the basis of clanship, for grease would be shared with non-clansmen. The structure of exchange, however, imposes a second line of determination in that it presupposes and entails a difference between exchanging clans even as it creates a similarity. Put differently, clans define themselves in terms of the sharing of exchange functions. Recall that collection and distribution of the bridewealth is a creative, salient index of clan identity. So much so that bridewealth is at the cutting edge of native awareness, clansmen characteristically framing their verbal ideology of clanship in terms of the sharing of bridewealth.

Hence, clansmen gain their identity from a sharing of clan grease or substance, coupled with a sharing of exchange functions. Within the orbit of practice, gardening and eating cooperatively generate a co-substance relation among clansmen, while exchange maps the limits of this substance relation. The crucial point is that although members of different clans utilize each others' substance, they do so by virtue of exchange rather than sharing. The sacrifice of pigs for the ancestors, with its ritual dedication and communion, and brideprice payments, explicitly enunciate this distinction.

A clan's substance has wider dissemination than its identity, though the two overlap and are organically connected. This overlap allows for a structured passage from the status of non-agnate to agnate. Individuals and groups may pass from exchanging agnatic substance – via land for example – to sharing the exchange itself. This transforms what was an exchange relationship – by definition non-agnatic – into a sharing relationship. The transformation of identity may occur at any level of the social structural hierarchy, from a lone individual up to the fusion of entire clans. This structure is the historical dynamic of Maring social organization: the modulation of grease and blood with respect to the practices of sharing and exchange.

A closing point about ideology: theirs and ours. Insofar as the Maring social order is inseparable from production, exchange, and consumption, the intricacies of clanship surface as commonsense statements about giving, receiving, eating, and planting. A result is that Maring social organization is deceptive to the Western eye, which interprets the remarks as so much economic rationality. The Western ideology inhibits analysis because Maring behavior appears so rational and comprehensible that the ethnographer is lulled by his own ideology into accepting Maring ideology at face value. In this respect, the ideological trap swings both ways; it encourages both an indigenous presentation and an anthropological reading of social life whose main function is to legitimize, by disguising in a culturally recommended way, the dialectic between structure and practice which produces social groups as historical products. In New Guinea especially, where the social and epistemological separation is so enormous, anthropology must account for and transcend ideologies by going beyond the impersonal, etic gathering of data to embrace a self-reflexive ethnography which begins by putting itself, as well as its empirical data-gathering procedures, into question. As Peng explained, giving and receiving, sharing and exchanging, and to this he might have added planting, eating, and burying, are never innocent, and no less so than in the practice of ethnography.

5 Marriage exchange

This chapter centers on marriage exchange and the various forms of compensation payments flowing from it. Where grease is the conceptual ground of agnation and clan formation, affinity rests on the movement of female blood via marriages. The drive towards reciprocity – the conviction that the best relationship is one that maintains balance – animates exchange. The same elements come into play here as with agnation, only this time land, food, pigs, magic, and money are part of the give and take among clans. The chapter sets out how marriage helps crystalize the clan and clan cluster, and how it is instrumental in their reproduction. Equally, it addresses how the clan's reproductive concerns, as culturally defined and implemented, inflect the structure of the marriage system. My general thesis is that marriage exchange is the basis of lateral structure and, as such, is as influential as agnation in the formation of the clan.

The perspective which guided the ethnography and guides the description is that marriage cannot be reduced to the bilateral relationship which allies clans via the exchange of women; more than this, it is a multilateral relationship which accomplishes social, economic, and political ends within institutional limits. These ends may be compatible or contradictory; they may serve the interests of the clan but not all of its subclans. My purpose is thus to define the social field within which the marriage occurs, both in terms of the clan's internal dynamics and the audience of past, present, and potential wife-givers and wife-takers who evaluate marriage as a relation of significance, and a commentary on the significance of prevailing relations.

Accordingly, I make no attempt to typologize Maring marriage as general or restricted, symmetrical or asymmetrical, immediate or delayed. The trouble with these formal distinctions is that they let ethnographers off the hook. That between immediate and delayed exchange, for example, allows ethnographers in New Guinea and elsewhere to ignore cultural concepts and strategies of time and tempo, rhythm and reciprocity, which imbue an exchange with meaning, and hence incite people to make the marriages that they do. Perhaps most of all, these distinctions tend to sanction the ideology of exchange, and thus to downplay the role of women who, at least in the Maring world, have an influence on practice which is not represented in the ideology.

The issue of exchange brings to the fore a critical though complicated point about the relationship between ethnography and theory. Exchange in New Guinea has both a social and economic moment whose interrelationship is not transparent and whose relative weight changes from one context to the next. This had led to an ethnographic distortion that is understandable in terms of the ethnographer's position within his own scientific culture, which demands that he produce an explanation which transcends his own experience, and his position within his "other culture" which is his experience. The ethnographer, inescapably a stranger, stands outside the social framing of exchange. Due to this separation, local exchangers – with the exception of those who mimic Western practice, usually because of exposure to Christian missionaries, kiaps, and sometimes anthropologists – have no reason to socialize the exchange. Hence, the character of the transaction emphasizes the economic moment at the expense of the social one. Moreover, the ethnographer has no means to construct the social dimension of exchange. The clansman, by recourse to his network of kin ties, can substitute a personalized, kin-based relation for an impersonal one, and create a social basis for exchange in almost any setting. The consequence is that the ethnographer experiences exchange as an almost purely economic affair. People seem most interested in using him to his full economic advantage (with the result that the ethnographer values as "friends" precisely those people who avoid the obvious implications of his status as outsider).

This de-socialized relationship to society resembles our own ideology of maximization and not accidently ethnographers have so attributed this economism to New Guineans. At the same time, however, ethnographers also realize that there is a social moment to exchange which they must account for. But this is a moment which enters experience often only from the standpoint of the observer, thus inviting the analyst to describe exchange as a finished and dyadic relationship ordained by the mechanics of custom. Forced, in other words, to construct the social dimension of exchange when they themselves experienced only the economic, ethnographers have fallen back on our own contractual theory. The end product has been mechanical theories of exchange whose underlying logic is instrumental. A good example is the theory that the inclusion of utilitarian and non-utilitarian goods in an exchange network is "really" intended to stimulate the production and distribution of the utilitarian goods.

Reciprocity

Maring perceive any type of illness, injury, death, or madness as the result of purposeful action by another being. Almost all misfortune must be intentional and thus must be caused by a sentient being (i.e., one that possesses *rawa* or spirit). Hence, inanimate objects, such as food, or non-sentient beings, such as mosquitos, cannot cause illness of their own accord, but must be directed by a thinking agent. So ancestor spirits and sorcerers are held responsible for food poisoning, malaria, and many other types of illness (see LiPuma 1986).

The purposive actions of other beings influence an individual's decision-making process, particularly their use of reproductive resources. Ancestors and affines are most influential; sorcerers are less dominant, though affines may become sorcerers, especially if normal political channels fail. Maring say that when they make decisions they feel the interests and the desires of ancestors and affines as an "invisible pulling" (*mu di*). All of the following beings influence, manipulate, or control the movement of substance: ancestors oversee the natural cycle and the continuity of passage of clan grease from one generation to the next; affines control the reproduction and transfer of female blood; and sorcerers use nail clippings and other personal leavings to disrupt the passage of food through the body or prevent crops from growing properly.

Clansmen attempt to offset the influence of affines and also to elicit their support and allegiance, through reciprocity. In turn, affines are eager to be compensated. The exemplary affinal relationship is one in which the demands of the wife-giver match the reciprocity of the wife-taker. No matter the size or prestige of the gift, it cannot discharge the claims of the wife-giver. Maring say that the more a woman becomes a part of her husband's clan, finalized in the burial service, the more her natal clan should receive in gifts, prestige, and other women: because her "natal clan raised her and made her what she is."

For Maring, total reciprocity would involve the exchange of sisters. In this sense, a wife is a replacement for a sister as epitomized in the ideal of sister exchange. Bridewealth is thus a form of reciprocity in which material goods are substituted for the woman in question. And, even in instances of direct sister exchange, wealth should be transferred because the value of each woman is still unknown, and hence there is no way to determine whether the exchange is equivalent. Bridewealth consists of a special category of material goods called *mungoi*. Speakers may use *mungoi* to refer to bridewealth or any object identified with an individual or group. *Mungoi* (pigs, money, cassowaries, plumes, etc.) may be substituted for social persons because such wealth embodies the reproductive potential of the clan.

Clanspeople view reciprocity as a means of settling claims, and restoring the balance (*kopla*) or equilibrium which is upset constantly by marriage, and occasionally by homicide. A woman given in one generation and returned several generations hence, a whole contingent of intermediate material transactions standing between these moments, erodes mutual obligations and brings the state of affairs into harmony. Marriage generates an exchange cycle between clans, opposing prestation and counter-prestation so as eventually to close and settle all claims. Hence, the marriage system does not structurally endorse a self-perpetuating relationship between wife-giver and wife-taker. This has two consequences. First, it allows the clan to forge a temporary alliance with distant clans (in some instances with different linguistic and cultural groups). Second, a clan that wishes to maintain an affinal tie must renew the exchange when blood ties lapse and the claims are settled.

Wife-takers try to offset their obligations to wife-givers in three ways. First, the wife-takers substitute pigs, money, land, and other valuables for the individuals themselves. Such reproductive objects are intrinsically less valuable than women because their reproductive potential depends on women's labor. Clansmen recognize that "without good marriages it is impossible to raise many pigs or make good gardens or have many children." Second, one marriage reciprocates another so that each clan both gives and receives a woman. The failure to "back" a woman ends the relationship, leads to bitter feelings, and in former times was the harbinger of future hostilities. Exchange in the opposite direction offsets the advantageous position of the wife-giver. Finally, every compensation payment, no matter what the circumstances or occasion, must be immediately reciprocated (often the following day) with a counter-prestation. Maring say that "it is impossible for two clans to meet as equals if one clan has nothing to present."

Involvement in marriage: clan and subclan

The clan and subclan have different involvements in marriage and the accompanying compensation payments. The clan functions as the unit of alliance and reciprocity, performing the political and social duties

Table 12 *Levirate – adoption*

	Sample number	Husband's brother	Husband's subclansmen	Husband's clansmen	Other
Levirate	16	8	5	3	0
Adoption	19	8	6	3	2

which arise because a co-substance tie links all clan members. The subclan, however, is the most active unit in Maring marriages, transferring women, bridewealth, child payments, and any counter-prestations on behalf of the clan as a whole. As noted, bridewealth and all other forms of compensation are raised from contributions from all members of the wife-takers' clan and distributed to all members of the wife-givers' clan (see Wagner 1967:152). A woman bestowed in marriage by a particular subclan may be "backed" by a woman from any of the subclans of the wife-takers. There are demographic as well as economic reasons which encourage this form of exchange, and although clansmen say they prefer direct sister exchange, it does not occur frequently (less than 15% of marriages).

People believe that an in-marrying woman belongs to the clan because all members have contributed the bridewealth. By the same token, children belong to the clan because they are formed from clan grease and any claims on them are settled with clan wealth. The subclan has similar though more powerful claims on women and children because members of a subclan are bound by blood ties. There is a clan levirate under which a clan brother will marry a widow of his clan brother, presuming that no stronger claim exists, such as one held by a "true" brother. Likewise, clan brothers of other subclans sometimes adopt orphaned children, especially if they have no children of their own. Table 12 depicts the transfer of women and children among the Kauwatyi.

As the clan is the unit of affinity and reciprocity, so its constituent subclans are the operational units which drive the marriage relationships. Maring say that a clan bears "the name of the affinal relationship" and stands "together in marriage exchange" while the subclan develops the "give and take of the relationship." These words capture the fact that it is the subclan which conducts the marriage negotiations, arranges the exchange and compensation, and generally sets events in motion. This appears pointedly in the practical flow of affairs, such as the loan of garden lands. Figure 22 illustrates how two intermarrying subclans act as intermediaries in the transfer of land rights. Formally, because A is an agnate of B, A can solicit the assistance of D to obtain land from C.

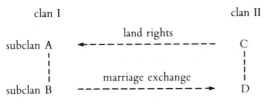

Figure 22 Transfer of inter-clan rights

In one such instance, a subclansman from A went with the father of the bride (from B) who ostensibly was visiting his daughter now residing with subclan D, to see how she was faring. On the second day of their stay, the subclansman from A made a small speech in which he remarked how well the marriage was working, noting particularly that the bride had recently given birth. Later in the conversation, he asked the father of the groom from subclan D if he could use a certain tract of land to plant some coffee. Subclansmen from C had traditionally used the plot in question, so D interpreted A's request as a request for D to approach C. This was indeed done, C ceded A use rights in the land, and when the coffee crop was harvested and sold several years later, A compensated C for the land by offering a percentage of the coffee money. C, in turn, shared a percentage of the compensation with D.

Especially within a clan cluster, such as the Kauwatyi or Cenda, each subclan will be wife-givers to some subclans of another clan and wife-takers from others. Clansmen recognize that the best cement to link subclans together and establish a balanced relationship – that is, one of complete reciprocity – is by direct exchange of women. A family or extended household can also forge the strongest relationship to a similar unit in the same manner. For this reason, among others, Maring advocate direct sister exchange between brothers; and informants, particularly unmarried men, declare that it is the preferred form of marriage. Copresent with direct exchange is a network of indirect exchange that implicates all the subclans in a criss-crossing pattern. A subclan will reciprocate the marriage of a woman given to it by giving a woman to any subclan of the wife-giver clan. Thus, each subclan welcomes a woman of the other clan regardless of which subclan she may have come from. For the most part, there is balance, or *kopla*, between clans in marriage exchange but not between individual subclans.

The operational relationship between intermarrying subclans has structural implications given local concepts of substance and reproduction. The subclans have a brisk interaction, typically exchanging land, co-gardening, trading planting materials, doing cooperative labor, and giving food. This creates a co-substance bond which brings the subclansmen closer together.

The connection between intermarrying subclans seems to vie with intra-clan ties between subclans. Especially when the intermarrying subclans have a long history of involvement, their relationship may seem to overshadow intra-clan relationships in many instances. In terms of warfare, subclans of the same clan have sometimes opposed one another across the battleline because one subclan was aligned with one combatant and the other subclan with the other combatant. Given the presence of co-substance links, and the traditionally close tie between cross-cousins, the isolation of subclans through direct sister exchange undermines the clan structure. Conversely, indirect exchange will integrate the subclans by retaining the clan as the unit of reciprocity. Moreover, the bridewealth demanded for indirect exchange is more than that for direct (in 1979, 7 pigs and 1,000 kina versus 3 pigs and 400 kina), making it relatively easy for the subclan to raise payment in the latter case but rarely in the former. The creation of such localized marriage exchanges functionally differentiates the subclans of a given clan. Statistically, although not preferentially, indirect exchange dominates the marriage system, even if all subclans make some direct exchanges.

Rights in women

Rights in women, and thus rights to the compensation wife-takers pay for female substance and fertility, derive from local concepts about the genesis of kin relatedness. The clan as a body holds the primary right in an unmarried female because the woman was born of clan grease. Within the clan, rights are graded following the contour of co-gardening, food sharing, and housing arrangements. In most cases, practice ordains that the oldest unmarried brother will have the strongest claim to arrange the marriage of his sister. This is based on the preference to marry off senior men first, and because the older brother has "cared for his sister and given her food" – both as part of his familial obligations and with an eye to eliciting her cooperation. There is an artful and sometimes tumultuous negotiation carried out between brother and sister over whom she will marry, for women are rarely bystanders in their own future and the chosen groom must be mutually acceptable to both siblings (LiPuma 1980). A woman's brother may curse her if she insists on an unacceptable husband. This curse is thought to cause sterility and thus to diminish her value. The brother receives the lion's share of the bridewealth and, in cases of direct exchange, has first right to marry the woman sent in return for his sister (Rappaport 1969:122).

For the wife-giver, the acquisition of reproductive wealth in the form of bridewealth is of great significance because "women are the planting material which make the clan grow." The objective is to obtain sufficient wealth to replace the woman given away. Hence, should one of its own women not immediately be forthcoming, a wife-taker should reciprocate enough wealth to "buy" a bride for a son of the wife-giving clan. The entire practice of accumulating and transferring bridewealth revolves around the impending marriage of the woman's brother. An express part of marriage practice is to try to align subclan brothers and sisters into marriage pairs. In the ideal situation, a brother will exchange his true sister, this being a major reason why parents prefer to have an equal number of sons and daughters. Families with a disproportionate number of brothers or sisters circumvent the problem in several ways.

Not uncommonly, a man who has no sons selects a subclansman as his daughter's "marriage brother". The young man usually has no sisters or his family has more brothers than sisters. The woman's father makes a garden with the young man, shares his personal heirlooms which bear his spirit, provides food and other amenities, and generally adopts the young man. The transformation of status from a subclan "son" to that of a "marriage son" is terminologically marked by a shift in the usage of *wai* (son). The father uses *wai* in all those contexts normally reserved for true son. This is ceremonially broadcast in the marriage negotiations when the "son" of the father and "brother" of the daughter is identified and his interests and plans are spelled out. Rappaport (1969:22) characterizes the relationship between the daughter and her "marriage-linked" brother:

At the time of his selection, or shortly thereafter, the young man presents to his marriage-linked "sister" a small gift of beads or an orchid-fibre waistband and gives her father a few valuables. Henceforth he cooperates with them as if he were a true son and brother, plants most of his gardens with them and helps in housebuilding and collecting firewood. He may also take most of his meals at their hearth. For his gifts and services the young man obtains primary rights in the disposal of his marriage-linked sister.

The cooperation, sharing, and common activity between father, daughter, and son is the Maring means of making kin relations close. Willingness to tighten the relationship is indicated by the transfer of the initial presents. What binds the kinsmen is the practice of engaging cooperatively in reproductive, substance-creating acts, such as the sharing of food. Note that the creation of marriage pairs and the exchange of a sister for a future bridewealth, tends to put all marriage exchanges in the form of direct sister exchange. In one case, brothers actually trade their sisters; in the other, brothers trade their sisters for the value of someone else's sister. So Maring try to transform all marriages into direct exchange between brothers, though the content of the exchange and its timing may vary.

Because bridewealth is payment for a woman's reproductive powers, substance, or planting material, any individual or group who has contributed to her powers has a right to a share of that bridewealth. Hence, those who have helped to raise and nourish the woman receive a share proportionate to their contribution. When a woman and her husband do not reside patrilocally it leads to plural claims. A bride's agnates will always receive a share because they contributed clan grease. If the bride has lived on the land of her mother's agnates and eaten their food, they too will be accorded a share of the bridewealth. In the past warfare tended to multiply rights. If a refugee family settled in with affines they, rather than his own agnates, claimed superior rights in his daughters; and "even if he returned to his own land, those who had sheltered him and provided him with garden land continued to claim some rights in his daughters" (*ibid.*:123). Plural claims are often resolved when the daughter is young, principally by a payment of pork. Records of forty-four cases indicate that non-agnates may receive anywhere from a joint of pig to half the bridewealth depending on their contribution and their current status in economic relations. An example will set some of the issues surrounding plural rights in perspective and illustrate how claims may be worked out.

Example of settlement of plural rights

Wana was married to Goli of the Kamjepakai clan and had a single daughter by him. When his daughter was three, Goli went to work on a coastal plantation, never to return. During this time, Wana lived with her eldest brother and his subclansmen from the Kambant'igai line. For seven years Wana waited for Goli to return, though reports from the plantation indicated that Goli had his mind set on remaining there. Disgusted, Wana divorced Goli and two years later married Ying, a man from the Kakupogai clan, as his second wife. Ying confessed that he was anxious to take a second wife because his first marriage had produced no children, though Ying had begun the process of adopting the son of his wife's brother (who, incidentally, had gone to the plantation with Goli, returning four years later only to re-enlist in late 1978). Ying's second marriage created a situation in which Goli's daughter, Kumb, could be paired with the son of his wife's brother. So the adoption process, however informal, accelerated. The young man, Mun, began to spend more time helping Ying with his coffee and house repairs, and eventually moved in on a permanent basis. Not wasting any time, Mun presented the daughter with a dress which she accepted. Soon after, Goli's daughter and Mun made a garden together, addressed each other as brother and sister, and ate from the same fire.

Mun's newfound sister, of long limb, a downturned nose, and a good disposition, was very attractive by local standards, and several suitors were interested in marriage. Mun told his sister, however, that she could not marry immediately, for he had to make payment to her father's line. Mun, in concert with Ying, presented four scooped nautilus shells, a pig, and 100 kina to the Kamjepakai clan of Goli, specifically to Goli's brother who made the following speech:

When Goli was here . . . he bought Wana and they lived at Kwia [a place name on Kamjepakai land], where they made [or carried] a daughter. For many seasons, Wana and Kumb [the daughter] ate *komba* [vegetables laced with pandanus nut oils], taro, and pig provided by my brother. Now my brother has forgotten about his wife and daughter, and being on the coast, neither provides them with food nor helps them to make a garden. Kumb has grown up away from Kamjepakai land and so it is not right for us to take the bridewealth. Mun has presented valuables for his claim to Kumb.

This speech, like others of its kind, legitimizes the transfer of rights in terms of Goli's failure to provide food and labor. At the same time, the reference to Kumb's birth explicitly states the Kamjepakai's original contribution. More, the reference to *komba*, which stimulates blood, and taro, the food related to breast milk, invokes the repayment of clan substance through the compensation of pork, money, and shells. Note again how Maring use straightforward practical talk about land, food, and gardens to describe the formation and exchange of substance. In the same vein, brothers cajole a strong-willed sister by vowing that should the sister run off with a husband of her choice alone, they would no longer accept food from her garden, eat at her hearth, or share valuables.

About six months after this compensation payment, Kumb married a man from the Baigai clan. Mun and the Kakupogai clan negotiated a bridewealth of 7 pigs, 800 kina, and 1 cassowary. At this point, it was essential to compensate Wana's eldest brother who had supported and co-gardened with Kumb during her formative years. At the formal

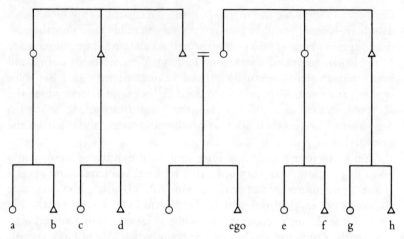

Figure 23 Co-substance relations

exchange, a delegation from the Kambant'igai subclan which supported Kumb stood next to the Kakupogai subclan, though slightly to the side of the main line of exchange. Once the pork and money had officially changed hands, Mun and Ying gave 200 kina and 4 flanks of bridal pork to Wana's brother who, in turn, further divided the pork among his own subclansmen. Thus, the transmigration of Kumb from the land of one clan to the next generated plural claims which her "brother" could discharge only by the payment of vital reproductive goods.

Co-substance and marriage preferences

Maring say that they marry two kinds of people. The first is *yindok ndemi* (literally, wild/undomesticated people), meaning those clans with whom no outstanding marriage relations exist. Clansmen commonly apply the term to groups which only exchange women, goods, and services infrequently. The second kind is *yindok wumbi* (literally, tame/domesticated people), meaning those clans which have a long history of intermarriage, and who are involved in an intricate web of exchanges of every sort. Within the second class, clansmen marry cross-cousins and almost never parallel cousins. This is true both statistically and normatively, and is understandable in terms of the lines of co-substance. A look at the distribution of co-substance relations will illustrate the point (see Figure 23).

The co-substance relations created by a marriage, and applicable to any ego, turn on the dual pattern of heredity: the local concepts concerning the transmission of substance. Recall that though men and women possess grease and blood, men transmit only grease and women only blood to their children. Thus a man does not share clan grease with his mother nor blood with his father.

In the figure, clan grease links ego to both his father's sister and brother. On his mother's side, blood ties link ego to both his mother's brother and sister. However, given the local conception of procreation and heredity, ego will not always bear the same substance relationship to his cousins as he did to their parents. Ego bears an unmediated co-substance relation to persons c, d, e, and f; c and d share clan substance with ego while e and f share blood through the mother's sister. By contrast, ego is related in a mediated way to a, b, g, or h, only through their parents. For ego, cross-cousins are fundamentally different from parallel cousins.

The kinship terminology follows the contours set out by the pattern of heredity. Cognatic kin terms differentiate cross- from parallel cousins. Ego calls his parallel cousins *ngut'e* (brother) or *at'a* (sister) depending on sex; he calls all cross-cousins *wambe* irrespective of sex. The terms for parallel cousins, *ngut'e* and *at'a*, do not observe clan boundaries. In marked and unmarked uses they may refer to both agnates and non-agnates. In contrast, *wambe* unambiguously specifies members of another clan. This surfaces in the generic or sociocentric use of *wambe* to refer to the lineage of potential spouses. In practice, given the configuration of co-substance relations it is rarely permissible to marry a first cousin of any type, though there is a manifest difference in the destiny of the cross and parallel lines.

For Maring, of course, the connection between kin terms and co-substance remains implicit, as individuals may divine concrete parts of the system as they appear in specific instances, but not the totality. What interests clansmen is that *wambe* represent the descent of alliance and reciprocity through the generations. This crystalizes in the use of the idiom of vegetable propagation; thus clansmen conceptualize *wambe* as "planting material" or "seeds" of future generations. In the figure, ego is the planting material or *wump* of the mother's brother's clan, for ego's daughter is the potential wife and the center of reciprocity for h and his clansmen. One informant explained it this way:

My mother came here [to his father's clan] long ago and now she is a mature woman (*ambra mai*). She was sent by the Kambant'igai line [her natal clan] and hence I am their wump [planting material]. When my daughter grows up she will be sent back to the Kambant'igai. There is a man there who had marked her [as his future bride].

The continuity inherent in the organic metaphor implies that the cross-cousin is an elementary linkage in the descent of the marriage tie. *Wambe* are the intermediate steps in the reciprocity and transmission of blood between clans. It is the absence of a co-substance relation in the presence of a demonstrable continuity which permits intermarriage in the second generation and makes the *wambe* relation so critical in the first. *Wambe* have a very large emotional, economic, and social commitment to one another. They embrace and support one another, and frequently a man's closest personal kinsmen are his true brothers and his *wambe*. Note also that recourse to the *mai/wump* metaphor again exposes the linkage between production and clan reproduction: *wambe* are like cultigens which have been exchanged back and forth between the land of two clans. Or, put differently, *wambe* are dimensions of the same generative scheme as land, gardens, women, pigs, and money.

First cousin marriages, which occur in very limited number (less than 1% of my total sample), illustrate the differences between the two types of cousins. The dual pattern of heredity in conjunction with the obligations of reciprocity skew first cousin marriages towards the FZD. In a sample, necessarily small, five out of seven first cousin marriages were with the FZD. Of the remaining two cases, one marriage was with the MBD and one with the MZD. The latter marriage led to a vociferous court fight and the couple involved were essentially living in exile on the Anglican mission station. Marriage with the FBD never seems to occur and people have a hard time even swallowing the idea, as they perceive it as not only incestuous but stupid.

The objectives of exchange

In contexts ranging from formal marriage negotiations to off-hand attempts to persuade a bachelor to marry, men will itemize the benefits of marriage, characteristically by reciting how women will bear children, help in the garden, and raise pigs. The explicit idea is that to give a woman is to bestow the gift of social potential upon another group, women being the indispensable resource without which the clan and subclan would cease to reproduce. In recognition of this reality, women, the children they bear, their labor, and the substance of their bodies (i.e., bones) fall under the heading of "that which we must compensate for." In the Maring scheme, pigs, money, land, and military assistance count as basic compensation, though a number of subsidiary goods and services may also oil the exchange. Outside European influence and the rise of the Papua New Guinea nation has affected the system in two ways: cash has been substituted for shells, although shells occasionally still figure in prestations to this day; and commercial assistance, especially in the establishment of a trade store or the cultivation of coffee, has replaced military help. These constitute the primary and definitive objects which flow along the marriage alliance axis.

Clansmen make clear that due to women's importance in social reproduction no amount of material goods can fully compensate the donor. So, the often unspoken, because non-negotiable, clause of any marriage agreement is that the recipient will refund a woman at a later date. To maintain its exchange credibility and thereby its powers to attract women – which from both a demographic and a social standpoint are in short supply – a clan must repay its debts.

The demand of reciprocity creates a tension between wife-giver and wife-taker because producing balance and evenhandedness is an ongoing, dynamic process. Some men pay bridewealth once, twice, even three times to compensate their in-laws; in other instances, wife-givers will return, usually circuitously, a portion of the original bridewealth. Whether the wife is exemplary or poor there is a drive towards reciprocity. The tension between wife-giver and wife-taker moves on two grounds: first, the taking clan does not know whether the woman will work in the interests of her husband, bear children, garden successfully, or remain faithful; second, the wife-giver does not know whether the receiving clan will proffer sufficient compensation during the life of the marriage or will eventually return a woman. The link between understanding and interest compound the difficulties. What counts as good gardening or sufficient compensation is a matter of debate.

Clansmen are quite explicit about these concerns, which is one reason they are careful to calibrate the risks and rewards of a given marriage. An advantage of being heavily intermarried with another clan is that this reduces the uncertainties of reciprocity since interests, objectives, and activities become interdependent. Tension between in-laws finds voice in the formalities surrounding the serving of food and a set of prohibitions on their interaction. For example, it is taboo for in-laws to address one another by name or even to mention each other's name in conversation. Thus affines usually call each other by kin terms or terms which otherwise index the relationship, perpetually underscoring that this relationship between individuals is also a relation between groups.

If a dyadic description does poor justice to the link between individual in-laws, it is still less adequate to the clan level. Each marriage plays to an audience of other clans, who are also marriage and trade partners, monitoring the terms and execution of reciprocity with consuming interest. Affines of both the wife-giver and wife-taker evaluate the marriage using it as information to guide their own impending plans, and implicitly confer more or less social prestige on the clan in center stage. Maring say they are keenly aware of the "other eyes, other thoughts" which review the exchange, and keep a sharp ear attuned for the innuendo and gossip which serve as a running public commentary on the actions of the exchanging clans. Public comments center on reciprocity and the virtues of the individuals who are involved.

A second and complementary objective of marriage exchange is to generate kinship relationships based on the sharing of blood. In the generation of marriage, the exchange of substance against vital wealth is the link between intermarrying clans. In the first descending generation, the terms of the relationship become co-substance. Blood ties relate sister's son and daughter to the mother's brother. This link is transitive and relates sister's son and daughter to all members of the mother's brother's clan. The relationship is based on what may be called cross-substance ties and follows this logic: if ZS and ZD are related to MB by blood, and MB is related to his agnates by clan grease, then ZS and ZD are related by substance to all members of their mother's natal clan. Mother's brother not only mediates the relationship but serves as the source of local consciousness about the cross-substance tie. When someone wishes to specify their connection to a particular clan, they will say that so-and-so is my mother's brother. The relationship extends in the other direction as well to all the agnates of the ZS and ZD. Through the ZS (and ZD) and MB there is a continuity of substance connecting the intermarrying clans. In this way, clansmen can always translate cognatic ties into clan ties. This serves as the ground for the transfer of land, food, labor, and planting material which strengthens and animates the relationship. Thus the differential properties of blood and grease allow Maring to transform co-substance relationships between individuals into co-substance ties between groups.

Marriage also generates a second line of relationship which flows through the mother's sister. By the laws of heredity, the offspring of two sisters will share "one blood," this co-substance often inspiring a strong, well-maintained practical relationship. For any person, there are less obligations and expectations built into their relationship to MZ children, at least as compared with the sons and daughters of their MB. Maring make a distinction between relationships that are customary and pre-packaged, saying such relationships "have a name," and those which flower mostly through individual initiative and the conjunction of interests. Stated differently, the indexical value of an action, such as gift-giving, is inversely proportional to its necessity. People treasure most those gifts (defined broadly) which are not called for. Recall that MZD and his clansmen figure prominently in the making of exchange relations, as men often call upon their MZS for hospitality and introductions. Healey (1979) remarks that Maring have a penchant for exploiting a sister's son in trade relations.

Observe that by the second generation a single marriage will relate a wife-taker to at least two other clans, sometimes more, depending on the number of sisters the wife has. Hence, whether a woman has sisters and where they are married concerns wife-takers. This is one reason why clansmen are unenthusiastic (in most cases) about receiving two sisters from the same bloodline. In practical fashion, they note that such redundancy chokes the clan's capacity to develop exchange relations.

Because women alone transmit the blood ties created by marriage, such ties are inherently transient from the standpoint of the intermarrying clans. In the absence of renewal, blood ties between clans will lapse thus terminating their relationship. This will occur if two clans wind up on opposing sides of the battlefield or, what to Maring amounts to the same thing, a homicide takes place. Figure 24 traces the descent of the bloodline and its implications for the renewal of the alliance.

In the first generation, both male and female children (e and f) inherit the blood of their mother (d). As a result, they share one blood with her brother (b) and cannot marry into his line (clan B). But this relationship does not endure more than one generation because men cannot transmit blood to their children (f and i are not one blood). Therefore, consubstantiality is severed altogether by the second descending generation; a woman's granddaughter will bear no kinship with her natal line (i and b are unrelated). This means that intermarriage is again possible and that to uphold the alliance the respective clans must again intertwine the bloodlines. As will become clear, this is not the only means to clear the debt or renew the blood tie.

The final objective of any marriage is to satisfy a range of economic and political concerns. Maring do not need to be told the sure advantages of having a stable of enduring and deeply rooted affinal ties; ancestor spirits, by counseling their descendants on which allies to cultivate, sanctify this practice. But enduring and hence relatively repetitive relationships are not necessarily the best strategy when the

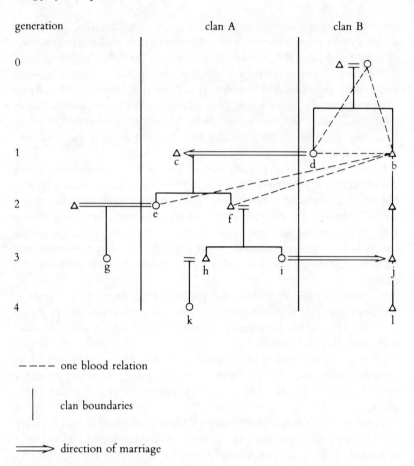

generation   clan A   clan B

– – – – one blood relation

clan boundaries

⟹ direction of marriage

Figure 24 Bloodlines – exchange

objective is both to clear the marriage debt and advance the interests of clan reproduction. While a debt is the memory of past exchanges, current interests invariably point towards the future, time conspiring with need to throw the pair out of synchronicity. The clan's interests change in response to the state of regional affairs, such as political turmoil or closure of an important exchange route; to demographic fluctuations, a sharp decline in numbers or a sudden influx of non-agnates hardly being atypical; to transformations within the clan, particularly in the structures and uses of power and authority, today shifting away from the older men towards the younger and more worldly-wise; and

164

to the impact of external agencies like the Christian mission and the national government, over whom the Maring can exercise little or no control. So clansmen, now more than ever, must continually revise their marriage policies to adjust to transformation and at the same time repay their creditors. Moreover, though I have laid stress on the accelerating pace of change, oral history makes clear that the clan was always condemned to an eventful life, modernization being perhaps just a bit more disruptive than war.

The form and practice of marriage

Maring practice features a variety of alternative plans that tailor the marriage to its social context. All marriages seek the three objectives of establishing reciprocity, interweaving bloodlines, and meeting the demands of clan reproduction. Nonetheless, the making of a marriage is like a winding road, to borrow a local metaphor; clan objectives are weighted by situation and success is generally mixed, at least judging from the swirl of pre-marriage opinion. Alternative plans are less a conscious review of possibilities than simply letting clan interests develop within the limits of practice.

Maring recognize and name three forms of marriage exchange, though they place no emphasis on classifying individual unions. The recognized forms are sister exchange, returning the planting material, and bride payment exchange. These forms, because they derive from local concepts of co-substance and marriage, do not conform to standard anthropological distinctions, such as generation and collaterality.

Especially for men, the most sought-after form of marriage is sister exchange: that is, two brothers exchange their sisters or women who count as their marriage sisters. The simultaneous (or nearly simultaneous) transfer of sisters is the ideal method, but it is not constitutive of the practice. Brothers will exchange a sister for the promise to return a sister. As much as a decade may divide the actual movement of the sisters, with the average in the vicinity of a year. Sister exchange usually involves only token bridewealth – 2 pigs and 500 kina, for example – because it is likely that the exchange will be balanced. Informants note, however, that this is not always the case, for some women work hard and bear children while others don't. History may prove that the balance and reciprocity are only an illusion of the exchange. In the case of delayed sister exchange, the comparatively small bride payment counts as a promise of the wife-taker to return his sister. Thus, during the exchange ceremony the wife-taker makes an explicit pronouncement that "we are rich in pigs, land, and are very strong; we have given such a small payment because our sister will soon go to your house." Sometimes, the timing of the sister return is set (roughly) in pre-marriage negotiations. Occasionally, a delayed exchange will go awry, the promised sister rebelling against the marriage, usually by running off with another man. In such cases, the wife-taker augments the original bridewealth by making a second payment nearly equal to the first. Brothers who have promised their sister to another, what Maring call "marking" the woman, show an unusual amount of anxiety about who she visits and where she goes, their anxiety heightened during festival times.

Brothers prefer a sister exchange because it streamlines the process of obtaining a wife. The built-in reciprocity simplifies pre-nuptial negotiations, as there is little to decide with regard to the form and quantity of the bridewealth. More, since the bridewealth is considerably lower, sister exchange does not entail the same accumulation of pigs and cash. Men feel that this puts them in a stronger position because they are not so dependent on more distant clansmen. They can accumulate the bridewealth with little assistance and thus avert the political posturing and in-fighting which often accompany the collection of bridewealth. By the same token, sister exchange takes the decision-making process entirely out of the hands of women, who are notoriously strong-willed about marriage. In this sense, the community recognizes sister exchange as the ability of a brother through skill and wisdom to "manage" his sister, and hence to exercise authority in a manly way.

For the clan, sister exchange meets the goals of marriage in some very positive ways. It generates a tight-knit set of social relationships, since the distribution of blood relations will be the same on both sides of the marriage exchange. The transfer of goods, land, and services will possess an unshakable foundation. Maring aver that the brothers will be *mbapa* (mother's brother) to one another's children and that all the children will be *wambe*. Sister exchange also perfectly satisfies the terms of reciprocity, in principle if not practice. Clansmen especially favor sister exchange when the intermarrying clans are geographically far apart, a circumstance that has become increasingly common with cessation of war and the development of a more regional political identity (e.g., Jimi Valley people). In essence, clansmen will endorse sister exchange because it maximally interlinks the bloodlines and creates certain reciprocity.

Note from Table 13 that sister exchange, although desired by most men, occurs less frequently than other forms of marriage. There are two outstanding reasons for this. The first is that while sisters recog-

Table 13 *Forms of marriage exchange*

Category	Number	Percentage
Sister exchange	48	12.7
Reciprocal exchange	194	51.2
Bride payment	127	33.5
Other	10	2.6
Totals	379	100.0

Note: I should make it clear that insofar as the sample comes principally from interviews, it represents how Maring classify marriages after the fact, not what originally motivated the marriage or its intended form. For example, time and ideology may transform what was originally meant as a sister exchange into a bride payment.

nize an obligation to assist their brother in his quest for a wife, they are active, sometimes decisive, forces in the determination of the marriage. Sisters will repeatedly exercise veto power on the mate selected by the brother until he happens, no doubt urged by their prompting, to select a man they are already fond of. Hence, it is not easy for a brother to either convince or pressure a sister to accept a husband of his choice alone. So most attempts at creating a sister exchange seem doomed to failure, a fact that most brothers are not wont to admit given the local ideology of male dominance.

The second reason is that sister exchange often does not meet the reproductive needs of the clan. Thus, a young man who is endeavoring to arrange a sister exchange may run headlong into opposition from the elders within his clan. This opposition is expressed as concern for the immediacies of social reproduction. A man's agnates may complain – in louder or softer voice – that a sister exchange would not assist the clan in meeting its debts to wife-givers, who it turns out are usually anxious to receive a woman and are busy lobbying for reciprocity. Clansmen may also argue that it is more important to make a marriage which repairs trade relations or permits access to productive land, such as for raising pandanus. In their discourse on sister exchange, Maring recognize (though without any attempt to sustain the abstraction) that this form of marriage limits the possibilities for creating alliances, and thus for achieving reproductive goals. Moreover, sister exchange tends to occur between clans too far apart to conduct any meaningful commerce – women nowadays marrying as far away as a day's walk – or between clans so intermarried that further ties have no marginal value. Several men reported that they had received negligible support from agnates in their efforts to consummate a sister exchange. A young man would typically relate how his "fathers" were opposed to the marriage because they had already "marked" a woman. It should be no surprise that given the numerous diverse interests in play, many attempts at making a marriage end in stalemate.

Much more common than sister exchange, and more an express part of reigning strategy, is what Maring refer to as bride payment exchange. Such marriages serve to initiate or, more frequently, develop a relationship between clans by accelerating their degree of inter-marriage. In bride payment the woman in question is very explicitly exchanged against reproductive goods, with the implicit proviso that the wife-taker will return a woman at some unspecified time in the future. If bridewealth is not given, a daughter of the marriage will go and reside with her MB and he will collect brideprice for her as a substitute. In nearly half (47%) of the cases of bride payment, the men claiming rights in the woman arranged the marriage.

Notably, in the majority of cases (53%) the bride was, in local terminology, "stolen" by the wife-taker. This refers to marriages in which the woman picks out a man and approaches him independent of her brother's consent. It is the woman who has orchestrated the flight to the house of the man and she is mainly responsible for her "theft". People compare "stealing" a woman to unlawfully raiding a garden or pandanus patch. It is theft regardless of the attitude of the woman or her role in the affair, for what is at issue is the removal of clan substance without clan consent.

Rappaport notes (1969:129) that "bride stealing frequently follows the all night dances which occur during festivals." At the dance, girls

are presented with eligible young men of local groups with which they may otherwise be unfamiliar. The context, moreover, permits the young women to discriminate among the young men in terms of strength (shown by how vigorously and how long a man continues in the competitive dancing) and social relations (signified by the magnificence of his shell and feather finery).

Male relatives invariably set out in pursuit of the woman when they discover what has happened. When the relatives arrive at the house of the prospective groom the theft can be resolved in a number of ways. In some cases the young man has no real interest in marriage, and is more than willing to renounce his claim. More often, the two clans regularize the marriage. Rappaport (1969:129-30) describes:

After the girl's relatives have ranted sufficiently to demonstrate a proper amount of belligerence and ferocity, they permit themselves to be persuaded that the marriage is not intolerable. Often they are influenced by the promise of a bride in exchange in the future or by the promise of a large and prompt payment of bridewealth.

Brothers sometimes have an inkling that their sisters will elope, but allow the theft to take place because they don't see it as materially harmful to their own marriage plans. This is especially true if she intends to marry a man in an already allied clan close to home.

But the encounter does not always end on such a sanguine note, particularly when the relationship between clans has been strained for some time. Before pacification, dispute leading to all out war could ensue when a stolen woman was not returned forthwith. Today, such thefts lead to bitter court decisions that sometimes annul the marriage, but more often rule in favor of the woman on the grounds that an individual's will should predominate in this Independence era. The courts also stipulate the bridewealth which should be paid by the wife-taker, a very handsome settlement of 8 pigs and 1,000 kina not being atypical.

Of major approaches to marriage, the last and most frequent (see Table 13) is reciprocal exchange. In practice and speech about practice, people refer to this as "returning the planting material." One clan, for example, will exhort another to provide a bride by saying that it should return planting material. The metaphor is of plots of garden land between which gardeners transplant material in a continuing cycle. In its many uses, "returning the planting material" signifies not only the making of balance (*kopla*), but the continuity and certainty of exchange. The abiding idea that there will be a continuous and equivalent flow of women between clans because each recognizes and supports the reproductive interests of the other.

Reciprocal exchange illustrates that the forms of marriage are more accurately characterized as approaches to social reproduction, presuming that we understand reproduction as the creation of the social order in which kinship and economy are separable only from the perspective of the observer and only for the purposes of analysis. The illustration unfolds in two ways. First, questioned out of context, Maring will recite what appears to be a positive marriage rule: one of a woman's granddaughters should marry back into her natal subclan. This is an ideological version of what happens and, strictly speaking, patrilateral second cross-cousin marriage is rare and few clans ever "return the planting material" in the strict sense. My survey indicated that it occurred about 11% of the time (LiPuma 1983), and Rappaport reported an incidence of 4% (1969:128). Nonetheless, Maring still count a wide variety of reciprocal exchanges as truly "returning the planting material" on the grounds that they satisfy the conditions of reciprocity and retie the bloodlines.

Second, when asked, clansmen were often unsure whether a certain marriage was initiating or reciprocating. They pointed out that clans who have been heavily intermarrying over a long period of time, creating what is called a pig-woman road, tend to describe all unions in terms of planting material because no one keeps a precise ledger on the number of exchanges, despite clans being relatively sure of where they stand in any specific exchange. As one informant noted: "when two lines give and take, they share land and pigs and help one another to make gardens; they do not think about this marriage or that marriage." How people describe an exchange relationship – as part of a continuing cycle of return or as fixed reciprocity – reveals whether they see the affinal tie as enduring, or as temporary and susceptible to failure. Clans within a clan cluster, by definition heavily intermarried, tend to describe all internal marriages as the simple circulation and return of women.

Clans may return the planting material in several ways. A common one is for the debtor to delay repayment for an additional generation or two. Intermarrying clans are generally involved in a complex web of exchanges, all in various stages of development, making delay an easier proposition because the debtor–creditor relation is rarely one-sided. As observed, a subclan may owe a woman to an affinal line who in turn owes compensation to this subclan's brother line. When this delay occurs, it is customary to present a gift, usually a third of the bridewealth, in the intervening generation as a show of good faith.

Another of the more common options is to substitute another woman from the same line. This is a particularly favorable and legitimate option when the woman is of the same bloodline, though this is neither a necessary nor sufficient condition for such an exchange. In this way it is possible both to satisfy the exchange and restore blood relations. In most cases, the two clans merely concur on the substitution of another woman; or, more precisely, the clans count as reciprocity a marriage motivated by other reasons.

Reciprocity also evolves into a triangular arrangement where debtor repays creditor through an intermediary line. Clan A gives a woman to clan B who gives a woman to C who returns a woman to A. This interweaves the bloodline across three clans and thus serves to interrelate them more forcefully. Maring do not consciously plan such arrangements, but they do recognize them as they develop. People perceive that the marriage between A and C cancels C's debt to B and B's debt to A. This surfaces in the proper (i.e., balanced) distribution of rights and obligations and privileges.

This form of marriage surfaces at the level of cognatic kin terms as the understanding that a man should marry the children of *mamia*, or what in genealogically defined space would be the patrilateral second cross-cousin. Such an exchange would, of course, return the planting material. For Maring, however, the constitutive ambiguity of socio-centric and cognatic cross-cousin terms permits all members of the appropriate clan to fall into the proper kin category. Ego's *mamia* are his father's *wambe* and his father's *wambe* is the entire range of cross-cousins. Hence, any woman in the clan of the FFZS fits the description, although clanspeople never bother with such categorizing since it has no bearing on the production of marriage.

Ideology and exchange

An implication of the foregoing analysis is that exchange is not produced by a set of rules (see LiPuma 1983). Still, analysis must account for the fact that the form of marriage, "returning the planting material," is more conspicuous and transparent than other forms and gives rise to local statements that appear to take on the coloring of a rule, especially when refracted through the lens of exchange theory. Why do Maring characterize reciprocal exchange as the ideal way for clans to interact when they see no merit in its realization apart from the goals of clan reproduction? The issue is how to account for a subordinated ideology which has no official role in the indigenous representation of practice. For example, the concept that a clan should offer compensation for failing to "return the planting material" privileges this form of marriage. Yet, it is equally clear that a clan may reciprocate the marriage in many ways, and that clans who do not rarely surrender payment. Moreover, the compensation itself presupposes that other marriages and other strategies are available.

The virtue of reciprocal exchange over bride payment is that it resolves the chronic uncertainties of exchange. Clansmen talk tirelessly of the failures and deceits of exchange, and litigants parade such cases through the local courts. In place of an open-ended exchange, this marriage form creates one which is both local, the circuit being insular and short, and also presupposed. Where bride payment leaves reciprocity at risk, reciprocal exchange establishes a near-perfect reciprocity by seeing any marriage as a temporary loan of substance. The clan which offered the woman becomes, by generational turns, the wife-taker. In this respect, these marriages parallel sister exchange which, recall, is also an ideal. In contradistinction to bride payment, it "invariably" fulfills the aims of reciprocity and institutes balance.

Reciprocity is a self-fulfilling prophecy insofar as each additional

revolution of the marriage cycle augments the moral and social interdependence of affines. But more, reciprocal exchange also creates harmony between the different structural levels. It constitutes an
ideological refusal to recognize the relationship between family lines
within a subclan, and subclans within a clan, for what it truly is: a complex of very competitive relationships. Reciprocal exchange has the
virtue of simultaneously satisfying the interests of family lines, subclans and clans. And by settling the score on all levels at once, it avoids
the contentious debate which ignites when marital interests and fortunes diverge.

Maring do not use this form of marriage to regiment exchange,
although the fact that it is an ideal, a strategy, and an ethical norm
would make it eminently suitable for such purposes (Bourdieu
1977:43). Hence, reciprocal exchange does not enjoy an exalted position in local or anthropological accounts. More broadly, one of the
ways in which Maring exchange differs from certain Indian, African, or
Arabic systems is that it is much less enamoured with privileging a particular reading of marriage. That is, it is less interested in rendering an
official account and thus in suppressing alternative pathways of
exchange. I would suggest further that a main difference between
Maring exchange and exchange in these other systems is that the latter
creates an official, ideologically fixed version of marriage, and thus
projects a marriage pattern which anthropologist and native may represent in terms of preferential/proscriptive rules; by contrast, the
Maring ethnographer faces a system uninterested in giving an official
account. Indeed, what seems to have often thrown Highland analysts
off the scent is that their ideological bias encountered systems where
marriage ideology was relatively bare.

Marriage negotiations

A given marriage may be made to reciprocate a wife-giver, to attain
some economic goal, or perhaps merely to raise sufficient bridewealth
so that a brother can afford a wife. The characteristics of the marriage
rest on the emerging strategy of the clan involved. The clan does not,
of course, set its objectives in a vacuum but depends on the means at
hand. Certain marriages are "good" or "bad" only given certain conditions, a fact implicit in Maring judgements about the value of proposed unions.

The making of a marriage rides on several factors. First, wife-givers
and wife-takers review each other's material wealth and thus socially
productive state. The current state includes other outstanding mar-

riages and the clan's reputation for reciprocity. Second, clans assess how well they may capitalize on each other's resources and services. The wife-taker may have available large tracts of arable land, but this is only of value if the land is needed and accessible without hardship. Third, the skill of the clansmen who negotiate the marriage does much to determine its outcome. Certain clans, as almost any Maring will attest, are better or worse at creating favorable marriages and impressing their affines.

The clan's marriage strategy results from the combined and various interests of its membership. This normally embraces all members of the intermarrying subclans and the senior members of the corollary subclans. The weight accorded to any particular interest turns on the emergence of factions or lines of opinion. The views of senior clansmen are taken more seriously, but only infrequently do they all line up on the same side of an issue, in part because they are competing with one another for influence. Each subclan rarely has a consensus of opinions and undivided interests. Yet, where marriage is concerned, clansmen pride themselves on doing what is best for the clan as a whole. This injects a measure of individual freedom into any argument since a man can always claim that he was acting in the best interests of the clan. There is further incentive to take up this broader stance, especially for young men, because it characterizes the big-man.

Marriage negotiation involves the participation and animates the passions of all clan members, be they senior men acting in their official capacity as heads of the subclans or women acting as the concerned voice of other affines (i.e., their natal clans). As every person has a vested interest, and a part to play at the appropriate moment, each contributes to the negotiation's measured success. In Maring fashion, a negotiation has no fixed points, or narrow topics, or necessary participants; there is no ceremony or formal gathering of the clansmen or business-like demeanor. A negotiation continues publicly and privately, between individuals and groups, formally and informally, discussions not infrequently wandering off onto only remotely related topics, the participants coming and going as they see fit. Yet, communication succeeds and gradually a consensus crystalizes, both within a clan and between clans. The negotiation is less a fixed event than a process in practice. Discussions continue right into the early days of the marriage, what does progressively change being the terms and certainties of the talks.

The negotiation of marriage is rooted in the understanding that clans direct their efforts toward their own reproduction. There is no thought to the production of assets *per se*, which is really quite alien to the belief that the world measures a clan's strength in terms of the practice of its members: their ability to make acclaimed social exchanges or to fight successfully. The marriage negotiations, by orchestrating concepts of men, women, land, pigs, food, money, and history in the interests of clan reproduction, bring together and objectify the principles of substance and exchange. Depending on their position in the clan, different clansmen may pursue contradictory interests, to which they assign a certain value based on their beliefs, desires, and judgements about a given marriage. Clansmen who have cultivated one set of affines may find disagreement in that a woman is not being returned to these affines. More typically, young men see less advantage in repaying old debts than in creating marriages that will enhance their ability to grow coffee or operate a trade store.[1]

The foregoing description of sister exchange, elopement, and bride payment illustrates that people may initiate marriages in numerous ways, although the mutual consent of brother and sister seems essential. Once the real possibility of marriage emerges, the immediate relatives of the bride and groom hold preliminary talks, at first to discover the truth of the other's intentions. "It is necessary to peel away the skin of the discussion so that we are not blinded by the 'grease' or carried away by our greed": this according to a man famous for his ability to arbitrate. The negotiators begin by setting the stage: "we have [or have not] come far and are gathered here together" is a common preamble from the bride's kin, who then go on to name themselves by subclan. The discussion then detours through a variety of topics, the speakers oscillating between demonstrations of independence and strength on the one hand and solidarity and politeness on the other. By this circuitous route the negotiations return to their epicenter, the terms and acceptability of the marriage. The relevant lines of inquiry are as follows:

a. Whether the woman is a hard-working gardener and successful in raising pigs. This is not only important in itself, but embodies the general perception of the status of the woman in question.

b. Whether the man is a hard-working gardener who shares food generously, and more centrally, how well and successfully he makes exchanges and wields influence. These summarize a man's status.

[1] One cardinal requirement of running a successful trade store in a remote area is maintaining good supply lines. Since the goods are shipped from Mt Hagen to Koinambe and then to local areas, it is best to have affines or other relatives at both transshipment points.

c. The composition of the family of the bride and groom, and thus how much bridewealth and in what proportions. If, for example, the woman has an unmarried brother, the size of the bridewealth and the inclusion of cash become central. Or if the woman has other sisters who are already married, this enhances the value of the exchange (since the union will immediately increase the groom's clan's range of alliances manyfold in one move).

d. The age difference, if significant, between bride and groom. This is especially the case when the man is considerably older than the woman, and possibility of the levirate, or some variation, is imminent.

Sometimes preliminary talks break up in disarray and the two clans renounce the union. Inability to reach a consensus usually signals a deeper division, and in times past must have been a harbinger of conflict. But often the immediate relatives establish the grounds for marriage, returning home to present the matter to the entire clan. People also consult their affines, who feel free to express their opinions however much they may possess vested interests. Clan members then pursue a second, broader line of inquiry and debate which broaches the following issues:

a. The land, pigs, and other forms of wealth at the disposal of the opposing clan and subclans.

b. The quality and extent of the alliance and trade network that the opposing group is part of.

c. The existing marriages between the clans and the value of an additional exchange.

d. The big-men of the opposing clan and their relative prestige and political position.

e. How this marriage fits into the future objectives of clan and subclan.

Discussions about a proposed marriage are usually by turns bitter, funny, and calculating. They are kaleidoscopic: diverging angles and points of view are expressed, cleavages occur and are repaired, the composition of different factions changing rapidly. To the ethnographer, it sometimes appears that just when complete disarray has taken hold, a consensus emerges. Maring themselves are often at a loss to explain how a consensus was forged from the fire of dispute. Ethnographers of New Guinea have had an especially difficult time with practices, such as negotiations, which, being highly pragmatic, are founded on a native mastery of the history and interests of intermarrying clans and the semiotics of social interaction. Just to grasp that a marriage negotiation is going on takes mature social skills because it does not announce itself with formal markers (such as a social space or time set aside for negotiations). And, because negotiations are not clearly bounded events, that is, they are not segmentable, informants have great problems reporting about them in interview situations. They will tell the ethnographer of the outcome of the negotiating but never how this outcome came about. The upshot is that the *modus operandi* for creating marriages or for recruiting allies during warfare is underreported in the New Guinea literature despite its emphasis on warfare and exchange.

For Maring, marriage negotiations constitute the clan in two ways: (1) the intra-clan disputes presume the existence of the clan because what is good for the clan as a whole is perceived as the highest and most rational form of argument; and (2) the process of agreeing to disagree establishes the terms of intra-clan discourse: where the style, issues, principles, and purposes define that clan as a clan unlike all others. Or, to put it differently, the clan forum can tolerate different points of view because it presupposes and creates a common ground about which there is no question. In large measure, the social persona of the clan – how it appears to other clans – is based not on what clansmen do and say (*per se*), but on this characteristic common ground about which there is no talk. The tendency to turn New Guineans into rough and ready empiricists forgets that clan itself is an abstraction removed from empirical reality.

The marriage process

Maring conceptualize marriage as a process of binding, whose final moment is the woman's burial on clan lands of her husband, in the sacred grove where the spirits of the dead dwell. In this light people perceive marriage as flexible, open to ambiguity, and admitting no easy definition. Whatever its attributes, marriage is not a jural process which simply generates and transfers a handful of rights, liabilities, and obligations.

Importantly, there is no social ceremony with the powers to create a legally valid union. Especially in their early stages, marriages may be awash in ambiguity. For the ethnographer and no less for indigenous observers, it is often difficult to fathom whether a recent couple is truly married or not. For the Anglican Church and ethnographers wedded to our jurisprudential tradition, the local concept that marriage is a process has proven difficult. So both have tried to regiment the facts to fit our understanding of there being a decisive change in statuses. The problems, one might add, inherent in the use of "marriage" are not indigenous to New Guinea as Murry's (1976) study of Sotho marriage and Camaroff and Roberts' (1981) analysis of Tswana unions show.

Attempts to regiment Maring marriage are misguided. Maring has no performative verbs set in institutional contexts, whose proper use signifies the passage from one status to another. For Maring, the crucial elements are the pragmatic interplay between duration, fertility, bride payments, and community recognition. There is no event which bridges pre- and post-marriage statuses. Marriages crystalize as time passes, children and other indices accumulate, bridewealth is given, and the community recognizes the marriage and the couple so presents themselves to the community.

In the early stages of a marriage – before, after, or during the negotiations – a woman begins residing with her husband's mother and unmarried sisters. When the negotiations wind down, and often they seem just quietly to evaporate, the husband will sometimes give a small payment to the bride's kin to signify that both parties agree to proceed with the marriage. Even at this point, men rarely begin to have intercourse with their wives, as there is a deep-seated fear that sex drains off a man's powers and virility, especially if performed too early and too often in his life. In some instances, newly married men head straight for the coast to do a stint of plantation labor, hoping to raise some cash and avoid contact with their wives for several years. For the woman, the time spent in her mother-in-law's house is a testing period to determine whether the woman works hard and faithfully, can mesh with other personalities, and truly desires the marriage. The next phase of the marriage is when the man builds a house for the woman. Traditionally, the man would continue to sleep in the men's house, making daily visits to his wife's residence. Nowadays, men tend to build a single dwelling to establish a conjugal home. However, the house essentially replicates on a smaller scale the organization of the compound. The house is divided down the center, with the front door situated so that the women's quarters are downhill on the left and men's quarters are uphill on the right. The crucial difference between old and new housing, and one recognized by Maring, is that the conjugal home embodies the growth of individuality because each man is now master of his own compound.

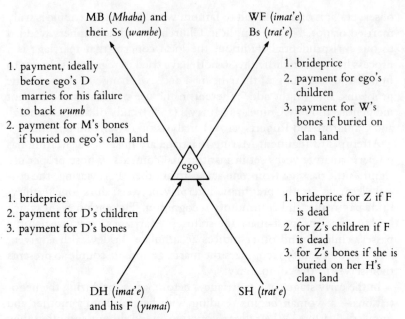

MB (*Mhaba*) and
their Ss (*wambe*)

WF (*imat'e*)
Bs (*trat'e*)

1. payment, ideally
   before ego's D
   marries for his failure
   to back *wumb*
2. payment for M's bones
   if buried on ego's clan land

1. brideprice
2. payment for ego's
   children
3. payment for W's
   bones if buried on
   clan land

ego

1. brideprice
2. payment for D's children
3. payment for D's bones

1. brideprice for Z if F
   is dead
2. for Z's children if F
   is dead
3. for Z's bones if she is
   buried on her H's
   clan land

DH (*imat'e*)
and his F (*yumai*)

SH (*trat'e*)

Figure 25 Compensation payments for Maring male received from and given to affines

As the woman becomes progressively assimilated into the man's family and establishes herself as wife and gardener, the marriage begins to crystalize. At this point, a man may decide, often at the urging of his wife, to arrange the payment of the major bridewealth. This may come many years after the original negotiations, men delaying the payment until they have several children. It is not unusual for a man to make both a marriage and child payment on the same occasion. Often bridewealth deviates from the original estimate, being greater if the woman has been an outstanding wife and less if the marriage has been unfruitful. Recall that people almost invariably blame infertility on the woman. It is in early stages of a union, before bridewealth is paid, that marriages are most brittle. With good reason, divorce (more accurately, what counts as divorce) is exceptionally high during this period. Of the twenty-two marriages initiated during my field stay, seven had disintegrated, or were on the verge of doing so, by my departure. Young men often jest by saying they are trying the marriage out to see if it breaks or takes root. After payment of bridewealth, divorce is less frequent and more serious, in many cases leading to court action.

The final marker of marriage is public recognition. Such public acknowledgement matters most before bridewealth is paid, since the

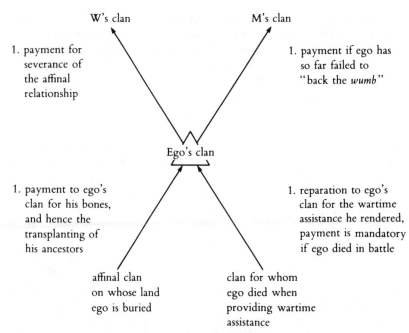

W's clan   M's clan

1. payment for
   severance of
   the affinal
   relationship

1. payment if ego has
   so far failed to
   "back the *wumb*"

Ego's clan

1. payment to ego's
   clan for his bones,
   and hence the
   transplanting of
   his ancestors

1. reparation to ego's
   clan for the wartime
   assistance he rendered,
   payment is mandatory
   if ego died in battle

affinal clan
on whose land
ego is buried

clan for whom
ego died when
providing wartime
assistance

Figure 26 Compensation payments made on death of a Maring male

bride payment is unequivocally definitive of marriage. Nonetheless, informants aver that a couple may be married even if bridewealth has never changed hands. Court decisions about the status of a union not defined by bride payment look to public wisdom to render a verdict, although sometimes the community is hotly divided over whether the union is truly a marriage. The general sentiment seems to be that it is not until the couple have produced children that the marriage makes roots.

In essence, marriage is a process of binding in which none of the stages are absolutely necessary. Under varying conditions, any and all may be dispensed with, though it is only in instances of direct sister exchange that no bridewealth is ever paid. It is also clear that the purpose of bridewealth is not to legitimize the conjugal relation. Rather, it is the conjugal relation which legitimizes payment of bridewealth.

Compensation payment

Every gift of a woman, being enmeshed in a web of clan and subclan interests, runs the risk of not being reciprocated. This reciprocity is made extra urgent by the shortage of marriageable women, a shortage which clansmen bemoan but which is inevitable given a natural im-

179

balance in sex ratios (more men than women) and an ideology which exalts polygamy. It is no secret to any Maring bachelor that a reasonable bridewealth for his sister will be less than her value to social reproduction. This is all the more true because the clan's internal power structure and the goals forged by the meeting of collective interests mediate between the bachelor and a potential marriage partner.

It is in this sense that a set of inequalities surround the equality of exchange. On one hand, the woman's clan has the upper hand in any exchange (except maybe that involving an older woman). Wife-givers possess the most valuable and scarce resource for which there is always a real demand. This affords the wife-giver the privilege of choosing somewhat more freely, of being slightly less anxious to consummate the exchange, of being more certain of the benefits that will accrue. It also allows small clans, who can offer little to large clans in the way of military assistance or exchange partners, to intermarry with them. On the other hand, the wife-taker overcomes this inferiority at the moment of the exchange. For however grandiose the bridewealth, it is less than a woman is worth in a system of reproduction so dependent on women. Compensation pay is a promissory note on future social reproduction – the exchange of a woman and the series of exchanges that should follow – whereas the woman is the keystone of successful reproduction. This lies behind the Maring words that "children replace the dead, gardens make us strong, and pigs raise our name."

Compensation payments are centers of attention because clansmen arrange them in light of their prevailing interests. They are never fixed or certain, but involve a measure of risk insofar as circumstances change and people reorder their reproductive paths. Contrary to the standard wisdom which seems to permeate accounts of Highland exchange, gift and counter-gift, marriage and counter-marriage are never a mechanical sequence of relatively obligatory acts, triggered by the inaugural prestation or marriage.[2]

[2] A particularly explicit and coherent example is Kelly's study of Etoro marriage which assumes that the "major exchange relationships entail a mutual obligation to provide wives as they are available and in accordance with the needs of the other lineages" (1977:121). This formal reduction strips away the pragmatics of exchange by presuming in advance the very practice which it needs to explain; namely, how Etoro marriage exchange so effectively harmonizes the different, changing interests, motives, and positions of the lineages within the exchange system. I would argue that the regularities or consistencies of the exchange system do not derive from an implicit contract between the lineages in question, if for no other reason than that such a contract could never accommodate the economic, political, and social changes which every society must weather to survive (that is, socially reproduce). Rather, there is a set of known strategies, embodied in practice, constructed on the basis of cultural categories and principles, which allow the group to reimburse its affines without sacrificing the interests of social reproduction.

In his lifetime, a man will be indirectly involved in all forms of compensation, and likely directly involved in most. The main set of compensation payments are roughly correlated with the reproductive cycle of the family, specifically the transfer of women and the use of their substance to produce children. At some point after his marriage takes root, a husband will decide to give bridewealth. In 1979, normal bridewealth among the Jimi Valley Maring ranged from 3 pigs and 500 kina to 10 pigs and 1,000 kina in cash, with the majority falling somewhere in between. In the twenty-one bridewealth payments I witnessed and/ or participated in, the average prestation was 6.8 pigs and 670 kina. The quantity given and the timing of the exchange depend on several factors: the woman's fertility, the value attached to the particular exchange relation, the current need to broadcast clan wealth for some political purpose, the perceived needs of the wife-giver, the ceremonial calendar, plus the response to all the other gifts (e.g., land) given by the affines in addition to the woman. Recognizing the influence of these factors on bridewealth, clansmen invoke them to explain its quantity. For example, during the early days of my fieldwork when the Kauwatyi anticipated holding a *kon't kaiko*, the bridewealth shrank in size, men explaining to their affines that the upcoming pig slaughter forced them to cut back on prestations.

The bridewealth, like all compensation for female substance, divides into two moments and involves a double reciprocity. The first is on the plane of exchange itself where a woman is given in return for reproductive wealth; the second lies on the plane of the transaction where every prestation elicits a counter-prestation. Maring call *nogai kon't* (literally, sweet potato-pig) that portion of the bridewealth which the groom presents to the wife-giver in exchange for female blood, labor, and skills. The sweep of the metaphor is that sweet potatoes are the staple of the Maring diet, being less seasonal and more resistant to bad weather than taro or yams, and thus circumscribe what is fundamental or basic. Pork, by contrast, is ceremonial food offered only to affines and ancestors. It signifies the social qualities of the gift: that it is an elective generosity and a precise compensation for the woman given. Moreover, the notion of *nogai kon't* explicitly aligns the purviews of men and women, for the context of exchange associates men with pigs and sweet potatoes with women. It says that the clan exchange a woman, the basis of reproduction, for the transactable signs and substance of men.

The *nogai kon't* is some portion of the total prestation of wealth. If the bridewealth consists of 7 pigs and 700 kina in cash, a common figure, *nogai kon't* will be in the neighborhood of 3 or 4 pigs and 300 to

400 kina. Negotiations only roughly determine the size of the basic payment, and disputes sometimes arise when the wife-giver claims a larger share than the wife-taker feels conditions justify. Wife-givers reimburse, usually the next day, what they do not claim as *nogai kon't*. Wife-givers will kill and present several pigs as well as return some portion of the money. So of the 7 pigs and 700 kina given, 3 pigs and 400 kina may be returned. This counter-prestation, particularly the gift of pigs nurtured on clan lands, balances the transaction.

Clansmen consider payment of initial bridewealth mandatory because it would upset the social order to appropriate blood and women's fertility without rendering compensation. Nonetheless, it would be an ethnographic distortion to see bridewealth as an obligatory response which seals the marriage contract. This is not only because men may delay bridewealth for many years, but because it is perpetually infused with motive and opportunity. There are rightfully no terms in Maring to differentiate optional from obligatory payments. The gift of pork and money responds to the more general economic discourse between clans. In the case of bridewealth, what counts pragmatically is: the amount of the gift, its composition, when and where it is given, and its place in the constellation of compensation payments outstanding. Sometimes, a clan may twice pay bridewealth to a favored clan before it has made a first payment to another. Men occasionally make two, three, and in one instance four bridewealth payments. Extra payments are usually smaller than the initial one – though certainly there is no rule to this effect – and wife-takers use them frequently to repay wife-givers for rights in garden land, pandanus groves, or primary forest in which to hunt for cassowaries and bird plumes. Secondary bridewealth runs in the vicinity of 2 or 3 pigs and 200 to 300 kina.

Usually, but not necessarily, a man makes a key payment to his wife's father to celebrate and compensate for the birth of his first child, and sometimes the second or third. As many things motivate the gift besides the birth itself, compensation is as likely for a female as for a male. The compensation is for the blood and bones of the child, direct contributions of the woman. The ceremony of the child payment (*wamba mungoi*) spells out in symbolic form the wife-giver's contribution of substance. As the men make speeches, present the pigs and line the money (i.e., lay it in rows of 2 kina notes), the child sits with his mother's natal clan.[3]

[3] All compensation payments are prestations where the arrangement of valuable "for the eye to see" in precise detail and order indexes the value and significance of the gift. It is essential to have as many valuables as possible; for example, 2 kina notes as opposed to larger denominations. Men make disparaging remarks about bridewealth which includes 10 and 20 kina notes, as they do not properly represent the worth of the gift.

When the presentation is over, the father and his clansmen align in ritualized war formation while the wife's clansmen form a barricade, ostensibly to defend the child. The husband and his clansmen then charge into the camp of the wife-giver, and after a brief struggle, carry off the child (this can sometimes become quite cumbersome and thus comical when the child is fifteen or sixteen).

Clansmen are seldom reluctant to combine child payments and bridewealth. This may result in a larger prestation, but usually the payment covers both because the gift-giver announces that that is the purpose of the ceremony. In such instances, the woman's clansmen may claim a larger share of the payment than they might otherwise, although this is not certain because the prestation is part of the many-sided social and economic mediation of inter-clan relations. The character of the payment is set from the inside in terms of visible objectives and in relation to the totality of simultaneously possible prestations, especially to other affines. Each payment, by its realization and attributes, is a commentary on the state of the given affinal relationship, and implicitly on all others. Generally, child payments indicate strong relations. When offered separately, usual payments are similar in size to a second bridewealth, about 2 or 3 pigs and some 300 kina.

Due to the various social forces at work, child compensation is not always paid. Statistically, compensation was given for first born children in 68% of the cases, the figures dropping to 35% and 7% for second and third born children. Whether a father does or does not offer compensation, the MBS always has the option of making a payment of his own – that is, putting himself at the "inside of the payment." MBSs did so in 32% of recorded cases, although here there is no correlation between birth order and compensation. Young men most often make the prestation when they are "close" to their mother's brother, residing perhaps part time in his house and likely helping in the harvesting of the coffee crop. The payment is "because we are of one blood" and more strategically in response to the varieties of transaction and influence which shape the relationship. Payment is even more likely if the MB is a big-man who has accumulated significant social credits by making gifts and extending services to the coterie or young men who surround him. A payment in this context is especially important for the young man, for it is integral to restoring balance and hence a measure of equality to the ongoing relationship. It allows the young man to say ceremonially, and with the full performative powers of the gift, that he is standing in succession, and standing moreover from a position of strength rather than simply riding the reputation of the big-man. In one case, a man in his early thirties, endowed with a gift for oratory and a sense of theater, made a munificent prestation of 4 pigs, 400 kina cash, some traditional shell valuables, and 5 bushknives to his mother's brother. The local community interpreted the display as a sign of political acumen and personal strength which could lead to future status.

A man may also offer compensation to his MB or, in the event of the MB's death, to the MBS if he does not reciprocate one of his daughters to his mother's natal clan, and thus "return the planting material." From a statistical viewpoint a subclan which did not "return the planting material" compensated its affines in only 23% of the recorded instances. The percentage because compensating affines is only one member of a family of strategies for managing exchange relations. In some cases, wife-takers make no payment whatsoever to demonstrate their dissatisfaction with the affinal relationship. They will contend, sometimes forcibly in court, that the original bridewealth was sufficient compensation because the woman was not a good gardener and mother, and the relationship did not generate a respectable traffic in goods and services. Compensation can also be foregone when the substitution of another woman (planned or unplanned) satisfies the wife-giver's demands. Wife-takers may offer compensation whether or not they offer a substitute woman, for they may use the opportunity to repay wife-givers for other debts. Finally, wife-takers also offer compensation when they desire to continue the relationship, but to postpone returning a woman for another generation or two. All these possible options, which culturally recognizable situations call for, represent a strategic drive towards reciprocity which draws a balance between social credits and credibility on one hand and more immediate reproductive interests on the other.

The last compensation payment a man usually makes during his life is when he "buys the bones" of his wife. Such payments are made when the wife has lived patrilocally for all of her married life. Conversely, a man rarely offers payment when he and his wife have resided with her kinsmen, or when the woman returned to her natal lands early in the marriage. The "bones" here are a metonym of the body and substance of the wife. For, as the corpse lies on the outdoor burial platform, all of its bodily substances, with the exception of the bones, return directly to the land. They return in this case, however, not to the land of their origin but to the land of her husband and his clansmen. This is possible because years of living on his clan lands have transformed her substantively. All that needs to be done is to finalize what was begun many years earlier with the payment of a bridewealth. In a sense, with the payment of *gio mungoi* (bone payment) a man signals that his wife has been recruited to his clan, and that like all agnates, her spirit (*rawa*) will reside on his clan lands as one of its ancestor spirits. Compensation for the wife's bones is around 2 pigs and 200 kina. In contrast to other payments, it frequently includes a variety of traditional wealth items, such as kina shells, no doubt because the couple were likely married in pre-contact times when such valuables were key symbols of marriage. Clansmen recognize that "bone payments" have a broad strategic significance because they very much solidify an affinal relationship, for essentially the two clans have interconverted their membership.

Compensation payments have a dual and conflicting character. It is as if the gift had two sides, each with a distinct vision of its purpose and the functions it was meant to serve. On one side, people maintain that gifts should be given truthfully. Once the recipient peels away the skin of the gift, he should see that the intentions of the donor are pure, being free from calculation and manipulative interests. The true gift is, according to this way of thinking, an elective offering or a gift given freely in response to a previous gift. This vision of compensation discounts all the pragmatic elements of giving; for it erases the elements of time and tempo and the contrast of this gift to gifts given to others, although all of these are important in the determination of the meaning of the gift. It is the most common rhetorical device for the donor to say as he proffers the gift: "I give you this gift without gift desire" or, in the Pidgin idiom, "I give you this nothing." In short, such ideological representations of exchange are embodied in language as well as a variety of other social forms and norms.

On the other side, the fact that compensation payments feature such a wide variety of options disposes clansmen to create, shape, and redefine an affinal relationship on the basis of its reproductive merits. Clansmen accomplish a general redefinition by (a) reproducing some affinal relations and not others; (b) emphasizing the value of some relations by offering a large prestation and downplaying others by offering a meager one; and (c) fiddling with the timing of the gift. In a sense, the self-interest which Maring exhibit is even more profound than that which materialist-minded investigators give them credit for, since this interest is never limited to material gain, but spans the panorama of social reproduction, sweeping under its wing everything from acquiring garden land to acquiring pigs to augment male substance; and in so doing recognizes that land and pigs, as well as men and women themselves, are all elements of a unitary reproductive cycle. The distinction between material and symbolic interest cannot be applied to a Maring system which does not sanction such a distinction, nor could it give its own principles of reproduction. So what confronts the ethnographer is that people use an economizing strategy, such as the assistance of ancestors, to attain symbolic ends, just as they use a symbolic strategy, such as garden magic, for economic ends. In this way, one side of the compensation payment can underwrite social relations even as the opposing side pursues economic interests, where we understand economic in the broad sense of social reproduction.

For example, a clansman and his brothers may arrange to make a second bride payment to an affine who has been generous in his loan of garden lands (or, nowadays, has helped to finance a trade store). There is a meaningful difference between the gift given for production and the exchange of the gift. Where the land is loaned unceremonially and in the past, the compensation payment is the highest form of ceremony in the present. In this way, by the separation imposed by time and context, bridewealth can be an unsolicited prestation which, given with no overt demands, is true to its purpose, and also direct reproductive compensation for the rights in land. Compensation payments, by the cultural regimentation of meaning, can be true and generous, revealing the social spirit of the gift, and at the same time, calculated self-interest. It is for this reason that there exists no distinction between obligatory and optional payments: for all gifts are obligatory at the level of reciprocity and optional at the level of sociality. This calculus of the gift is embodied in pragmatic representations of exchange which expose the self-interest behind the prestation, dramatically in a recipient's condemnation of a proffered gift because it makes immediate and undisguised demands.

Marriage and compensation: a case in point

Just more than a decade ago, Gou married Awa with the full consent of both clans. It was a good marriage in the double sense that Awa "chose" Gou, and her brother, Amp, was much in favor of the union. Gou's clan, the Kauwatyi Kamjepakai, was plagued with chronic land shortage, and the land they did possess was situated mostly in the high ground. This not only created noticeable land pressure, especially with the introduction of coffee cropping, but offered scant opportunity to cultivate valuable, warm-weather crops such as pandanus. Moreover, without access to foreign lands, the Kamjepakai would find it difficult to raise enough pigs to meet the demands of compensation payments. The feeling among Kamjepakai, now as then, was that without greater access to land it would be hard to preserve their preeminent position among clans. Over the past decades, the Kamjepakai have evolved several strategies to deal with their problem, and people currently consider them to produce extremely high quality pigs, have sufficient resources of pandanus, and to be excellent allies.

Awa's brother, Amp, and more specially her father's oldest brother, Wunt, were powerful men who controlled clan-wide support. In the early years of the marriage, which were admittedly shaky (due to Awa's "infertility"), Amp and Wunt, as well as other clansmen, frequently gave gifts of pandanus to Gou and his father. On one occasion, which has apparently settled deeply into people's memories, Wunt's subclan was making a child payment (long overdue) to the other Kamjepakai subclan (i.e., not Gou's). During the ceremony, Wunt and Amp presented Gou and his subclansmen with a subsidiary gift of twenty pandanus and two piglets. The Kamjepakai were certainly the most powerful clan in the area – historically monopolizing three of the four elected political posts in the clan cluster, including that of Councilor, and having the greatest number of big-men. Wunt and Amp were taking the opportunity to fortify relations, as they might expect that Gou and the Kamjepakai would reciprocate their offering with pork and political support.

About five years into the marriage, when coincidentally Awa was pregnant with her first child, Amp suggested that Gou maintain and harvest "as his own" one of Wunt's pandanus groves. That pandanus is a substance-bearing food stimulated interest in the use-rights and in turn made the gift of pandanus all the more valuable. Moreover, there had already been a growing confluence of interests and the building of a co-substance relation, for Awa assisted her brother in making gardens and was entitled to a share of their produce which she naturally distributed to her family and relatives. The reappropriation of Awa's labor by her natal clan, the ease of this co-gardening being one reason Amp so heartily endorsed the marriage, resulted in the creation of a co-substance tie between affines, and simultaneously counted as partial compensation for the gifts of pandanus land and pigs.

About a year after Awa gave birth to a son, she began urging Gou to give bridewealth to her brother's line. Gou's subclansmen had recently completed a major compensation payment, and he averred that the time was not right. The quasi-official explanation was that Gou was postponing payment until his sows had weaned their young, the dry season had arrived, and the boars were fat enough.

Of at least equal import was the push and pull of domestic politics which defined the ordering of the compensation payments. The major payment in question had been made on behalf of Gou's FBS, or brother, who had taken a bride from a clan located on the far side of the

Jimi River, near the district headquarters at Tabibuga where local council meetings are held. Given the wider political and governmental aspirations of two of the Kamjepakai big-men, there was pressure first to nurture this distant alliance. The big-men phrased their maneuver typically, saying at a public meeting "that it was bad that when they went to Tabibuga for council meetings there was not place to stay or food to eat" (literally speaking, this wasn't accurate, though it was true with respect to lacking kinsmen). In essence, the two big-men felt that they could exert greater leverage at council meetings if they had a safe base in Tabibuga, which was no doubt an accurate assessment. The strategic ordering of compensation payments also played on the opposition between distant and proximate alliances. The reasoning was that the clan could sustain a proximate alliance by dint of interpersonal affinity, an infinity of smaller exchanges, and the more common interests and interdependence which emerges from working and gardening together. By contrast, distant alliances are more dependent on formal indexes. Affines would be more forthcoming with support if the bridewealth was of major size and speedily delivered. In this fashion, the two big-men created an outpost and lined up support in Tabibuga.

Gou offered as bride payment 7 pigs and 800 kina cash, by any standards a healthy bridewealth. Ostensibly, the generous bride payment indicated that Gou and his clansmen were making a substantial gift to Amp and his agnates. Its public face was that Gou's clan was powerful and that Amp's clan was important. From the prestation, Amp's agnates claimed a large *nogai kon't*, 5 pigs and 500 kina, recognizing their right to compensation for the pandanus and pigs given previously. The value of the gift was somewhat offset by the delay in payment, although this turned out to be relatively unimportant given the size of the payment and the value of the alliance to Amp's clan. Clanspeople on both sides downplayed strategic considerations, the official view seemingly that the bridewealth was a munificent gift. Wunt and Amp had also been generous in their gifts, and thus the goodwill maintained on both sides had brought balance to the relationship. In this way, the gift conveyed its generous, elective spirit, even as it maintained its rigorous reciprocity and strategic value.

As a final point, consider that the relative ease with which the affinal relationship unfolds belies its actual complexity, a complexity which is not revealed in either ideological representations, or, what in a different idiom is the same thing, simple descriptions of overt social relations. The sequence of events develops in such an accepted, comprehensible manner because of local mastery of the semiotic forms and possibilities animated by exchange. Actions and reactions rest on a wealth of presuppositions and dispositions about the value of pandanus in generating substance, how people accumulate prestige, the social effects of sharing food, the relationship between clan numbers and social power, the place of land in the reproductive cycle, the available strategies given the spatiality of the clans, the socially authorized perception of the gift, the influence of time and tempo on the value of the prestation, and much more.

Bloodlines and clan cluster formation

The perpetual flow of women across clan lines and the production of children creates inter-clan bloodlines. Maring refer to such bloodlines as *ambra kongipo* (women's line). The term captures both the notion that the line descends over time and that it threads its way through the male lines. One man, to illustrate the idea, pointed to a Christian cross – one of many crossed set of sticks remaining from the now-defunct Anglican mission station – to demonstrate how the descending male line, rooted in the ground, was intersected by a female line, the individual being the point where the two sticks meet. In contrast to the male line, the female line has no "home or base" but is *wump* which moves from one garden to the next.

People say they trace bloodlines for two generations above and below ego, after which it peters out. They express this in the idea that memory shadows salience. "After two generations the blood dies and so we forget the names of the woman line." This is a normative statement insofar as clansmen can always move distant kinsmen closer by emphasizing the similarities, either an intermediate blood relative or one related by grease. The possibility of establishing both same-substance and cross-substance ties exponentially increases the power to constuct relationships. Recall that a man will specify his link to a clansman of his MZS by virtue of his blood relation to the MZS and the MZS grease relation to the clansman in question. A blood tie thus dies in the absence of other creative, countervailing measures. In local humor, people laugh about the ingenious man who swindles an ingenuous stranger by fabricating a blood tie.

It follows from this that blood is the structural basis of lateral relationships and the construction of women-based ties is the generative scheme for building exchange networks. A man's exchange network begins with his wife's clansmen and those of his mother's sister's son (and daughter once she marries). Given the laws of heredity, an individual will have blood relations in four clans, and more likely twice

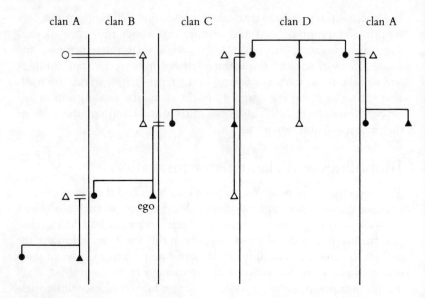

● bloodline

Figure 27 Bloodlines

that number. Figure 27 is a simple diagram taken from almost any genealogy.

Before examining Figure 27 it is worth noting that relations based on women's blood appear in Maring language, action, and consciousness as relations among men. Just as land, labor, and food may stand for (index) relations grounded in male substance, so concrete relations among men may stand for, and thereby mask, relations grounded in blood. The reasons for this are well known to Highland anthropology (see M. Strathern 1978 and 1981 for a sophisticated interpretation). Briefly, women are part of the household, procreation, and domestic production, not of exchange and inter-clan relations. They live in a society which does not officially recognize their public presence, even if their control over production accords them practical recognition. The Maring clan defines its reproductive interests as the interests of its men. It reinforces this to the point where women appear to know less and be less willing to talk about social order and exchange (Lowman, personal communication). As opposed to verbal exchanges about men's relations, talk about blood ties belongs properly to the domestic domain where its "domesticity" divests it of "social" function. In this sense, the culture represses the constituting powers of blood ties, recasting them as male relations based on men's skill in crafting good exchanges and productive marriages. As a footnote to affinity, recognize that stepping behind this ideology which rests on the practical interdependence of concepts of male dominance and clanship is problematic for the male ethnographer – and to Maring all ethnographers are male by virtue of the power and wealth at their disposal.

There are several structural keys to the organization of blood ties. First, a bloodline forges a co-substance bond among members of two or more clans, creating the cultural basis for a sustained relation. Second, given a normal frequency of intra-cluster marriages, a clan will intermarry with the same bloodline from two different directions. This sets up the possibility of overlapping ties. Third, from the standpoint of any ego, the ban on (what translates as) first cousin marriage divides the universe into four quadrants. The terms of reciprocal exchange reinforce this division, especially as clansmen are motivated to support this pattern because it supports their interests. To the extent that members of the clan cluster intermarry in this way, the fourfold division will exist at least in profile on this level.

An example of the empirical forms of marriage relations can be seen in Table 14 which maps the distribution of marriages for one major Kauwatyi clan, Kamjepakai. Note the clear distribution pattern of a high concentration of intra-cluster unions combined with a wide assortment of extra-cluster marriages. Table 14 includes a sample of marriages of both incoming and outgoing women.

A marriage alliance finds its "base" in the children of the union because the children embody the grease of their father's clan and the woman's blood. But the substance relations are not equivalent. The agnatic tie marches on a group level linking the offspring to all members of their father's clan; the blood tie passes through and links individuals. So children are related to their mother's clan by virtue of the blood tie with her brother. People say that blood ties come in pairs whereas agnatic ties surround the person. One side of this relationship, to recall earlier discussion, is the constitutive basis of patrilineality; the other of inter-clan relationships. And with the prohibition, at once conceptual and inscribed in practice, on marrying someone with whom one shares substance, the bloodline will gravitate in a smooth diagonal across clan lines. Its filial basis bestows a certain autonomy to the bloodline, giving it a relatively narrow and precise definition. Thus, the inter-clan relationships which derive from blood (women) are roughly proportional to the degree of intermarriage. Clansmen recognize that their "women based" relations are strong with some clans, weak with others, and always temporal. From the local standpoint, what is important about reproducing an affinal relationship, and so

Table 14 *Distribution of marriage exchanges: a Kauwatyi Kamjepakai example*

Number of exchanges	Clan cluster	Clan	Percentage of total	Geographical relationship
47	Kauwatyi	Kakupogai	27.0	Bordering
29		Kambant'igai	16.0	Bordering
21		Baigai	12.0	Bordering
14		Angengbogai	8.0	Bordering
1	Manamban	Kundemagai	0.5	Adjacent cluster
3	Tukmenga	Kondagai	1.7	Distant
4		Bomagai	2.3	Distant
1		Amangai	0.5	Distant
2		Mokai	1.2	Distant
2	Irimban	Wendakai	1.2	Distant
1	Yomban	Komaiwo	0.5	Distant
1		Mbro	0.5	Distant
2	Kandambiamp	Koromb Markai	1.2	Distant
2		Wendakai	1.2	Distant
2	Amberakwi	Ambogai	1.2	Distant
2		Wendakai	1.2	Distant
2	Kundagai	Mbaigai	1.2	Adjacent cluster
4		Tyembogai	2.3	Adjacent cluster
6		Wendakai	3.5	Adjacent cluster
3		Koromb	1.7	Adjacent cluster
3	Tsembaga	Merkai	1.7	Distant
4		Tsembaga	2.3	Distant
1		Kamungagai	0.5	Distant
2	Tuguma	Raweng	1.2	Distant
3		Kongakai	1.7	Distant
1	Kanmb-Kaul	Mepai	0.5	Distant
1	Cenda	Nenbenong	0.5	Adjacent cluster

reproducing a set of blood ties, is that it maintains a particular axis or "road" of exchange.

For this reason also, no bloodline is a relation unto itself; it accrues value from its position within a constellation of other blood ties. A man who marries from the same subclan as his brother usually creates a situation in which the whole is less than the sum of the parts; and practice discourages such marriages. Having diversified blood relations gives individuals social leverage, people considering impoverished those who have descended from small families and thus have a constrained set of blood relations. Moreover, the value of a bloodline is inseparable from the imminent possibility of creating new blood ties and using existing ones in particular ways, such as gaining access to garden land or a trade connection. Exchange strategies find their logic and motive in the interplay between domestic (e.g., intra-clan politics) and external (e.g., political allies) considerations, as such an interplay develops against the existing inventory of blood ties. To start from the individual perspective, a man from a family that has married well is in a favorable position because his agnates will utilize his bloodline, imbuing it with practical significance. His agnates will continually mobilize the link for reproductive purposes, treating it as the clan's patrimony made possible by the work of "this" man. And although there are no official honors bestowed on the man with good connections, all the avenues of prestige and status lie before him. To use a local metaphor, a man stands in the line of importance by the importance of the lines which pass through him. Similarly, a clan is an important and desirable ally if it promises a strong set of bloodlines or affinal linkages. It is this characteristic which makes the larger Kauwatyi, Tukmenga, and Kundagai clans desirable allies. From another angle, this helps to explain why Maring equate clan size with strength and wealth. The larger clans have the luxury of marrying their women close to home and far away. They can exchange women within the clan cluster to reinforce integration and commitment, and marry into other clan clusters to extend their range of political connections and trade alliances.

The clan faces two major problems to which the formation of the clan cluster appears to be a solution. The problems surface in practice as norms and objectives. The first is achieving reciprocity or balance so that the clan's inflow and outflow of women are advantageous. That women are the lifeblood of fertility and production means that people place high value on enduring, stable exchange relationships. Accordingly there are norms and pragmatic motivations for reciprocity which results in a closed circle of clans with self-renewing exchanges. For these reasons, Maring ideology exalts the pig-woman road and the clan which faithfully "backs" its exchanges.

The second problem is the defense of clanspeople and lands, both of which are (literally) the substance of the clan. The land and all its products are not separable from the ancestors and clansmen who live by this land. All possess the same personalized quality, and an attack on a clan's land (e.g., theft or destruction of crops) is an attack on the clan's body. Maring state that "our land is us" and use place names and clan names interchangeably because "no one could think of a clan without thinking of its land." It is no wonder, then, that Maring war parties, after having killed or routed the defenders, expend a great amount of time and energy killing the enemy's pigs, cutting down the pandanus trees, and uprooting the taro. Murder and the destruction of land are different versions of the same offense, especially when symbolically aimed against substance-producing goods because, pragmatically, they are most significant to clan reproduction. Therefore the clan cluster appears as a strategic solution to problems of defense and marriage.

But ends are distinct from means only from a point alien to the system itself. It is equally true that the principles of exchange and substance generate the clan cluster. First and most constitutively, the cluster is based on a high degree of endogamy. Statistically, this means that in excess of 60% and sometimes as high as 75% of marriages are made with other clans in the cluster. More meaningful is that no matter the precise and variable number of in-house marriages, these marriages occupy a privileged position. Structurally, they exemplify reciprocal exchange and hence the formation of a permanent relationship. Practically, they are maximally useful in that the doors of exchange are wide open. This endogamy results in a flood of intersecting, overlapping bloodlines. Any two members of a clan cluster can easily trace a kinship (co-substance) relationship to one another.

A secondary basis for clan cluster formation is the flow of agnatic material along the marriage route. Clans which are in close proximity and intermarried are in the best position to form a closed circuit through the exchange of land, labor, etc. The making of the clan cluster as a territorial unit thus depends on both a high degree of continuing intermarriage and the corollary flow of agnatic material along this axis. In this way, the clan cluster, constituted by relations through women, takes on the character of a higher level of the social structural hierarchy. The key point is that a clan's compulsion to improve its lot in the social order, using the cultural means at hand, compels it to reproduce the structure of exchange in such a way as to reproduce the clan cluster. The lines of intermarriage and blood are concrete possibilities that dispose and invite clansmen to seek their objectives within these limits and along these (blood)lines. It is this give-and-take of people acting in their own interest by using cultural concepts and materials (particularly the manipulation of land and people), and, simultaneously, cultural concepts of social relation and exchange acting on people which produce the clan cluster.

It is worth reemphasizing, as a conclusion to this chapter, that exchange must be grasped in terms of how material relations and practices are culturally constituted, yet pragmatic and part of social reproduction. The fault of ecological anthropology as practiced on Highlanders is that by separating form from content, material reality from symbolic trapping, it isolates itself from the cultural rationality embodied in practice, and imposes in this vacuum its own rationality; namely, our rationality. By contrast, symbolic anthropology, by severing itself from strategy, action, and ultimately practice, reduces life to series of symbolic forms which are far from experience and can never account for social reproduction, however much the analysis of symbolic forms is the necessary first step. Maring exchange reveals especially clearly that description and analysis must transcend these theories to give an account adequate to its object.

6   The making of the local group

This chapter describes the formation of local groups. It centers on the principles of local group organization and the social practices from which they emerge. My description flows culturally from the foregoing analysis of clanship and marriage exchange. It aims to construct a theory which explains local groups and the theories of local groups found in the literature. How Highland social groups appear "on the ground" continues to be the testing ground of theory and (equally although not as self-consciously) of method.

My analysis tries to show how the interplay between lineal and lateral structures determines the composition of local groups. It begins by focusing on the relationship between agnation and locality, and then relates the local group to residence practices. The connecting theme throughout is the Maring practices which, by producing co-substance relations, create the bridge between landedness and locality on one hand and agnatic identity on the other. To relate concepts of residence to practices of residing, I develop a notion of social marking – that is, the value and acceptability which a society places on certain structural possibilities, given specific economic, social, and political facts and conditions.

Central to the analysis is the thesis that the clan and the local group are logically separate, though intrinsically linked by the practices of clan reproduction. The argument, no more than an extension of the ethnography, is that the composition and transformation of Maring local groups obey a cultural logic of practical necessity. This is inevitable because the process of reproduction places clansmen in novel relationships to other clansmen and to objects of reproduction. The local group takes on a determinate form by virtue of the interaction – embodied in the strategies of reproduction – between cultural values (e.g., those placed on land), generative schemes (e.g., sharing vs exchange), and the "objective" world (e.g., increases or decreases in population, pacification, etc.) as culturally valued. Although the local group is a response to the "objective" situation, it is never directly determined by that situation. To give an example known to Maring history, the breakup of a clan into constituent subclans due to depopulation, and the subsequent assimilation of these subclans into different clans, can never be grasped in terms of that depopulation; for the perceived cause of depopulation (e.g., sorcery), the lack of sufficient numbers to conduct successful exchange relations, the gardening and land transfer patterns which generate co-substance relations and thus motivate accretion to other clans – all of these stem from the cultural logic of reproduction even as depopulation demands the practical necessity of response.

Agnation and local group formation

Agnation is the point of reference from which practice defines the principles of local group formation. What complicates local group formation, and what has proven difficult for analysis to master, is that agnatic concepts operate on two separate levels and serve two separate functions. First, they define the clan as a category of social people by creating a classification based on the sharing and exchange of substance. Second, common grease constitutes a basis for local group membership. All clansmen have the birthright to reside on their natal clan lands because they embody the same substance as the land. Even those clansmen who have lived extra-locally for many decades always retain the right to return to their native land. Local courts have ruled that men have the right to return whether or not their own agnates approve.

The extra-local residence of such men is an illustration that clanship is a sufficient though not a necessary condition of local group membership. The logical distinction between clanship and locality is the basis for a variety of practices which assimilate non-agnates to the local group. The most important of these practices is marriage. The Maring concept of clanship dictates that agnates should be raised on their own soil. From this flows the conception that women should reside on the land of their husbands. Anything less would push the system in the direction of matrilineality, and indeed this tension is inherent in the compensation payments that a father offers his wife's brother. In the absence of countervailing interests – crucial to the overall structure – a married couple should reside with his clan. This means that the inclusion of foreign women is a structural condition of the Maring local group as constituted. The clan can reproduce only if the local group assimilates non-agnates; the more successful a clan is, the more female non-agnates enter.

Marriage exchange is but one dimension of a larger reproductive scheme. The clan has a political and economic interest in organizing the local group so that some of its members live elsewhere while some outsiders live on its lands. The heart of this highly generative scheme is the connective logic which links food, land, and clan identity. It allows clans to construct inter-clan relationships by moving people from one locale to another. This means that a clan can negotiate its fate not only by dealing in food, pigs, seed taro, land, and eligible women, but in men and children as well. Hence, in addition to marriage exchange, there are a set of corollary practices, such as child exchange, dual residence, men's house co-residence, full-fledged emigration. Such residential moves have few preordained limits; they always give rise to the possibility of creating a new clan identity, a fact not lost on temporary residents or their hosts. Whether a given non-agnate becomes an agnate is a pragmatic issue which is resolved through ritual mediation and the struggles of domestic clan politics.

The upshot of this, and the point I wish to establish at the outset, is that the local vision of social organization dictates that local groups embrace many non-agnates. Clansmen worry about current practices only when land shortages or domestic squabbles push the issue to the fore. Orthodox questions on the percentage of non-agnates or the degree to which promiscuous recruiting will dilute the clan's purity miss the point. The ethnographic problem is what the structural conditions and means are that allow a clan to generate a particular mix of agnates and non-agnates, and to what ends. Non-agnates are a problem only for those who have a residual faith in lineage theory: the Maring do not.

Child exchange

The transfer of children from one set of clansmen to another is a primary way of creating and enhancing relationships. It is also a way to offset the claims of an affine. In short, it is a strategy of kinship and exchange.

There are two major permutations to child exchange. Either a child is raised by cognatic or uterine kin until he/she becomes of marriageable age, and then returns to the father's natal clan with all the position and powers of any other agnate. Or, less often, the child becomes permanently attached to another clan, thereby virtually transforming his/her agnatic identity. In such cases, the influence and grease of the child's father is offset by a compensation payment of money and pork.

The most famous local case – because it is the most peripheral – has been the adoption of a Kauwatyi infant (a female twin) by an Australian bible translator from the Summer Institute of Linguistics. Following the literature (Meggitt 1965:25–6), I could distinguish here adoption from fostering, introducing a semantic distinction where Maring act on a practical one. They perceive "adoption" and "fostering" as two variations on the theme of child exchange. Their critical cut is between intra-clan adoption – which is common, but for which there is no specific name – and inter-clan adoption which they call *wamba awa wela* (literally, child/we give/we take). The key point is that locality is important because persons retain a consubstantial tie with their natal clan even as they construct a co-substance tie with their adopting one. Clansmen say that this is simply a matter of degree. When, for example, a child is adopted at a very early age, and lives until adolescence with the adopting clansmen, it is equally consubstantial with both clans in some fundamental sense. Maring know this from the way the person behaves. In essence, the exchange capitalizes on the difference between the formation of a child through procreation and its bodily development through the eating of food.

A woman's brother maintains a vital link to her children by virtue of shared blood. In practice, his sister mediates this link insofar as her influence over her husband and her children facilitates this relationship. Thus, the death of the sister can sever the brother's influence. The mother's brother can partially rectify this by making special trips to visit his sister's children and inviting them to visit him for extended stays. A compromise may evolve where he adopts the children, or at least one of them, until they come of age.

It sometimes happens that a husband dies, or, more frequently, goes off for a long stint to a coastal plantation, and his wife returns with her children in tow to her natal clan. In such cases, the youngsters will usually live with their mother's brother until their mother remarries or father returns from the plantation. Many young husbands spend up to eight years on coastal plantations, making this form of adoption common. This explains from another vantage point why the most usual type of reaffiliation is to the mother's brother's clan.

When a widow marries out of her late husband's clan, perhaps after having temporarily lived with her brother, her children, especially if young, will sometimes reside with her new husband. Another possibility is that a widow will move into the household of a married sister, making it likely that the sister's husband will adopt the children. In times past, the hardships of war also contributed to the relocation of women and children.

When an adopted boy, perhaps now a teenager, returns to his true natal clan he will often give a small payment or series of informal gifts to his father-by-adoption. He may offer the gift by himself or in concert with his father and/or father's brothers. If the adopted child is a girl, a portion of her brideprice will usually be presented to her father-by-adoption. Both payments are expressly for "feeding the child" and sharing food. The oratory which surrounds the payment dwells at length, and emphasizes by repetition, how the foster parent nurtured the child. Listen to one such speech:

When you were no longer than my arm, you and your mother came to my house, my land. I made many gardens for your mother. I gave you food: taro, yams, bananas, pandanus, sweet potatoes ... When I had pig, I gave you some and said "Eat this, this is yours." Some foods were taboo for you, and I did not eat them. When you grew up, you remembered that you had a father living in Kwiama, and you said that you wanted to return to him. I told you that you should go, that your land and your father were in Kwiama. Now that you have settled down in Kwiama you give this gift to me, for the food that made you grow.

The style and content of this speech is almost ritual. Thus, it seems to paraphrase not only other speeches which I recorded, but a speech recorded by Rappaport (1969:124) nearly two decades earlier. In all cases, there is a virtual link between gardens, labor, food, housing, and reproductive wealth, a connection which participants do not recognize as significant precisely because it is an unquestionable "fact" of social reality.

For clan and subclan, child exchange generates relationships between units that parallel and supplement those made in marriage. Clanspeople view it as another strategy for orchestrating social relations and resolving some of the problems they confront. In a larger sense, practices which allow children to be removed from clan lands are, like marriage exchange, means by which the clan creates cosubstance relations beyond its borders to insure its perpetuation as an independent and self-sufficient entity. An immediate result of this practice is that all local groups include a variety of adopted children. It could never be otherwise in a society in which the local group is the point where the principles of exchange intersect those of agnation to produce a system of social reproduction.

Land rights and residence

The principles and strategies of marriage exchange induce clansmen to extend gardening privileges to select affines. Changes in residence often march in step with the transfer of land rights. This is true for most Highland societies and Brown's (1978:119) general description applies well to the Maring:

In the eastern highland village communities, as well as the western highlands homestead settlements, individuals, married couples, families, and sometimes larger groups ... use unclaimed or long-fallow land ... the territory of a relative. If this land is in the residential locality, it may require no new building, but if it is too far away for daily convenience, a temporary or long-term move, and new houses, may be involved. The move may be instigated by a need or desire of the host ... Good relations between host and immigrant are essential when the move is made, and the arrangement does not outlive ... mutual satisfaction. But the relationship may outlive the host, as when the couple become active participants in the locality of a wife's father and stay on when he dies.

As an addition to this description, the location of the garden land in question is part of the strategy of exchange, especially for clans who wish to attract outsiders to enlarge the membership of the local group.

The gift of garden land authorizes the recipient to live near this land if he so chooses. Practically, land rights and the right to reside nearby come as a package and are never in their own right controversial. From the perspective of the social relationship, the gift of land is no less than an invitation, offered on a trial or permanent basis, to entwine the reproductive activities of those involved. It is common for host and recipient to co-garden in such cases. Participants set the terms of a given relationship, though the inalienable connection between clanship and landedness dictates that the actions of clansmen take on clan-wide significance. Thus it is inevitable that agnates of host and recipient will exploit the relationship, or, more fairly, see it as a social resource.

The Maring habit of making gardens in widely dispersed locations (for social and ecological reasons) leads to dual residences for some men. They have house sites or what they consider to be semi-official residences on the territory of more than one clan. And while this is not widespread, it is yet another custom which contributes to the admixture of non-agnates and agnates which comprise the local group. The key here is to see that land and residence are themselves objects of exchange and mediation. Like women, food, labor, and planting material they are transactable signs of clanship.

The exchange of men

One of the most influential though least acknowledged modes of exchange in the New Guinea Highlands is the circulation of men. It is not only the exchange of women, goods, and land which allies clans, but the exchange of men. This has been reported from the earliest days of post-war ethnography, but not understood as such due to genealogically based theories of descent and exchange: and thus very narrow views of social reproduction which assumed that the exchange of women allied clans while the non-agnatic residence by men undermined them. So as ethnographers were first turning their attention to social organization, Brown (1962:61), wrote that "although about eighty per cent of the men . . . live on the territory of their natal subclan, garden patrilineally inherited land, and participate in the activities organized by leaders of their natal subclan and clan, we found very few men who had not at some time in youth or adulthood resided with non-agnatic kin or affines." Precisely so.

At the level of locality – where clanship is inseparably tied to landedness – the exchange of men among the Maring parallels the exchange of women. As modes of exchange, they are complementary, though different, and the structure of clan reproduction couches each in its own terms. Where women interrelate clans by virtue of blood and fertility of procreation, men interrelate clans through the kinship of co-production. By eating foods which he has helped to produce on the land of another clan, a non-agnate establishes a link between his clan and that of his host.

Traditionally and still to some degree in the most modernized of settlements (such as those of Kompiai and Togban), men's houses embody – literally and symbolically – the exchange of men. Today, however, incoming residents may live in the men's house, the house of a kinsman, or share time between them. Introduction of Papuan-style family dwellings which put men and women under one roof has not materially affected exchange. Maring settlements are characteristic of this region of the Highlands. There are compounds or clumps of houses distributed over the clan territory, usually in the vicinity of a main thoroughfare or road. Prior to contact, a compound consisted of anywhere from two to a dozen women's houses in an uneven semi-circle around a men's house. Each married woman had her own house where she lived with her young children, pigs, and perhaps an aging relative. A man might spend a considerable amount of time in his wife's house, but would sleep and store his belongings in the men's house. Today, Papuan-style houses have been added to this arrangement so that many compounds include all three types of dwellings. The Papuan houses are divided into a men's side and a women's side, essentially moving the distinction between male and female dwellings indoors. And the men's portion of the house is sometimes transformed into a *de facto* men's house. Thus the house of a leading big-man had five separate chambers in the male portion in which lived his brother's son, his sister's son, his wife's brother's son, and his own son.

Maring explicitly associate men's houses with specific clans. They so identify them in speech and action, and every member of a clan holds an inalienable right to use its men's houses. To quote one informant: "if a fellow clansmen comes to this men's house [i.e., the one in which he was currently living] and wants to stay here, that is his prerogative, for the house does not belong to anyone." However strong this agnatic claim, the members of the clan who own the men's house rarely exhaust the membership of that house. There is always a variable proportion of non-agnates in the larger houses. All Kauwatyi men's houses have members of at least one other clan, and most have two or more. One of the central functions of larger houses, whether traditional men's dwellings or Papua family houses, seems to be the accommodation of outsiders. Among the Kauwatyi, larger men's houses have an average of four non-agnates or approximately 25% of the residents.

Within terms of their conceptual and institutional resources, clansmen have practical ideas about how to act strategically in their own interests. There are thus many personal reasons why men want to reside with non-agnatic kin, although the bottom line for most is access to particular lands. This may allow a man to raise better pigs, for example, and thus to make more prestigious exchanges. Significantly, access to land is the standard reason men give for having relocated, although they may also move because they bristle under the authority of senior clansmen or have been losers in an intra-clan power struggle. Given the symbolic power of food, the lines of affiliation between clans, and the concept that residence is a means of social reproduction, there will be a flow and counterflow of individuals between local groups. This gives rise to a pattern of male exchange which residence in the men's house symbolically, if not practically, institutionalizes. What is crucial is that male exchange crystalizes as a practice in its own right, taking on the capacity to create relationships between clans. An understanding arises that it is useful to have clansmen placed in other clans, just as it is useful to marry out and have women placed abroad.

A man who is the agnate of one clan and lives on the territory of another, mediates the relationship between the two clans. Like relations based on marriage, such men become conduits for transactions between members of the opposing lines. This may occur very informally, as when a non-agnate invites one of his own clansmen to join

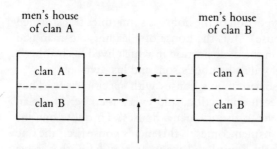

Figure 28 Organization of relationships in the new house food ceremony

him in making a garden. A more formal example comes from the baptism of a new men's house.

When the house is completed those who have assisted in its construction, their wives, and often other kinsmen, warm the new house by bringing net bags laden with food. The senior man who presides over the house welcomes the food with ceremony and then returns food from his own garden and those of his agnates. As one expects, taro and yams, the signs of the garden, figure prominently in these presentations. The gifts of vegetables, moreover, do not redistribute any limited resources as the amounts exchanged are calculated to be equal and differences are not in any case counted as meaningful.

The ceremonial exchange divides the house against itself. Members of the same clan share food whether or not they live together, and those of distinct clans exchange food even if they are co-residents. Several vectors of social relationships are articulated and cross-referenced in this context. To give a one-line review: sharing of food binds the members of the same clan and differentiates the residents of the men's house, while the exchange of food differentiates opposing clans and so binds respective men's houses. The manner in which clansmen share and exchange food is a means of indexing the social persona.

When the exchange between clans is based not only on the marriage of women but the residence of men, the alliance takes on a new and stronger character. To a greater and greater extent, the relationship between the clansmen moves closer to sharing and away from exchange. The social side increasingly comes to dominate the economic side of the transaction. When the exchange between clans moves towards this totalizing interdependence – there being a constant interflow of men, women, children, pork, garden land, labor planting material, foods, political aid, money, etc. – the two clans regard one another as "brother" lines. In the Kauwatyi clan cluster, the Kakupogai and Kambant'igai clans see themselves as "brother" lines, although the intimacy of their relationship seems to have relaxed in recent years.

Maring recognize that men circulate from one local group to another. And though people are sensitive to who uses clan lands, they perceive this as an unexceptional aspect of social life. In the words of one clansman: "I was not concerned when my *wambe* came to stay with me. Nor were my clan brothers. They saw that he was a hard-working man who made good gardens and good exchanges." By "good exchanges" the speaker meant that his *wambe* had engineered several excellent transactions. Essentially, the circulation of men develops on two levels. On the first, individuals make use of their egocentric networks to maneuver themselves into favorable positions; they acquire the land, pigs, or support they feel they need to "raise their name." On the second level, male exchange is one of the practices defining and shaping the relationship between clans.

From an ideological standpoint, male and female exchange are very distinct. In contrast to marriage, Maring ideology does not officially recognize the residential shifts made by men as a form of exchange. Males are never perceived as being given in exchange for males. Such an ideology would subvert the concept of clanship by acknowledging that grease can flow across clan boundaries, men living on foreign soil simply counting as another type of planting material. But the concept of clanship is built on the conflation of grease, males, and land. So the ideology of reproduction must deny the structural implications of male exchange: that clanship is always in jeopardy because over the long term a clan may exchange all of its members, men as well as women. The result is that the Maring do not have an ideology of male exchange, even if exchange surfaces implicitly in practices like the dedication of the men's house. Clansmen think of and phrase residential shifts in terms of localized, practical concerns (e.g., obtaining more land or living with a sister). This practical, down-to-earth ideology of extra-clan residence mediates and masks the social contradiction between exchange and lineality. It also makes it hard for ethnographers, who are prone to accept this practical ideology at face value and not inquire further, thus overlooking both the structure of male exchange and the functions that the practical ideology serves.

A case history

Te, who is a man of renown, was born to a Kakupogai father and an Angengbogai mother. His father lived on Kakupogai land until Te "left his mother's house" (probably at around the age of seven), at which time he lived for several years with his wife's clan. However, when Te's father returned to his own land, Te stayed behind with his mother's brother. While living with his mother's brother, Te continued to make gardens on Kakupogai land, not only helping his own parents in the construction of gardens but assisting the wife of his youngest brother – his youngest brother having gone to the plantation. In addition, Te made gardens over the years with Kakupogai clansmen who were using Angengbogai land. As Te stood between the clans, and especially between respective subclans, he used his position "to help" his clan brothers and members of his mother's clan. Not incidentally, of course, in doing these good deeds Te was also beginning to establish his own reputation.

When Te was in his mid-twenties, he went off to the plantation for two years. On his return, he settled down on Kakupogai ground and shortly after married a woman from the Baigai clan. The Kakupogai clan does not have extensive landholdings in the low ground and thus depends on other clans, such as Angengbogai and Baigai, to help secure cultigens which grow best in a warmer climate (e.g., bananas and pandanus). Te began using some of the land belonging to his wife's subclan and in so doing built up a close relationship to her unmarried brother. A short time later the brother moved in with Te in the men's house belonging to the Kakupogai. What attracted the brother was not only Te, but the fact that two other Baigai men were also living with the Kakupogai. When Te's brother returned from the plantation, he obtained, via Te, the right to use some Baigai land in the low ground. On the urging of Baigai men, Te's brother eventually made a house on Baigai land "so that he could be close to his garden." Like Te, he continued to make some gardens on Kakupogai land and to make gardens with other Kakupogai on Baigai land. To further enhance his social position, Te has helped his mother's brother's son carry coffee to market by enlisting the aid of Baigai relatives.

The point I stress here is that the principles of exchange syncopate the circulation of men and women. The orientation of exchange creates conditions in which men are very likely to form a close association with their mother's brother. That Te went to live with his MB is extremely common. This accords with concepts of blood and with the fact that men most often reaffiliate to the clan of the MB. That men will take up residence in their mother's clan implies that men will tend to flow in the opposite direction of women and in the alternate generation. In the simplest case, a man from clan A will reside in his mother's clan, B. His son, in turn, will tend to reside with his MB in clan C. In essence, the circulation of men follows one step and in the

Table 15 *Structure of local clan groups for the Kauwatyi clan cluster*

	Kamje-pakai	Kaku-pogai	Kamban-t'igai	Bai-gai	Angeng-bogai
Marriage	59	56	37	42	33
Men's house co-residence	17	14	17	11	12
Adoption	9	11	8	8	4
Reaffiliation	17	11	19	15	13
Land use	2	2	4	9	8
Other	4	6	3	6	2
Percentage of total in local group	38.3	39.5	46.5	60.3	49.4

opposite direction behind the exchange of women. There is no explicit norm regimenting the movement of men, but the one blood tie between ZS and MB, the practices of adoption and land tenure, the emotional bond and compensation payment all push exchange in this direction. Note, furthermore, that the circulation of men adds flexibility to land tenure by providing a structural route for practical action.

Table 15 gives an overview of the composition of Kauwatyi local groups. The categories are not mutually exclusive and it is not always easy to regiment people's reasons for living outside their own native grounds. Moreover, in some cases the categories appear to represent a progression: an individual who originally resettled simply to be near his garden may eventually reaffiliate. What is important is that the table gives a statistical picture of the structural means used to create the local group. The Baigai and Angengbogai have the greatest number of non-agnates because they have the lowest population densities while other clans are suffering from land shortage. Coffee growing has aggravated land shortage in recent years, forcing clansmen from the larger groups to migrate, at least temporarily, to the land of the Baigai and Angengbogai. The figures for the Kauwatyi are very similar to calculations by Cook (1970) for the Manga phratry which resides immediately east of the Maring. Cook (1970:192) estimates that 21.23% of those who are members of the local group – territorially co-resident – are non-agnates. He excludes wives from his calculations (because he was working with the concept of descent group); if wives are excluded, the Kauwatyi figures are actually slightly lower than those reported by Cook. In any case, it is clear that there is a vast difference throughout the Jimi Valley between who is a clansman and who is embraced by the local group.

Ethnography and residence patterns

In word and deed, Maring imply that clansmen may reside on land to which they possess no birthright, and that smaller clans will actively recruit men from larger ones. No stigma attaches to the man who lives with his wife's kinsmen, though such moves have definite social and political consequences. Nevertheless, it is equally true that though clansmen may reside on foreign soil, most men live patrilocally. It is clear that their socialization and sense of clanship disposes clansmen to plant their roots in their own soil. This raises the issue of what precisely are residence practices and how are they embodied in talking about residence.

The problem Highland theorists have had in formulating this issue is their inclination to see residence in terms of residence rules. Because people "as a rule" reside patrilocally, analysts reach the conclusion that there are residence rules, albeit ones which practical interest breaks at will. Local statements, when filtered through the perspective of our own linguistic ideology, appear to support this interpretation. On the one hand, people tell the ethnographer (in the interview situation) information which appears rule-like in its certainty. For example, informants told me that "when a woman marries a man she should come to live with his clansmen." On the other hand, the informants who made such statements rarely see anything illicit or out of the ordinary in matrilocality. Ethnographers have interpreted this apparent contradiction as indicating the presence of a rule of patrilocality which people bend, break, or ignore when faced with hard material realities.

But for the Maring, there are no rules of residence, though residence certainly has an underlying structure determined by the interplay of clanship and exchange. Rather than a rule, there is a sense of clanship that creates a logic of residence. Everything in a clansman's life and the life of the clan invites him to live patrilocally, as long as this enhances his own social reproduction and that of his clan. Hence, men reside with their own clans in the absence of special economic or political considerations which will influence production, exchange, and consumption (as they are culturally defined).

The Maring evidence states that what has passed as a rule is merely, in terms of the clan's internal operation, the unmarked case. It is the clan's official representation which disavows the influence of exchange because exchange is constituted by the female principle. In asking a question out of context (e.g., where should a couple reside once they marry?), an ethnographer predisposes the speaker to refer to the unmarked situation. The informant is saying that given a situation with no further specification, a woman should live with her husband's clansmen.

Clearly, however, exchange is often fundamental to a clan's reproduction and thus there are many sound reasons for residing with affines or cognatic kin. For Maring, the cardinal idiom for conceptualizing this reproductive relationship is access to land – necessary for gardening, pig raising, pandanus, etc. In Maring eyes, a need for quality land justifies 'a shift in residence. It presents a special circumstance which legitimizes living on non-natal lands.

When an ethnographer points to a particular situation – such as a man who is living matrilocally – and asks an informant about that situation, the informant, possessing a native mastery of his own culture and aware of the history of the relationship in question, sees that special circumstances pertain and notes that such residence is perfectly legitimate. In a sense, the legitimacy of the move is judged by its strategic value; namely, how well it has enhanced a man's reproductive situation. By virtue of identifying a concrete instance (the exception to the rule), the ethnographer has pointed to a marked situation and the informant has responded to the presence of additional information. There are really only two forms of local residence: living with one's own clansmen and living elsewhere, as broken down into structured, exchange-based, specific relationships (e.g., adoption).

The argument is that patrilocal residence is not a type of residence unto itself. Nor are there "rules of residence" to be obeyed or broken. Patrilocal residence is both the ideal, hence unmarked, form of residence and simply a type of residence among others recommended in certain situations. There is a fit between residential possibilities, as defined by the structure of social organization, and any specific practical context. Such meshing is part of residential practices that derive pattern and meaning from the relationship between types of residence and what commitments they call forth from the individuals and groups involved. Maring residence has three dimensions: (1) an underlying set of structural possibilities based on cultural concepts of substance and exchange; (2) clansmen choose from among these possibilities according to their reproductive interests (these interests themselves defined in terms of the cultural valuation of land, pigs, etc.); and (3) an ideology which portrays residential shifts in purely practical terms. The notion of a rule and its violation only impedes theory and ethnography from a proper understanding of the structure and practice of residence.

Warfare and local group formation

In a society of limited arms and where men preside over the cycle of war and peace, men become the political and symbolic might which protects clan lands, and everything such lands represent. Before the "taming" of pacification, the practice of war meant serving well as an ally, preserving the manhood of the clan, and protecting the land and people from invaders. Today, inter-clan relations have taken on a new tone as men wield political influence in the councils of government.

For Maring, the reproduction and continuity of the clan must overcome four threats: disease, warfare, infertile women, and fragmentation. With these fears in mind, clansmen believe that the most crucial factor in a clan's long-range success is an increase in numbers. Accordingly, a clan's objective is to produce as many clanspeople as possible, and, where necessary, attract kinsmen from outside. Strategically put, one way in which a clan can help to insure its continuity is to situate itself in a large local group. This has led smaller clans especially to adopt whole families and subclans, with the result that the membership of the local group outruns that of the clan. Adoption, reaffiliation, marriage (particularly polygamy), and land grants are all mechanisms for expanding the local group. Clans use them for this purpose.

Maring view aggression and competitiveness as aspects of manhood. Through ceremonies such as competitive all-night dancing, socialization, gift exchange, gambling, and (formerly) warfare, the clan aims to direct male aggression outward. At trials involving intra-clan violence, occurring infrequently, and at compensation payment for intra-clan homicide, big-men lecture against the harms of internal conflict. The implicit understanding manifest on such occasions is that competitiveness and aggression could lead to the fragmentation of the clan if it is not carefully checked. Within the clan, men's "hotness" and anger should not be allowed to overpower the logic of social reason which preaches that clan unity is essential to the well-being of its members.

Clan pressures from within and without create a contradiction causing an endless source of tension for Maring society. As a clan increases in size and becomes secure from external threat, competition for resources within the clan generates the possibility of internal division. A clan's commitment to allies, such as the Kauwatyi's commitment to their Tsembaga kin when they were defeated and sought refuge, tends to complicate this problem. This is particularly true because outsiders gain refuge by virtue of cognatic ties. Contrary to Kauwatyi ideology the admission of Tsembaga created a division within several of the clans (e.g., Kamjepakai). Fortunately, the Australian administration intervened and restored the Tsembaga to their homeland more rapidly than would have normally occurred. This probably headed off a crisis in some of the Kauwatyi clans.

The social system does possess means to resolve this contradiction – at least partially and temporarily. The more crowded clan land becomes, the more practice inclines clansmen to share labor, land, food, housing, and other resources. As settlements become more densely packed, as the internal pressure grows and competition heightens, so do the bonds of kinship which suppress intra-clan violence. Given the ideology of war, it is hardly surprising that a clan often directs violence outwards towards those neighboring clans unrelated by marriage. Hence Lowman (1980) can demonstrate that there is a positive correlation between population density and frequency of warfare, though victorious clans do not appropriate any appreciable amounts of land. And it is in this context that we can understand why Maring warfare always seems to be triggered by some minor, though symbolic, incident. Recall that people describe wars as being instigated by a man stealing a pandanus nut, wife, or some other symbol of clan reproduction.

Ironically, the same forces which unite the clan internally and suppress violence also prevent the clan from appropriating the social and material resources of the enemy. As land is part and product of the production of kinship and the clan, the alienation of another clan's land or pigs or pandanus is the appropriation of its kinship system. That the enemy's ancestor spirits can never be driven from their homeland symbolizes this reality. Thus, Maring warriors destroy the pigs, houses, children, pandanus, and land of the enemy rather than appropriate them. To use the land or eat the food of the enemy is anathema because it would destroy the basis of kinship. It expunges the instruments of similarity and difference upon which clanship itself is founded. In essence, the internal logic of this system destines the cycle of war and peace to repeat itself, as indeed it did until pacification. What I have presented here suggests that to account for the "facts" of Maring warfare, analysis must initiate from the standpoint of social reproduction.

Given the social cycle of war and peace, it is evident why a major policy of smaller clans was to recruit new members to the local group. In many instances, practice transformed what began as a co-residence or co-gardening relationship into one of agnation. This is also the mechanism for the production of new clans and clan clusters – such as that at Fogaikump in the far eastern Simbai. It explains why such production takes place at the frontier where the Maring are pushing out into virgin forest. As members of a given clan move onto new territory and break new garden land, they create a new cycle of reproduction which effectively differentiates them. Since land is available at the frontier, this may encourage people in neighboring clans to move in with the new local group.

The development of the local group arises from the distinction between local groups and clanship, the processes of social exchange orchestrating movements of men between local groups, and the link between production from the land and the production of agnation. These three aspects, all of which stem from the embodied relationship between exchange and co-substance, allow clansmen to respond to local changes – such as a population surge or the presence of an ethnographer – in a way defined by the structure of practice. The practical necessity of obtaining more land, for example, is built (1) on the principles of kinship which permit certain kinsmen to pass through the semi-permeable boundary of the local group; (2) on the cultural understanding that land, pigs, food, etc., are valuable because they are the symbolically charged material of the structure of clan reproduction; and (3) on strategies for action which are themselves symbolic elements in a system of strategies. For the Maring, there is a cultural logic of practical necessity which defines in precise and meaningful ways the nature of clanship and the terms of its transformation.

One further comment about Maring warfare. It has repeatedly served as an ethnographic example of how warfare adjusts man/land ratios (see Vayda 1971). The social and historical evidence tells that this view is incorrect, no matter how much analysts force-fit the data. It is marriage relations that permit the exchange of land in an organized and productive fashion. Because warring clans do not intermarry, warfare disrupts the social process of redistribution – a process which Maring see as important to the reproduction of the clan. In addition, when warfare does occur and one clan cluster is driven from its land, the victorious cluster does not alienate the loser's land in any significant way. Clansmen refuse to use alien land because such land is alive with hostile spirits. The victor cannot enter into the enemy's reproductive cycle without a kinship with that enemy. Hence, what small appropriation of land may take place occurs on the margin of the loser's territory, on ground left uncultivated for several generations. The result is that from the standpoint of the total society, war redistributes the same total population over a *smaller* amount of used land. An example is the Tsembaga–Kundagai war, sometimes cited in support of ecological theory. The war had two consequences: (1) Tsembaga territory became uninhabited and uncultivated and would have remained so for years had not the Australian authorities intervened; (2) many defeated Tsembaga took refuge with the Kauwatyi who were already laboring under a land shortage. The Tsembaga–Kundagai war moved a small Tsembaga population blessed with substantial lands onto those of the most densely populated clan cluster. What is truly important is that the Kauwatyi took in the Tsembaga on the strength of blood ties and were willing to sustain a material loss to improve their social standing. The Kauwatyi's acceptance of their relatives was perceived as a sign of their strength. As one Kauwatyi elder put it: "We [the Kauwatyi] are everything; our name is foremost among all clans because we are not only the fiercest, having driven the Mananbant and Cenda from their land, but because we support our affines when they seek refuge. We say proudly: 'this is our land but you may garden with us.'"

Local groups in perspective

Strathern (1972:44–5) eloquently summarizes the problem which traditional thinking cannot resolve and thus must present as a paradox:

there is a *strong contrast* between the native model of the clan as a unit founded by a single father, where sons . . . found subclans, and the apparent *realities* of subclan formation . . . I have the impression that informants are themselves aware of the *discrepancy*, but that it does not trouble them much [my emphasis].

But there is no way that this standpoint, that is outside the system peering in, can be adequate to its object. For Maring (and I suspect for Melpa), it is the cycle of reproduction which links the "realities" of clansmen crossing clan lines with the model of the clan as a social form. The link between the history of the subclans and the model of a set of brothers is the production of kin relations: the eating, procreating, sharing, and dying on clan lands which defines people as part of the lineal flow of grease of a given clan. Outsiders become brothers because descent was never the issue either in the model of brotherhood or of reaffiliation. Why clansmen are not troubled is that there exists no discrepancy between model and reality, rather two separate, yet entirely compatible, perceptions of clan formation.

Note that the presupposition to Strathern's remarks is the analytical contrast between the ideology of patrilineal descent and the composition of descent groups (in terms of genealogical links). Two major positions have been developed from this presupposition. The first, more orthodox, view contends that agnation is the real structuring principle of local groups. However, Highland descent groups, beset

213

by warfare, the turbulence of an unpredictable and sometimes punishing environment, disease, and demographic fluctuations, never achieve perfect organization. Despite the ideal of a perfect fit between the descent group and the local group, the reality is one of descent groups rampant with non-agnates. The opposing view holds that local groups are formed from the solidarity and togetherness which derives from sharing food, co-gardening, and in general doing things cooperatively. Descent is an ideological category constructed after the fact to justify and legitimate a group built up on different principles.

Both these viewpoints notice important facts about the nature of local groups. The first grasps, albeit implicitly, that the lack of isomorphism between clan and local group is significant. The second realizes, equally implicitly, that food, co-gardening, and common labor are charged with significance. Both, however, falter on the same grounds. First, they fail to see that the clan and the local group represent different, though integrated, levels of social organization. For Maring, and I would argue for other Highland societies also (e.g., Wagner 1974; Watson 1983), there is no such thing as a descent group. The concept is a *non sequitur* because clanship circumscribes a class of social persons (such as those who share one grease or come from one penis). By contrast, the local group uses the principle of exchange to circumscribe a variety of non-agnates. Second, neither view understands that the relationship between the clan and the local group is not one of independent and dependent variables. Rather, they are linked in practice by the structure of clan reproduction. The relationship is always one of mediation. So, as the ethnography indicates, a man from clan A may, by virtue of a blood tie, move onto the land of clan B and by eating the food from this land, co-gardening, etc., change the agnatic identity of his children.

The formation of the local group requires that the reproductive cycle of one clan interacts with that of other clans. It is for this reason that Maring society appears to be "fuzzy" at its borders; there is no barrier which marks the transition from Maring culture to Kalam or Manga culture. Indeed, the clan cluster at Kandambiamp is an admixture of Maring and Kalam clans. In effect, the structure of inter-clan exchanges integrating Maring society begins to break down on the periphery as the reproductive cycles of Maring clans interface with those of neighboring societies.

Accounts of Maring social organization

It is appropriate to review received accounts of Maring social organization in the context of local groups, for all take the local group as the primary unit of analysis. Despite being the subject of heavy ethnographic interest, the Maring social system as a whole has been analyzed mostly in passing, usually as means of grounding ecologically inspired studies. One result is that the concepts and presuppositions of descent theory – the standard points of reference for kinship investigation – have dominated the presentation of local social organization. As in other cases (e.g., Reay 1959; Newman 1965), the description of the social system is really a description of how this system deviates from the descent model. That Lowman, Rappaport, Buchbinder, Clark, Manner, Healey, MacLean, and Vayda center their discussions on "territorial groups" or "local populations" encapsulates this perspective. Specifically, the presence of numerous non-agnates, the inter-clan transfer of land, and the general disinterest in calculating descent dilutes the value of concepts such as clan and subclan. Rappaport (1969:119) comments that "as the agnatic ideal is violated in land holding," thereby undermining the corporate powers of the descent group, "so it is violated in marriage," thus blurring clan boundaries. The ethnographic feeling has been that Maring are "putatively patrilineal" (Healey 1979:105), clanship being an ideology which is never fully realized in practice. Therefore, the real goal of analysis is to determine how etic forces outside the province of social structure – particularly economic and ecological interests – constitute the local group. For most part, the concept of local or territorial groups is less an explicit analytical category than one derived by default from the conspicuous failure of descent theory. Moreover, the ecological analyses of the Maring stimulated other Highland analysts (e.g., Lindenbaum 1971) to use ecological interests to capture the considerable amount of social life which fell through the holes of descent theory. It became commonplace to see studies which explained the transfer of land rights between clans as an instrument for adjusting man–land ratios. Note, however, that this type of explanation demands the view that the social organization is unorganized, for the objective effects of land transfer can never specify the structure of the exchange, the value and role of land in social reproduction, or the organization of the exchanging units.

Quite by accident, these weaknesses inherent in descent theory articulated with the interests of ecological anthropology. So analysts such as Meggitt, who began in the Fortesian mold, gradually incorporated more and more ecological theory into their understanding of social organization. In retrospect, the territorial group was really a category of compromise, suggesting some form of organization lying between the unilineal corporate descent group on one hand and the group constituted by practical, fleeting, and immediate interests on the other. De Lepervanche (1973) complained about the unrefined state of the art, showing that social groups were defined every way but successfully.

Focusing on territorial groups and local populations inherits the opposition between social organization and economic infrastructure from descent theory. And, if Maring social organization were separate from land tenure, patterns of exchange, production of pigs and crops, or procreation, then it would be unfair to criticize those whose main concerns were ecological rather than social. But, as I have argued, the unity of the Maring social economy is its elementary structure. What characterizes their social system is that social and material reproduction are intrinsically united and totally engaged. The explanatory power of a theory based on social reproduction lies in its comprehension that the social and economic are two sides of the same practices. In other words, the problem with the concepts derived from descent and/ or ecological theory is that they impose a division between social and material interests that is ethnographically wrong for Maring society. Being good ethnographers, Rappaport, Lowman, and Clark sense that something is awry, and thus all of their accounts contain passages implying the unity of the social and material.

It is possible to see the problems surrounding the concept of territorial group and the written insight of Maring ethnographers by reviewing a passage from Clark (1971:26–7) who in analyzing the ecology of a Simbai Maring community sets out social organization as follows:

the coherence and continuity of the Bomagai–Angoiang as a social group rests more on common residence within a bounded territory than on actual kinship ... In any such corporate group, economic and social organization are intimately connected. Questions arise to which is primary. Not surprisingly, the Bomagai–Angoiang creed is somewhat different from my outsider's view. They feel, for instance, that kinship is a condition from which flows the right to use corporately owned land, their instrument of sustenance. I believe, inversely, that their way of reckoning kinship is a method of distributing resources and describing who owns clan land.

Certainly, ... clan members are those who use and own or come to own land within the clan territory. Both the Angoiang and the Bomagai clans have recruited non-agnatic males who, once their right of access to clan land has been accepted, become, if not clan members themselves, the fathers of clan members. That is, ownership of clan land can create kinship. And despite their patrilineal ideology, the Bomagai–Angoiang will sometimes acknowledge this possibility, saying that it is acceptable because their group needs more men.

Clark is perceptive in noting that the ownership and use of land can create kinship. However, he does not use this observation theoretically to create an account of social reproduction, and thus sound footing for an ecology of the Bomagai–Angoiang. Rather, his description becomes progressively disorganized as a series of misunderstandings lead him further and further from the reality of Maring social organization. His assertion that the social group rests more on common residence than on actual kinship betrays a double misconception. First, it does not see that common residence on clan lands is a means of creating actual kinship through the production of co-substance relations. There is, for the Maring, no actual versus fictive kinship. There is only kinship based on the sharing and exchange of substance, as generated and embodied in practices such as co-residence. Second, Clark fails to see that the clan and local group are differently constructed and situated on separate levels of social organization. This is disguised by the term "social group" which may simultaneously refer to the clan or local group. As I have shown, however, there is an ethnographic and logical difference between clan and local group, a difference which can never be captured by the presumption that the two would be identical but for the intervention of material interests. In this way, Clark and other Highland ethnographers divide what must not be separated and conflate what must always be kept distinct.

Given this understanding, Clark must now decide whether social or economic organization is primary. To do this, he opposes the emic view of the Maring, who perceive kinship as a means of gaining access to land, to his own etic view, which sees kinship as a means of distributing land and other resources. But both viewpoints are simply different and incomplete perspectives on the same unified structure of clan reproduction. In ethnographic terms, what Clark reports as the emic view is really nothing more than one piece of Maring ideology. It is a decontextualized statement of the type usually gleaned from interviews rather than from practice itself. Presenting the ideology as if it were a structural principle, Clark is then forced to contradict himself. So immediately after stating that the Maring creed is that only agnates may use clan lands, he notes that clansmen also say that they actively recruit men from other clans. What Clark has uncovered is that in very different contexts people will reveal various ideological and pragmatic representations of social practice. Maring are keenly aware that they obtain land through kinship and create kinship through land. This is what the strategies, aims, and interests of social practice are all about. Clark sees that land can create kinship, but does not grasp its significance. Steeped in the presuppositions of descent theory, he has no way to make sense of the fact that living on clan land can lead to the assimilation of non-agnates, other than to assume that the social system is (1) unstructured and (2) driven by external economic and ecological forces.

The problems that skew Clark's analysis invade those of the other Maring ethnographers as well. Hooked into the categorical presuppositions of descent theory, even as they disavowed its analytical power, they were forced to adopt a weak notion of the local group, one that had little structural basis, and then to account for its formation through the abstract functions of ecology. But there is really no way to move from material interests, such as a desire to acquire more land, to the formation of a determinate form of local group or clan without a theory of social substance and reproduction. The major perception of Maring ethnographers was to notice that co-residence, common consumption, sharing land, etc., do create kinship. Nonetheless, they were not able to develop a concept of the local group that understood that this occurred not because the social system was loosely structured, but because this was the structure of the system.

7 From ethnography to theory

The Maring social system has been the ethnographic source of a theory of social reproduction, a theory centering on how the clan reproduces itself in and through practice. The reproduction of the clan is based on co-substance relations as they develop in terms of sharing and exchange. The ethnography details how local practices concerning food, land, labor, marriage, ancestors, sex, and death generate kinship and clanship, allowing Maring society to reproduce at once symbolically and materially in the continuous routines of everyday life. The result is a unified description of the social order which encompasses the full range of observed practices and comprehends how these practices are systematically interrelated.

The theory of social reproduction is rooted in the integrity of social practice. It stands in opposition to theories which factor out structure and practice, ideology and behavior, or emic and etic, and then treat them as separate phenomena. My analysis is simultaneously an ethnography of Maring practice and a theory of social practices that takes account of interests, strategies, and events without losing sight of their cultural construction. Thus, the description of agnation, marriage exchange, bridewealth and other forms of compensation, men's house residence, land tenure, ritual sacrifice, food taboos, co-gardening, kinship terms, etc., probes the cultural basis of a practical logic. Most of all, the theory of co-substance and reproduction stands out because it is a New Guinea Highlands theory, finding its strength in the basic characteristics of these societies.

The concept of reproduction developed here is not simply a replacement or specification for the traditional concept of function. A society does not reproduce itself without alterations, least of all Maring society. Central to my analysis is a theory and ethnography of structured transformation: how the principles embodied in practices permit Maring clans to maintain structural continuity while continually transforming. Insofar as cultural principles engross new people and revalue outstanding relations, the clan is simultaneously innovative and conservative. The flow of individuals from one local group to another (via co-residence, transfer of land rights, or whatever), and the redefining of their agnatic identity, are ordered processes grounded in the structure of exchange and agnation. Clan members use these processes to pursue their interests and strategies of social reproduction. The ethnography reveals that Maring social organization is not structurally flexible or variable as Highland analysts have come to use these terms. Rather, people define and redefine themselves agnatically by entering into the reproductive cycles of particular clans. The sharing of gardens, work, food, ritual, etc., are acts of clanship which determine co-substance and hence clan identity. In short, Maring know unquestionably that certain practical acts and practices create clanship. But it never ends there as the empiricist view of Highland societies seems to assume; ethnography must come to terms with the cultural construction of these practical acts and practices.

The structure of Maring clanship and the possibilities for transformation are only obscured by reusing the categories of descent theory. Clanship is not based on descent or the existence of corporate descent groups as such and can only be misunderstood from this perspective. So ethnographers have written that the coherence of social groups rests more on common residence, land-holding, and consumption than actual kinship without realizing that all of these are elements of actual kinship from the Maring standpoint. The acceptance of descent theory – mostly an implicit reliance on its presuppositions and categories – makes it difficult to understand the structure of social transformation. As a result, the movement of people between clans appears as a frequent moment of disorganization. The marvel of Maring society, and the societies of the Highlands in general, is that they have mastered the means of reorganizing the clan without sacrificing its structure. They possess generative structures which cannot be reduced to rules of descent, material interests, or any combination thereof. I would argue that what is ethnographically compelling about much of the research done in the Highlands is that it implicitly reveals the mechanisms of social transformation. They reveal the part land, food, co-residence, co-gardening, exchange, and mutual aid play in the local organization of clanship, even if they often reduce them to economic or ecosystemic facts. For the Maring, this generative structure rests on social reproduction – embodied in the flow of grease and blood in the reproductive cycle – and group formation grounded in the opposition between sharing and exchange.

What is especially appealing about this theory is that it is not only more theoretical than many previous accounts, being able adequately to encompass and explain a greater range of data, but is also more immediate and closer to social life. It is fully situated within the practical concerns of eating, gardening, raising a family, love-making, and speaking about the world. Its point of departure is not an abstract set of rules, but the tenor of everyday actions and emotions.

The substance of sharing is shared substance, each clan member possessing clan grease. This exists in both physical and spiritual states. Within the category of sharing and thus within the limits of clanship, the practices and actions of men transmit grease through a cycle of reproduction. The flow of substance from the bodies of clansmen into clan lands, from there through use of labor and magic into the taro, pigs, and other foods, and ultimately returning to people defines the relationship between these elements, creates their value, and makes them the practical terms in which the culture conceptualizes clanship. A crucial reason co-substance relations are so powerful is that they are embodied in objects and practices, especially those focusing on the human body. Maring are conscious of the embodiment of substance only incidentally, when for example blood passes between boundaries. Their sense of substance is not conceptual or given over to explicit formulations that bridge different contexts and practices. What people know explicitly is that those who eat food from the same land or participate in a variety of other practices share kinship. They know the practical dimensions and the consequences of co-substance relations without being able to formulate the relations systematically or articulate the principles. This in mind, my analysis illustrates how many ordinary statements, such as those about gardening and physical appearance, are grounded in principles of substance. Ethnographers have been collecting such information for decades of course, though I would submit without realizing its significance for the study of social organization.

Clan identity is based on the co-sharing of clan substance rather than descent from a common ancestor. It is participation in the same reproductive cycle which defines membership. Thus, clansmen conceive of their relationship in terms of brotherhood, rendering the calculation of precise genealogies and biological connections entirely beside the point. Brotherhood means a co-sharing of grease and thus refers to the relationship between sons of the same father, between clansmen in general, and between subclans of a clan.

A clan's natural cycle can never stand alone and reproduce itself independently. The structure of reproduction ordains that clans must exchange men, land, labor, pigs, food, and, centrally, women if they are to survive economically and politically. There is a dynamic relationship between the cycles of different clans as clansmen mobilize a variety of strategies to produce the clan against the odds of environmental conditions and in accordance to a cultural image of clanship. It is in the domain of marriage exchange and the flow of vital wealth that practice defines the external limits of the clan through the contrast between exchange and sharing. In this way, the constitution and evolution of the clan are as much dependent on inter-clan relations as they are on internal relations. So the ethnography illustrates that lateral relationships within the clan and outside the clan are equally as important as lineal ones in defining the significance of agnation and clanship.

A principal dynamic of the social system is the interrelationship between substances and social exchange. The interrelationship unites and orients many domains and practices, including those that ethnographers have treated as removed from social organization. A crucial strength of a revised position is that it can encompass and account for such practices as burial rites and food taboos. For it shows that they are squarely within the frame of social organization in that they define social relations through the movement of substance or taboos on such movement. Similarly, it is clear that the ordinary aspects of production – planting, harvesting, fence-building, etc. – generate social relations not merely because they promote solidarity and cooperation, but because they are based on an underlying structure of clan reproduction.

The heart of Maring social relations is a sense of kinship based on co-substance relations. The use of genealogical concepts would only distort the character of Maring kinship; for such concepts privilege forms of inheritance and social relationships not found in Maring practice. The circulation of male and female substance – as embodied in people, goods, and services – defines and motivates the circuits of exchange. It is not only the flow of substance directly between people, illustrated by procreation, that engenders relatedness; exchange also acts as a transformer for turning all instances of social production into occasions of social definition.

Opposition between male and female is a pervasive generative scheme for the construction of social relations. It appears as a major subdivision of Maring society into a line of men and a line of women. More, it founds the particular pattern of inheritance and thus the way Maring understand lineal relationships. From a sibling perspective: a brother inherits his mother's blood and father's grease, but can transmit only grease to his sons; his sister inherits only her mother's blood but transmits it both to her sons and daughters. The result is two descending lines of substance or relationship that form a dual pattern of heredity. However, transmission of semen, in marked contrast with blood, creates clanship because all members of the clan share substance derived from a common source.

The connection forged between food, land, and substance is the cultural logic which interconnects practices from discrete domains. So Maring burial procedure, where the corpse is left to rot on a raised, outdoor platform, becomes intelligible when we recognize that the motive is to separate flesh from bone and to return the substances of the deceased to the land. Similarly, the organization of the garden production and the value people place on certain crops derive from their efforts to produce the appropriate substances. The connection clarifies why Maring are so emotionally and intellectually involved in the history of land use and ownership, such that disputes over land can easily incite violence and necessitate court action. It also sets terms for understanding how the human body, through a series of mediations, manifests the reproductive power of the clan. Indeed, one of the main functions of Maring art, dance, and body decoration is to index the clan's power and strength.

An organic and instrumental link exists between garden and clan florescence, not only because success in one breeds success in the other, but because the same principle of fertility and growth operates in each. Maring ethnotheory locates the dynamics of growth and development in the exchange of female substance and fertility against the backdrop of fixed male assets (e.g., land, semen, and ancestors). Clansmen transplant women from their natal clan, importing the fertility to enrich the clan's growth. From the perspective of cultivation, growth depends on the marriage of female crops and labor to male lands. This entails transplanting cultigens from one garden to the next. The explicit link is that just as the transfer of women fertilizes the clan over successive generations, so the transplanting of cultigens fertilizes the land over seasons. Human ingenuity consists in bringing the principle of exchange to bear successfully. Essentially, by focusing on the transfer of planting material and extending the parallel to marriage, the ethnotheory creates a general account of clan growth and development.

Because food produces and renews the substances which create kinship, the structure and development of kin ties are inseparable from the management of production. The bonding of kinship to cultivation is the nature of Maring culture; it is their commonsense perspective on people and gardens. Thus, subclansmen disperse their gardens throughout clan territory, the interdigitation of gardens being one mechanism of clan unity. In this way, slash and burn agriculture opens up many avenues for cultivating social relations as practice encourages the diversification of gardening pairs and allows men and women to gain assistance along many kinship lines. Between husband and wife, gardening affirms the complementarity of sex roles in production and reproduction. Among agnates, cooperative gardening transforms an official clan link into a practical one with greater consequences for future concerted action. Among non-agnates, cultivation affords the chance to create co-substance bonds across clan lines.

That clansmen share a common substance inherited from their paternal ancestors forms the basis of lineality. Archetypically, a clan ascends from a founding set of ancestors who are fatherless brothers. The concept is that the original subclans were founded simultaneously and are genealogically equivalent. This view of origins produces the conceptions that all clansmen are brothers just as their ancestors were, and that a clan's subclans are co-equals. The point of differentiation is whether they are autochthonous or immigrants who have joined by integration into the clan's reproductive cycle.

The notion of ascent meshes with the understanding that a clan's growth and development parallels the model of vegetative propagation. Maring characteristically trace their origins to a territory rather than an individual, and people generally know little about their genealogical origins. The crucial point is that current generations reproduce the same clan relationships as their ancestors because they perpetuate the natural and social cycles. The continuity of landedness is the local measure of clan continuity; it bespeaks the lineal transmission of clan substance from one generation to the next.

The basis of agnation is that a child shares a common identity and heritage with all of his father's clansmen, but shares blood with his mother's clansmen only on a filial basis. The central and founding condition of recruitment is the origin of the father's grease. Hence, if a man lives and renews his grease from the land of clan A, his children belong to clan A no matter where he or his father may have come from.

Clan identity centers on the flow and transmission of male substance over time. There are two dimensions to this process: the practices by which a father replenishes his bodily substances by sharing food, land, etc., with kinsmen, and procreation by which a father creates an individual bearing a definite clan identity. This process implicates the practices of land tenure, gardening, food taboos, commensality, and other means of cycling substance. Here, the kinship system and the formation of clanship articulate with the structure of production.

The external limits of clanship are set through the opposition between sharing and exchanging. It divides the world into those who share reproductive resources; those who exchange them; and enemy

clans with whom all social exchanges are tabooed. In this way, the opposition between sharing and exchange represents the dual dimensions
of social reproduction: internally through the perpetuation of a shared
identity and externally via the exchange of reproductive assets.

Marriage exchange specifies the origin of a man's substance, for the
system of payment, more than demarcating clan membership,
generates co-substance bonds through the sharing of pork. Wife-
givers and wife-takers exchange gifts of pork which are divided and
shared among clan members. It is this dual nature of bridewealth
which imbues it with such formative powers, and also determines that
all bride payments must include pork if they are to be counted as such.
The criterion of clan identity is that clan members share exchange functions, giving and receiving together as a unit. The principle is that
those who share substance share bridewealth; and those who exchange
substance, be it women's blood, male labor, food or planting material,
exchange bridewealth.

Between proximate, intermarrying clans an entire complex of co-
substance relations are in process. Such affines are related not only by
the reticulation of bloodlines, but by the exchange of land, food,
taboos, planting material, and the other male/agnatic resources. It is
here that reaffiliation becomes a structural fact of organization. That is,
it is strategic action working within the lines of an objective structure
which organizes reaffiliation. Thus, the most profound links are between a mother's brother and his sister's son and this is the most frequent form of reaffiliation. Moreover, the process is both
straightforward and harmonic with principles of clanship because it is
based on the production of co-substance ties. A non-agnate's children
become full-fledged agnates because – like every other member – they
were created and reared from substances gleaned from clan lands. They
are fully integrated into the clan's natural cycle. And when their father
dies and is buried on the land of his new clan he enters its corps of
ancestor spirits which the entire clan will propitiate. This appears dramatically in the various rituals of integration, as when clansmen plant
their *min* or sacrifice pigs to the ancestors.

The ethnography indicates that kin terms and their use play a very
significant part in the construction of agnatic identity and the structured passage from non-agnate to agnate. The terms are an organized
semantic field of reference involving categories which emanate from,
and reflect, lines of co-substance. There are two principal levels of terminology in play. The first is agnatic terminology, those terms which
operate on a sociocentric or clan level to define relations of clanship of
alliance. The second is cognatic terminology, those terms which oper-

ate on the level of social persons, taking ego as the point of reference to construct a network of relations. The ambiguity which exists between levels was found to be a constitutive feature of the system of terms. So reaffiliation weathers the potential contradiction of being born into one clan and joining another by systematically manipulating the levels of terminology. It smoothes the reaffiliation by capitalizing on the overlap between levels, reading from one level to the next and then back again. Similar processes were seen to take place when clans merge or realign.

Marriage exchange proved to be a key element in the formation of the clan and the development of reproduction strategies. The central reason is that lateral relationships are the outgrowth of such exchanges and bloodlines they inspire. The same elements come into play as with agnation, only here land, food, pigs, magic, and money are part of the give and take among clans. Marriage preferences and rights in women derive from co-substance relations and the kinship they bring about. The orientation or dispositions of exchange had necessarily to start with consubstantiality. Clansmen derived the objectives of exchange from their general assessment and implementation of reproductive goals. Thus, the objectives of exchange were (1) to institute reciprocity; (2) to generate kin relations based on the sharing of blood; and (3) to satisfy a variable range of economic and political interests. The various types of marriage, from sister exchange to reciprocal exchange, were all ways to achieve these ends in certain circumstances.

Marriage exchange emerges from strategies – that is, the combined and various interests of the clan's membership – as these strategies unfold in terms of prevailing conditions and cultural principles. Wife-takers and wife-givers review each other's material and social productive state. They also assess how well they may take advantage of each other's resources, such as man power and land. The goal-directedness of marriage is also inscribed in its processual character. Thus, there is no event which bridges pre- and post-marriage status. Rather, marriages crystalize as time passes, bridewealth is paid, children and other indices accumulate, and the local community recognizes the marriage and the couple so presents themselves to the community.

The value of women in reproduction and the significance of exchange is expressed in the character of compensation payments. They constitute promissory notes on future social reproduction, the series of exchanges and exchange of women that hopefully follow, whereas the women are the keystone of successful reproduction. The major set of compensation payments are correlated with the reproductive cycle of the family, in particular the transfer of women and the use of their substance to produce children. Such payments are made in light of prevailing interests and depend on a range of social, political, and economic factors. Importantly, compensation payments have a dual character. On one hand, they must be elective offerings given freely and/or in response to previous gifts. On the other hand, compensation payments feature a wide variety of options and this encourages clansmen to create, shape, and redefine an affinal relationship on the basis of its reproductive merits. It is in this sense that the structure of exchange not merely guides behavior, but people's behavior and considerations produce a particular kind of structure.

The perpetual flow of women across clan lines and the production of children creates inter-clan bloodlines. These bloodlines are the conceptual underpinning of later relationships, and the construction of women-based linkages is the generative scheme for building exchange networks. For clansmen, what is important about reproducing an affinal relationship, and thus reproducing a set of blood ties, is that it maintains a particular axis of exchange. For this reason, the value of a bloodline depends on its position within a constellation of other bloodlines. And this value is inseparable from the possibility of creating new blood ties and using existing ones in very concrete ways. The integrity of the clan cluster as a territorial unit with a recognizable identity depends on a relatively high level of intra-cluster marriages and the corollary flow of agnatic material along these axes. In this way, the clan cluster generated by relations through women takes on the character of a higher level of the social structural hierarchy. The key point is that a clan's compulsion to improve its own lot within the social order, using the cultural means at hand, compels it to reproduce the structure of exchange in such a way as to reproduce the clan cluster.

Agnation is the perspective from which practice defines the principles of local group formation. Nonetheless, clanship and local groups are logically separate, clanship being a sufficient though not a necessary condition of membership. The distinction between clanship and locality opens out onto a variety of practices which assimilate non-agnates to the local group. Marriage exchange is the most significant of these though only one aspect of a larger reproductive scheme. The clan has political and economic interests in organizing the local group so that some of its members reside elsewhere and some outsiders live on its lands. The heart of this scheme is the cultural logic linking food, land, and clan identity within the opposition between sharing and exchange. In addition to marriage, such practices as child exchange, dual residence, men's house co-residence, and reaffiliation actively

227

recruit outsiders to the local group. The result of this process is that the local view of social organization dictates that local groups encompass many non-agnates. And certainly the Maring statistics bear this out.

The act of doing ethnography among the Maring and translating this ethnography into a description illuminates some of the ways in which ethnographic practice influences theory. My argument is as simple as the process is difficult: the ethnographer must transcend the social and epistemological divide between cultures so as to avoid the pitfall of reading into his object of research his relationship to that object. This is particularly true in exchange where theory, I argue, by taking a utilitarian and contractual perspective, is more a reflection of the social status of the ethnographer than a fact of ethnography. Similarly, the propensity of ethnographers to rely on decontextualized interviews slants the information they receive. It channels in ideological representations, referential material, and that which has discrete boundaries; it filters out pragmatic representations, the use of language, and the strategy and tactics of using cultural concepts (such as brotherhood) and objects (such as land) in the social context (such as a negotiation).

Finally, the Maring material reveals that there is a reciprocal relationship between structure and practice such that the reproduction of the social order entails its transformation. A consequence is that distinction between reproduction and transformation represents two moments or two perspectives of the same social system. For example, a social relation is understood in terms of cultural concepts of agents, relationship, and the use of words, objects, and actions by these agents in this relationship. Recall the rights, responsibilities, and obligations of a brother and sister towards one another, especially where marriage is concerned. But it is equally true that the realization and practical use of the relationship creates the conditions for its revaluation. Thus the end of warfare, government laws, and missionization have opened up new possibilities for exchange and new options for brother and sister which have served to reform the relationship. In other words, the interests and strategies of individuals and groups mediate the relationship between cultural concepts of the social order and the reproduction of this social order in and through material production, exchange, and ritual. The Maring, like other New Guinea Highland societies, show that anthropology must come to terms with the structures in practice and the practical reproduction of structures if it is to provide an account adequate to these societies.

Glossary

The Maring language is spoken as a first language by about 8,000 people. Even within such a small group of speakers there is marked internal differentiation for two reasons. The first is that some clan clusters border on and have extensive contact (including intermarriage and co-residence) with non-Maring communities. In one case, that of Kalam speakers in the Simbai, the two languages are extremely different. The second reason is that language is a culturally promoted and sanctioned means of establishing identity and difference between groups. Thus, Maring recognized even small phonological differences, particularly with respect to allophones of stops and prenasalized stops. For example, there is variation in the final consonant of the lexeme for pig, *kon't*, which ranges from a post-dental to a palatal stop.

Like all speakers of any language, Maring speakers refer and predicate, and, more generally, generate meaning in speech events by using all three communicative channels: kinesic (e.g., gesture and body postures), prosody (e.g., intonation, stress, tone), and verbal-grammatical. For example, *ana wundok* (or true father) can be referentially distinguished from other denotations of *ana* (e.g., all clansmen of a father's generation) by slightly lengthening the consonant. By the same token, the placement of a speaker's hand (e.g., on his stomach, ear, or opposite rib especially) can change the referent and/or meaning of his/her words. What follows then is not a list of the meanings or even referents of these lexemes; rather, it is the set of the most contextually general denotations and nothing more.

The glossary is also meant to contribute to the overall theme of the book. A review of the vocabulary shows that many words are used to denote both the growth and development of gardens, plants, and trees, and that of clans, people's actions and lives, the establishing of new practices, and much more. There is a reciprocal or dialectical relation between Maring ideology and the semantico-referential domain of language. Understanding this is critical in that ethnographers often cite lexemes as though they were always a direct reflection of ontological reality, rather than an important though second-order comprehension of that reality. For instance, that the Maring have no lexeme for family does not mean that they cannot distinguish what we would denote as a family; it means that because the "family" has no exclusive and ac-

Glossary

knowledged functions (although it can and does perform these functions), the family is not ideologically codified in a lexeme.

acek: formal or informal taboo or prohibition
ainyom: soft and dry
alome: highly valued type of taro
ama: kin type: mother; any female clanswoman of a mother's generation; source
amame: short, herbaceous plant, used ceremonially
ambanga: namesake
ambra: woman
ambra konch: bridal pork
ambra manga: single, unmarried woman
ana: kin type: father; any male clansman of a father's generation
ananga: grease, fat
anc: hard, firm, strong
Angengbogai: a clan of the Kauwatyi cluster
anginai: hardness, strength
apo: kin type: grandmother; female ancestor; any woman two or more generations above ego
aquia: a variety of red pandanus
arab: magic
at'a: kin type: sister; any clanswoman of a generation
at'mal: story
atemp: smaller
awo: to give; to take; to interact

Baigai: a clan of the Kauwatyi cluster
baka: short; adolescent stage of development; may imply transitional stage.

Cenda: a Jimi Valley clan cluster defeated by the Kauwatyi in 1955 and restored to their land by government officers in 1956: population 380

dong: taro

-gai: suffix, indicating base, root, or origin
gio: bone
golup: a favorite type of banana

imat'e: kin type: daughter's husband
imbana: grease, fat, semen

kai: base, root
kaiko: literally, dance; also festival involving the ceremonial slaughter of pigs
Kakupogai: the second largest clan in the Kauwatyi cluster
Kalam: the people and language of a group of western Simbai Valley clan clusters
Kambant'igai: a clan of the Kauwatyi cluster

Glossary

Kamjepakai: the largest clan in the Kauwatyi cluster
kangi: to grow something, to nurse, to raise by dint of one's own efforts
Kauwatyi: a centrally located and largest, Jimi Valley, clan cluster: population
    just under 1,000
kawi: sap; viscous liquid; semen
kekla: system, network
kinim: moist, watery; a woman's vaginal secretions; the mucous covering of an
    eel
koima: animals, animals used in brideprice and other compensation payments
koimp: witch
koka: kin type: grandfather; male ancestor; any male two or more generations
    above ego
komba: pandanus tree, the pandanus fruit; comes in red and yellow varieties
kongipo: a line; a set of intrinsically related things
kongong ri: to work
kon't: pig; pork
kopla: fairness, justice, balance; a balanced reciprocal relationship

mai: that which is mature and in a later stage of development; e.g. *ambra mai*, an
    older woman
mamia: kin type: a father's cross-cousin
Manamban: a centrally located, Jimi Valley, clan cluster; traditional enemy of
    the Kauwatyi: population around 700
manap: pitpit, type of vegetable
manga: a reply or retort; a young lady
manga awi: to pay back, compensate
manga ri: to exchange, barter, or trade
mangla: to tie, fasten, or link
mbapa: maternal uncle
men: seeds of a vegetable
min: life-force, bodily consciousness or awareness
moi: temporary food taboo circumscribing the nucleus of individuals related to
    the deceased
mu di: invisible pulling, or influence, of the ancestor spirits on a person
munga: new leaves; the flowering of something (e.g., an idea, an issue, a new
    practice)
mungoi: property; category of wealth items; the wealth items themselves; that
    which has an indelible association with its owner

na: to eat
nak: soft, not strong; immature and in the process of forming
Narak: the language spoken by people of the eastern Jimi Valley
ndemi: wild, untamed, uncultivated, uncivilized
nink: water
nogai: sweet potato; fundamental part
nomane: soul; culture, custom

231

nukmai: road, path; established practice
nukum: blood

pena: a not highly regarded variety of taro
pika: cucumber
-po: suffix, used to indicate a relationship between a dominant entity and a set
    of subordinate entities
poka: fork of a tree; payment creating a relationship

ra: to do or make; to perform or act
raku: sacred grove where sacrifices are made to ancestor spirits
rawa: spirit
rawa mugi: ancestor spirits of the high ground; red spirits
relya: absolute prohibitions against eating certain foods by members of a
    particular clan or subclan
rind: flower; outgrowth; a development of something
rombanda: hot, fiery, burning
rumbim: cordyline, tanket
rumpi: bad
rungyi: one; united

tap aingundo: something which grows from the ground; plants
tap wandundo: something which moves of its own volition; animals
trat'e: kin type: sister's husband
Tsembaga: Simbai Valley clan cluster: population 210
Tuguma: Simbai Valley clan cluster: population 230
Tukmenga: an eastern Jimi clan cluster; joined Kauwatyi in a rout of the
    Manamban in 1956: population about 850

wai: kin type: son
wainan: kin type: grandson
waiwa: type of vine
wak: bark; skin; the surface of an issue; what is revealed and known publicly
wamba: kin type: child
wambe: kin type: cross-cousin; term of affection and affinity
wambnan: kin type: granddaughter
wamb: kin type: female child
wamba: kin type: child; male child
watchi: highly valued type of taro
went: eldest
wo: to come; to approach; to arrive at a destination
wora: the lower portion of the environment, associated with cultivation
wumbi: domesticated, tame, having culture
wump: planting material, such as seed taro
wundok: truth, truthfulness
wunga: where the branch of a tree forks; where a line of descent forks or
    branches

Glossary

yik: branch, offshoot; an extension of something
yindok: people, humans, group
yondoi: large, mature
yondoi mai: very large, having completed the cycle of growth
yu: man
yu nim: many men; clan cluster

References

Barnes, J. 1962. African Models in the New Guinea Highlands. *Man* 622:5–9.
Berndt, R. 1962. *Excess and Restraint*. Chicago: University of Chicago Press.
Bourdieu, P. 1977. *Outline of a Theory of Practice*. Cambridge: Cambridge University Press.
Brown, P. 1962. Non-Agnates among the Patrilineal Chimbu. *Journal of the Polynesian Society* 71:57–69.
    1978. *Highland People of New Guinea*. Cambridge: Cambridge University Press.
Brown, P. and Brookfield, H. 1959. Chimbu Land and Society. *Oceania* 30(2):1–75.
Buchbinder, G. 1973. Maring Microadaptation: A Study of Demographic, Nutritional, Genetic, and Phenotypic Variation in a Highland New Guinea Population. Unpublished doctoral dissertation, Columbia University.
    1974. Where do Maring Pigs Come From? Paper presented at the Symposium on the Use and Management of Pigs in the New Guinea Highlands. Annual Meeting of the American Anthropology Association.
Buchbinder, G. and Rappaport, R. 1976. Fertility and Death Among the Maring. In *Man and Woman in New Guinea*, ed. P. Brown and G. Buchbinder, pp. 13–35. American Anthropological Association Publication No. 8. Washington.
Bulmer, R. 1968. The Strategies of Hunting in New Guinea. *Oceania* 38(3):302–18.
Bunn, G. and Scott, P. 1962. *Languages of the Mount Hagen Sub-District*. The Summer Institute of Linguistics, Ukarumpa, Eastern Highlands, Terrace of New Guinea.
Clark, W. 1971. *Place and People*. Los Angeles: University of California Press.
Clark, W. and Street, J. 1967. Soil Fertility and Cultivation Practices in New Guinea. *Journal of Tropical Geography* 24:7–11.
Comaroff, J. and Roberts, S. 1981. *Rules and Processes*. Chicago: University of Chicago Press.
Cook, E. 1967. Narak: Language or Dialect. *Language* 46:50–60.

1967–8. Descent, Residence and Leadership in the New Guinea Highlands. *Oceania* 38(2):124–89; 38(3):163–89.

1968. *Manga Social Organization.* Ann Arbor: University Microfilms International.

1970. On the Conversion of Non-Agnates into Agnates among the Manga, Jimi River, Western Highlands District, New Guinea. *Southwestern Journal of Anthropology* 26:190–6.

1973. Social Structure. In *Anthropology in Papua New Guinea*, ed. I. Hogbin, pp. 1–60. Melbourne: Melbourne University Press.

Cook, E. and O'Brien, D. (eds.). 1980. *Blood and Semen.* Ann Arbor: University of Michigan Press.

De Lepervanche, M. 1967–8. Descent, Residence, and Leadership in the New Guinea Highlands. *Oceania* 38:134–58 and 163–89.

1973. *Social Structure in Anthropology in Papua New Guinea*, ed. I. Hogbin. Melbourne: Melbourne University Press.

Fabian, J. 1983. *Time and the Other.* New York: Columbia University Press.

Fortes, M. 1945. *The Dynamics of Clanship among the Tellensi.* London: Oxford University Press.

1949. *The Web of Kinship Among the Tellensi.* London: Oxford University Press.

Glasse, R. 1968. *The Huli of Papua.* Paris: Mouton.

Healey, C. 1977. Maring Hunters and Traders: The Ecology of an Exploitative Non-Subsistence Activity. Unpublished Ph.D. Dissertation, University of Papua New Guinea.

1979. Assimilation of Nonagnates among the Kundagai Maring of Papua New Guinea Highlands. *Oceania* 50(2):193–217.

1985a. *Pioneers of the Mountain Forest.* Oceania Monograph No. 29. Sydney: University of Sydney Press.

1985b. Pigs, Cassowaries, and the Gift of the Flesh: A Symbolic Triad in Maring Cosmology. *Ethnology* 24:153–65.

Kelly, R. 1977. *Etoro Social Structure: A Study in Structural Contradiction.* Ann Arbor: University of Michigan Press.

Langness, L. 1971. Bena Bena Political Organization. In *Politics in New Guinea*, ed. R. Berndt and P. Lawrence, pp. 298–316. Nedlands: University of Western Australia Press.

Levi-Strauss, C. 1969. *The Elementary Structures of Kinship.* New York: Beacon Press.

Lindenbaum, S. 1971. Sorcery and Structure in Fore Society. *Oceania* 41(4):277–87.

LiPuma, E. 1980. Sexual Asymmetry and Social Reproduction among the Maring. *Ethnos* 1–2:34–57.

1981. Cosmology and Economy among the Maring of Papua, New Guinea. *Oceania* 61:266–85.

1982. The Spirits of Modernization: Maring Concept and Practice. In *Through a Glass Darkly: Beer and Modernization in Papua, New Guinea*, ed.

M. Marshall, pp. 175–88. Boroko, Papua New Guinea: Institute of Applied Social and Economic Research.

1983. On the Preference for Marriage Rules. *Man* 18:766–85.

1986. Medicine and Modernity among the Maring. In *A Continuing Trial of Treatment. Medical Pluralism in Papua New Guinea*, ed. S. Frankel.

Lowman, C. 1971. Maring Big-Men. In *Politics in New Guinea*, ed. R. Berndt, and P. Lawrence, pp. 317–61. Nedlands: University of Western Australia Press.

1974. The Slaughter and Non-Slaughter of Pigs for the Ancestors. Paper presented at the Symposium on the Use and Management of Pigs in the New Guinea Highlands, 1974 Annual Meeting of the American Anthropology Association.

1980. Environment, Society and Health: Ecological Bases of Community Growth and Decline in the Maring Region of Papua, New Guinea. Unpublished Ph.D. dissertation, Columbia University.

Maclean, N. 1984. To Develop Our Place: A Political Economy of the Maring. Unpublished Ph.D. dissertation, University of Adelaide.

Manner, H. 1976. The Effects of Shifting Cultivation and Fire on Vegetation and Soils in the Montane Tropics of New Guinea. Unpublished Ph.D. dissertation, Department of Geography, University of Hawaii.

Meggitt, M. 1965. *The Lineage System of the Mae Enga*. New York: Barnes and Nobles.

1969. Introduction. In *Pigs, Pearlshells and Women*, ed. P. Glasse and M. Meggitt, pp. 1–10. Englewood Cliffs, New Jersey: Prentice Hall.

Meigs, A. 1976. Male Pregnancy and the Reduction of Sexual Opposition in a New Guinea Highland. *Ethnology* 40:390–420.

Murry, C. 1976. Marital Strategy in Lesotho: The Redistribution of Migrant Earnings. *African Studies* 35:99–121.

Newman, P. 1965. *Knowing the Gururumba*. New York: Holt, Rhinehart, and Winston.

Rappaport, R. 1967. Ritual Regulation of Environmental Relations among a New Guinea People. *Ethnology* 6:17–30.

1968. *Pigs for the Ancestors*. New Haven: Yale University Press.

1969. Marriage among the Maring. In *Pigs, Pearlshells and Women*, ed. R. Glasse and M. Meggitt, pp. 117–37. Englewood Cliffs, New Jersey: Prentice Hall.

1971. Ritual, Sanctity, and Cybernetics. *American Anthropologist* 73:59–76.

1977. Maladaptation in Social Systems. In *Evolution in Social Systems*, ed. J. Friedman and J. Rowlands, pp. 100–45. London: Duckworth.

1979. *Ecology, Meaning, and Religion*. Richmond, California: North Atlantic Books.

Reay, M. 1959. *The Kuma*. Melbourne: Melbourne University Press.

Ryan, D. 1961. Gift Exchange in the Mendi Valley. Unpublished doctoral dissertation, Australian National University.

Sahlins, M. 1981. *Historical Metaphors and Mythical Realities*. Ann Arbor:

University of Michigan Press.

1985. *Islands of History*. Chicago: University of Chicago Press.

Salisbury, R. 1964. New Guinea Highland Models and Descent Theory. *Man* 64:168–71.

1965. The Siane of the Eastern Highlands. In *Gods, Ghosts, and Men in Melanesia*, ed. P. Lawrence and M. Meggitt, pp. 50–77. London: Oxford University Press.

Schneider, D. 1968. *American Kinship: A Cultural Account*. Englewood Cliffs, New Jersey: Prentice Hall.

1972. What is Kinship All About? In *Kinship Studies in the Morgan Centennial Year*, ed. Priscilla Reining, pp. 32–63. Washington, D.C.: Anthropological Society of Washington.

1976. Notes Towards a Theory of Culture. In *Meaning in Anthropology*, ed. K. Basso and H. Selby, pp. 197–220. Albuquerque: University of New Mexico Press.

Schwimmer, E. 1973. *Exchange in the Social Structure of the Orakavia*. New York: St Martin's Press.

Shaw, D. (ed.). 1974. *Kinship Studies in Papua New Guinea*. Ukarumpa, Papua New Guinea: Summer Institute of Linguistics.

Strathern, A. 1971. Wiru and Daribi Matrilateral Payments. *Journal of the Polynesian Society* 80:449–62.

1972. *One Father, One Blood*. London: Tavistock.

1973. Kinship, Descent, and Locality: Some New Guinea Examples. In *The Character of Kinship*, ed. J. Goody. Cambridge: Cambridge University Press.

1982. *Inequality in New Guinea Highland Societies*. Cambridge Papers in Social Anthropology. Cambridge: Cambridge University Press.

Strathern, M. 1978. The Achievement of Sex: Paradoxes in Hagen Gender-Thinking. In *The Yearbook of Symbolic Anthropology*, ed. E. Schwimmer, pp. 171–202. London: C. Hurst.

1981. Self-Interest and the Social Good. In *Sexual Meanings*, ed. S. Ortner and H. Whitehead. Cambridge: Cambridge University Press.

Street, J. 1967. Soil Conservation of Shifting Cultivators in the Bismarck Mountains of New Guinea. Mimeographed manuscript, Department of Geography, University of Hawai.

Turner, V. 1957. *Schism and Continuity in an African Society*. Manchester University Press for the Rhodes-Livingstone Institute.

1967. *The Forest of Symbols*. New York: Cornell University Press.

Vayda, A. 1971. Phases of the Processes of War and Peace among the Maring of New Guinea. *Oceania* 42:1–24.

Vayda, P. n.d. Pan Maring Survey. Unpublished report.

Vayda, P. and Cook, E. 1964. Structural Variability in the Bismarck Mountain Cultures of New Guinea: A Preliminary Report. *Transactions of the New York Academy of Sciences*, Ser. II 26:798–803.

Wagner, R. 1967. *The Curse of Souw*. Chicago: University of Chicago Press.

1970. Daribi and Foraba Cross-Cousin Terminology: A Structural Comparison. *Journal of Political Sociology* 79:91–8.

1972. *Habu.* Chicago: University of Chicago Press.

1974. Are There Social Groups in the New Guinea Highlands? In *Frontiers of Anthropology*, ed. Murray Leaf, pp. 95–122. New York: Van Nostrand Company.

Watson, J. 1983. *Tairora Culture.* Seattle: University of Washington Press.

Wurm, S. A. 1964. Australian New Guinea Highland Languages and the Distribution of Their Typological Features. In *New Guinea: The Central Highlands. American Anthropologist* 66:77–97.

Wurm, S. and Laycock, D. 1961. The Question of Language and Dialect in New Guinea. *Oceania* 32:128–243.

Index

administration, 20, 73, 82–3; Australian, 70–1
adoption, 122; child exchange, 198–200
adultery, 42, 65
affines, 7, 94, 97, ch. 5 *passim*, 162; and food, 85; marriage-making, 174–5; model of affinal relations, 57–8; offsetting influence of, 150–1; relations between, 161, 191
aggression, 42, 104, 210, 223
agnates, 9, 113–16, 197; defining, 119–20; disputes, 95; identity of, 100; land distribution, 23
alliance, 151, 161, 188; kinship of, 159; and marriage patterns, 110, 163, 175; and warfare, 154
ancestors, 7, 36, 52–6, 63, 66, 71; contact with, 67; retribution, 90, 150; sacrifices to, 128–9
animal husbandry, 23, 25, 55
ascent, 111–12, 224; as opposed to descent, 114

bananas, 66; gender of, 66
Barnes, J., 1, 12
big-men, 56, 71, 117, 134, 173, 183, 188, 210
bloodlines, 47–8, 57, 114, 116, 122–5; and clan cluster formation, 189–95; generation of, 162; perpetuation of, 164
Bourdieu, P., 4, 39–40, 172
bridewealth, 119–20, 151–6, 178, 179; qualities of, 182; quantity of, 181; for sister exchange, 165–6; variations on, 161
Brookfield, H., 12, 59
brother–sister relations, 51, 154, 166; marriage linked, 155, 157
Brown, P., 12, 59, 201, 202
Buchbinder, G., 17, 42n, 116
Bulmer, R., 28

Bunn, G., 14
bush (forest), 50

cash and cash cropping, 85; *see also* coffee
change (social and cultural), 53, 69, 71–2, 85, 164–5, 169, 210
children, 152, 182–3; conception of, 41, 43–4
Christianity, 53, 56, 88, 90
clan cluster(s), 10, 15, 86, 189–95; pattern of enmity and alliance, 109–10; size, 19
clan(s), 10, 129, 176; as allies, 193; boundaries, 118–21, 214; extinction of, 100; growth and decline, 140–5, 197, 210–11; landedness, 201, 224; nature of subclans, 114–16, 152, 224; reaffiliation, 134–9, 225; recruitment, 124, 184–5; substance (grease), 111, 113, 224
clanship, 48, 102, ch. 4 *passim*, 191, 211; as ideology, 214–15
Clark, W., 17, 216
coastal peoples, 45n
coffee, 70–1, 153, 207
Comaroff, J., 177
compensation, 32, 72, 99, 161, 226–7; for adoption, 122, 198, 199; for adultery, 42; for children, 182–3; death payments, 64, 94, 126, 184–5; for homicide, 73; for land title, 71–3; for marriage, 142, 150–1, 156–7; role of women, 57
contract labor, 199, 206
Cook, E., 15, 19, 133, 137, 207
cordyline, 63, 64, 66, 69, 95, 127
court, 45, 68–9, 71–2
crops: gender of, 66–7; *see also* under individual entries
cross-cousins, 125–6, 135; kin terms for, 130–1; and marriage, 133
curing, 79–80

death, 62–4, 179

239